The Long Road

to

Mount Kailash

By

Dominic J. Cibrario

July 7, 2017

Doug,
I hope you'll enjoy this novel.
Gratefully yours
Nick Cibrario

This book is a work of fiction. The characters and their conversations are products of the author's imagination. Their names and places are used fictitiously. Any resemblances to persons living or dead are coincidental.

Copyright © 2017 by Dominic J. Cibrario

All rights reserved. No part of this publication may be reproduced or transmitted in any form or by any means, electronic or mechanical, including photographs, recording, or any information storage and retrieval system, without permission in writing from the publisher.

ISBN 9781508550860

Publisher: Createspace
An Amazon.com Company
5341-Dorchester Road
North Charleston, SC 29418

Cover design: Kevin Flynn Minuteman Press

Typography and Book Design: Geri Cibrario

Dedication

Pilgrim, pilgrimage, and the road- was only myself, linked to the Universal Self, and the final arrival was but myself going through the Door into Eternity.

Sufi Mystic:

Jaial Al-Din Rumi (1207- 1273)

Other books by Dominic Cibrario

The Pomelo Tree (2004)

The Harvest (2005)

The Shamans (2006)

Murder in the Mountains (2011)

Secrets on the Family Farm (2008)

A Desperate Decision (2013)

Elmer the Octopus (2013)

Hester the Weird Witch (2013)
Geri Cibrario

Acknowledgments

I am grateful to my wife, Geri, for proof reading, editing and offering suggestions for improving the plot. I also want to thank John Brosseau for his editing while reading the drafts, and John Falk for his suggestions and help with the cover design.

I'd like to thank Genevieve Sesto and Briton Road Press for publishing my first novel and inspiring me to continue writing, and Dr. Shahid Ekbal at Rush University Hospital for introducing me to Rumi, the Sufi Mystic.

I'm indebted to Heather Bothe and Joe Schackelman for their suggestions at our writer's meetings, Doug Bingham for maintenance of my website, and the anthropologist, Jim Fisher, for reviewing my novel.

I am indebted to Ganesh Narayan for his weekly lessons in Sanskrit and his wife, Usha, for introducing me to the "Srimad Bhagavad Gita," at the Hindu Temple of Greater Chicago.

Lastly, I'm grateful to the readers of my novels, Nepalese friends, former students, relatives, Peace Corps volunteers, strangers, and acquaintances, who purchase my books at the local festivals and via Kindle and Amazon, or from my website.

The Blessing

I AM the Soul,

dwelling

in all living beings,

O Conqueror of Sleep.

I am the beginning, middle,

and end of all life.

The Bhagavad Gita 10:20

Meet the Characters

1. **Carl Brecht**, retired anthropologist
   Barbara, his wife, tour guide
2. **Mark Brecht**, their son, a microbiologist
3. **Corrine Brecht,** Mark's wife, filing for divorce
4. **Kathy Brecht**, doctor in residency, **Greg,** doctor.
5. **Sammy** and **Emily Brecht,** Mark and Corrine's children
6. **Margaret Porter,** grieving widow
7. **Nigel Porter,** Margaret's son, studying scriptures
8. **Rene Havlett**, Barbara's mother. **Sam Havlett**, Barbara's wealthy father
9. **Rama Narayan**, professor of history. **Samitra**, his wife, professor of languages
10. **Dipak Sharma**, Samitra's brother, civil engineer **Uma**, his wife, librarian.
11. **Hari**, tourist guide for pilgrims to Mount Kailash.
12. **Kesab** and **Lall**, drivers of vehicles in Tibet.

Map: Kathmandu to Mount Kailash

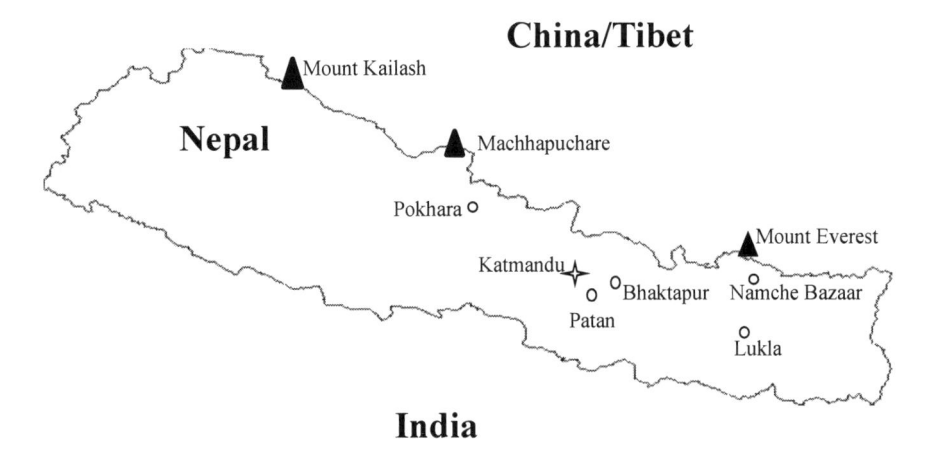

Chapter 1
"Slamming the Door"

Carl sat at the kitchen table in his underwear, drinking coffee and reading the "New York Times." He paused, listening to his wife coming from their bedroom with her high heels echoing on the stairs and in the hallway. When she entered the room, his jaw dropped.

"Barbara, you look stunning in that green silk dress! I thought you had the day off from work," he said.

"I don't work at the museum on weekends unless someone calls in sick. It's Sunday and I'm going to church," she sighed, opening the refrigerator door and removing a carton of orange juice.

"It's must be 90 degrees outside this morning," he said, glancing through the patio doors at the sunlight, illuminating the back yard.

"I didn't sleep very well last night," she yawned, her hand trembling as she poured the juice into a glass.

"Give me a few minutes to shower and shave, and I'll go with you to church. The last time we went to mass together was on Easter Sunday," he said, rising from the table and stretching, revealing his muscular arms and hairy chest.

"I'd rather go by myself," said Barbara, her hand shaking as she sipped her orange juice.

"Barbara, what's wrong?" he asked, worried because she turned away from him in bed when he tried to kiss her.

"I had three nightmares last night! They were all about

you going back to Nepal in August!" she snapped. "I woke up with a headache."

"Tell me about those dreams," he said.

"I don't want to talk about them right now. I wish you weren't going on that pilgrimage with your Nepalese friends to Mount Kailash in Tibet."

"Why don't you come with us on the pilgrimage? You really need a change of pace," said Carl, standing up and scratching his hairy chest.

"Absolutely not!" snapped Barbara, pacing up and down in front of the refrigerator. "You should put on some clothes because you're almost naked! Do you think you're Tarzan talking to Jane in the jungle?"

"I'll never forget when you and Mark came to meet me in Kathmandu," said Carl, trying to console with a hug.

"That was twelve years ago!" shouted Barbara, pushing him away. "You need to shave!"

"Why are you so angry with me?" asked Carl.

"I'm worried about you going back to Nepal. The last time you were there with Kathy, I didn't hear from you for weeks because of the assassination of the Royal Family by the Crown Prince," said Barbara with her hands clenched.

"That was back in 2001. I still don't believe that Prince Dipendra murdered his parents,' said Carl.

"I wish you'd cancel your flight to Nepal!" said Barbara, sitting down at the table. "I can't understand why you want to go there during the peak of the monsoon season. I read in 'Time Magazine' about the floods in the Himalayas where Hindu pilgrims are still stranded in India!"

"I already booked my flight on Qatar Airlines. I'm sure there's still room for you on the plane. I won't be departing from O'Hare until August 4th with Samitra and Rama. There's still time for you to get a ticket and come with us."

"You already told me you won't come back to Chicago until September 4th. You'll be gone a whole month," she said, frowning with disgust.

"Once we get to Kathmandu, we'll rest for a few days because of the time change. Then, I'll take you on a tour of the Royal Palace. The Maoists turned it into a museum after they got rid of the monarchy.

"We'll have plenty of time to visit the shrines before leaving on the pilgrimage because August is festival time. Besides we won't leave for Tibet until August tenth, and be back to Kathmandu on the twentieth."

"Carl, I can't go with you," said Barbara. "I promised Mark I'd babysit on weekends so that he and Corrine can have some time together!"

"Corrine shouldn't have let her mother, Margo, move in with them. It was a mistake! Mark's been talking about getting a divorce every time he comes here with Sammy and Emily," said Carl.

"I'm still working five days a week at the museum. I can't just take off. I must give them a six week notice to get a leave of absence," said Barbara, rising from the kitchen table. "It's already the second week in July and you'll be leaving in a couple of weeks!"

"I'll miss you while I'm gone," said Carl.

"No, you won't! You'll be busy visiting shrines and travelling with your Nepalese friends," she sighed, glancing at the front page of the newspaper. "What have you been reading in today's paper?"

"I just read that the Chinese government gave Nepal 1.8 billion dollars so their guards will be allowed to control the border to Tibet," said Carl. "They don't want Tibetan refugees taking asylum in Nepal or escaping to India.

"Last year only 400 Tibetans escaped from China due to

tight border control by their guards. They used to have about 4000 Tibetans refugees fleeing every year to India, where the Dalai Lama gave them asylum at his community in Dharmasala.

"Also during this past year a 100 monks poured gasoline onto their bodies, lit a match, and burned themselves to death in Tibet, protesting the Chinese occupation of their country," said Carl.

"The Dalai Lama doesn't approve of his angry monks, committing suicide," said Barbara. "He believes violence breeds violence."

"Earlier in the summer a Nepalese monk burned himself to death in Kathmandu because the Maoists don't want the Buddhists to celebrate the Dalai Lama's birthday this year. The Tibetans, who have been living in Nepal for several generations, are disturbed by the incident," said Carl.

"Oh my God, I'm going to be late for mass!" exclaimed Barbara, getting up quickly from her chair and accidently knocking her glass onto the floor.

"Now look what you made me do!" she screamed, staring at the puddle of juice and shattered glass on the floor.

Carl rose from the table and put his arms around his sobbing wife. "Don't worry about the broken glass. I'll clean it up in a few minutes."

"That's all you ever do is talk about Nepal and Tibet," said Barbara. "You don't understand that I'm stressed out because of my dreams!"

"Tell me about them before you leave for church."

"I can't because they're so horrifying. I tossed and turned the whole night because I don't want you going to Tibet! It's controlled by China!" she shouted, breaking away from him. "Just leave me alone! I've got to go now or I'll be late for church!"

"I thought we were taking Mark and Corrine out to lunch with Sammy and Emily today," said Carl.

"I don't want to go out with them!" she shouted, high heeling through the kitchen door and slamming it shut.

Carl opened the door and watched Barbara hurrying down the sidewalk toward the garage. A few minutes later she was backing the Toyota into the street and heading east toward Arlington Heights Road.

After returning to the kitchen, Carl swept up the glass, worrying about Barbara. He walked in his bare feet across the cool linoleum toward his desk and sat down, opening his email on the computer. A message was sent by Hari, the tour guide from Karnali Excursions.

He read that the departure from O'Hare was on the evening of August 4, 2013 and the arrival at Doha Qatar was on Monday, August 5th at 6:25 pm.

There would be a six hour layover in Doha before leaving for Nepal at 1:10 am and arriving in Kathmandu at 8:35 am, Tuesday August 6, losing a day by crossing the International Date Line.

Carl set down the itinerary and returned to the kitchen table, disturbed by Barbara's anger and her dreams. He was surprised that she was going to mass after not attending church regularly except on Christmas and Easter because their children were now grown up.

He knew that Barbara had been influenced by the new pope, who refused to live in the Vatican, but chose to reside at a small apartment in Rome, where he paid his own rent.

Carl paused, recalling the installation of Pope Francis, Jorge Mario Bergoglio, in March. When he was Archbishop of Buenos Aires, the pope visited the slums, travelling without body guards on the subway and walking several blocks to comfort victims of poverty and crime.

Pope Francis was totally opposite of Barbara's father, the president of Havlett Industries. Sam threatened to disinherit his daughter, Barbara, if she married Carl, who taught anthropology at the University of Pennsylvania.

When Carl was given a sabbatical leave to do research on Shamanism in Nepal, Barbara refused to go with him.

Carl would not give up teaching and departed for Nepal without Barbara.

He was surprised when she arrived in Kathmandu in the spring. Within a few weeks, they were married by Father Kent in the chapel at Saint Xavier's in Patan, Nepal.

After their wedding they moved to Pokhara with a grand view of the Himalayas. They lived on the university campus where Carl taught anthropology.

About a year later their son, Mark, was born. Because of Barbara's health issues, they left Nepal and returned to the United States. Carl returned to teaching at the University of Pennsylvania while Barbara stayed home to take care of their son.

Barbara's father, Sam, was pleased to have a grandson and offered to buy them a house in the suburb next to his mansion. When Carl declined the invitation, Sam was furious and refused to come to Mark's baptism. His wife, Renee, attended in spite of Sam's threats to divorce her.

When their daughter, Kathy, was born two years later, Carl was hired to teach at the University of Chicago. Once again Sam offered to buy them a house in Mount Pleasant. However they refused his offer and purchased a bungalow on Maple Street in Arlington Heights near the train station so he could commute to the university.

Carl glanced at the clock above the kitchen sink. He suddenly remembered that he had promised to go out to lunch with Mark, Corrine, and their grandchildren.

Chapter 2
"A Crisis in the Himalayas"

Carl rose from his desk when he heard the phone ring and rushed into the hallway to answer it.

"Hello, Mark! What's going on? I'm so glad you called because your mother isn't feeling well. No, she's not here right now. She left for church a half hour ago. Of course, you can come over with the kids. I'll see you soon," he said, returning to the kitchen, where he noticed a book on the shelf above his desk with an envelope protruding from it.

He picked up "Sherpas, Reflections on Change in Himalayan Nepal." Carl opened the letter and read an obituary about Sir Edmund Hillary, written by Jim Fisher. It was sent to him from Carlton College in 2008, where Jim taught anthropology.

The letter was written the same year as the Chinese Olympics, the beginning of the economic recession in the U.S., and the end of the Maoist revolution in Nepal, which enabled tourists and trekkers to return.

Carl began reading the obituary: "Many observers noted that the death of Sir Edmund Hillary last week marked the end of the classic age of mountaineering. That is true, but his work in Sherpa villages - building schools, bridges, clinics, air strips, among other things - to be more important than making the first ascent of Everest. I was privileged, as a member of one of his expeditions, to take part in that work, while we were chatting, walking along the trail, or sharing a tent.

"Ed, as he insisted on being called was the quintessential New Zealander: plain-spoken, direct, sensible, practical, and above all decisive.

"He was in his own authentic way, a populist. What he wanted to do was to simply extend a helping hand to people who, through no fault of their own, were poor, sick and uneducated. He wanted to do what he could to help because he was fond of them and genuinely admired them. It was just the right thing to do – pay back for all they had contributed to the successes he had achieved.

"Of course, he was also courted by the high and mighty royalty, but he spent only as much time with them as he had to without offending them…He turned down an invitation from Queen Elizabeth to celebrate the 50th anniversary of the first Everest ascent, because he wanted to celebrate it with his Sherpa friends."

Glancing at the kitchen clock above the sink, Carl hurried down the hallway and up the stairs to shower and shave, realizing that his son, Mark, would soon be there.

While shaving, he wondered about Barbara's disturbing dreams. Usually, they stayed in bed late on Sunday morning making love and then talking at length about their jobs and the grandchildren.

It was often noon before they came to the kitchen to have a late breakfast. Nearly every Sunday, they would go with Mark, Corrine, and their grandchildren to a restaurant for brunch.

While showering, he recalled an eleven day trek he had made to Gosainkund during the monsoon season in the summer of 1963. He stayed overnight in a Sherpa village, where he and his friends, camped in sleeping bags on the porch of the son of the Cini Lama of Nepal, who had two wives in his house at Helembu and five wives in distant villages.

He felt relieved now that he was retired from teaching fulltime at the University of Chicago. He still taught South Asian Anthropology part time, three mornings a week.

Barbara still teased him about looking like John F. Kennedy with grey hair. He also told her that she reminded him of Audrey Hepburn, which she denied.

He thought about travelling back to Nepal with his Nepalese friends from the university. Rama was now chairman of the South Asian Studies Department and his wife, Samitra, taught Nepali, Hindi, and Sanskrit.

The three of them had been talking about going on a pilgrimage to Mt. Kailash, the sacred Mountain in Tibet, for the past 12 years. They finally booked their flight on Qatar Airlines and would be departing on August 4.

Margaret informed Carl she was studying Nepali with Samitra via Skype for the past three months and would be joining them on the Karnali Excursion to Mt. Kailash. She also said that she was grieving the loss of her husband, Krishna, who had died nine months ago in an automobile accident in London.

Carl didn't tell Barbara that Margaret Porter sent him an email, mentioning her son, Nigel, was a Buddhist monk, studying Tibetan scriptures in Lhasa. She wanted to visit Nigel after returning from the pilgrimage.

Carl paused thinking that Barbara would be furious if he told her that Margaret Porter was now a widow and going on the trip with him and his Hindu friends to Mt. Kailash.

He recalled that in September 1976 after terminating a four year relationship with Barbara, he left for Nepal. When the plane landed in London, Carl met Margaret Porter, who boarded the jumbo jet with her unruly children, Christopher and Nigel.

Upon arrival in Kathmandu, Carl delayed his research on Shamanism to help Margaret get settled at her hotel, not knowing that she was fleeing from Yorg Schmidt, the leader of a London coven.

He also met Margaret twelve years ago when she came to Kathmandu to visit Nigel, a Buddhist monk, staying at the Royal Palace teaching yoga to Prince Dipendra.

Carl thought about his son, Mark, who met his wife Corrine in graduate school while studying microbiology.

After graduating they were married and eventually had two children. Everything was fine until Corrine's father, Arthur, died from a stroke and her mother, Margo, moved in with them grief stricken and penniless.

He wondered whether Margo was still making life a hell on earth for Mark, his wife, and his grandchildren.

Carl finally stepped out of the shower and got dressed. A few minutes later he hurried down the stairs, wearing a blue shirt, levis, and sandals. He went to kitchen to get the "New York Times," and then down the hallway to the porch.

He sat down on the swing, rocking back and forth while reading the headline of the New York Times, "Floods Continue to Delay Pilgrims in India." He read that 76,000 Hindu pilgrims were stranded in the Himalayas due to mountains collapsing and the destruction of the roads.

Although the Indian army and air force had rescued 12,000 people with helicopters, another 64,000 were still left behind in the mountains. The hardest hit town was in northern Uttar Pradesh where the flooding washed away roads, bridges, 365 houses, and 40 hotels.

Carl read that Prime Minister Manmohan Singh returned to New Delhi after an aerial survey of the flooded areas.

No wonder Barbara was having nightmares," thought Carl.

Chapter 3
"Family Issues"

Carl put the newspaper down on the porch swing when he heard the door of the taxi slam shut. He glanced toward Sammy and Emily, running up the sidewalk. Rising from the swing, he hurried toward his grandchildren.

"Grandpa! Grandpa! Our mom's mad at dad," yelled Sammy, giving him a hug before sitting down on the swing.

"Mommy told daddy to get out and never come back because he doesn't live with us anymore!" cried Emily, the tears flowing down her cheeks.

Carl gave Emily a hug and then removed a handkerchief from his back pocket to wipe her tears.

"Grandma Margo calls us spoiled brats," said Sammy, swinging back and forth. "She told Dad to take us with him so mom wouldn't have to go back to the hospital!"

"She said it's our fault that mom's so sick," said Emily.

"Mark, what happened?" asked Carl, turning toward his son coming up the sidewalk, carrying two suitcases and a black gym bag

"Hi, Dad," said his son, coming up the steps and setting the luggage down near the front door.

"It looks like you're coming here to stay for a while," said Carl, his brow furrowed from worry.

"Mommy doesn't love us anymore," pouted Emily.

"Grandma Margo's mean! She hits me all the time with her belt," shouted Sammy, jumping off the porch swing. He pulled up his shirt, showing his grandfather the bruises and welts on his back.

Carl gasped, shaking his head with disgust upon seeing Sammy's swollen back.

"Grandma Margo never hits me. She makes me stand in the corner," cried Emily. "She hates our daddy!"

Sammy blurted, "She told us that our mom made a big mistake marrying him."

"Corrine's stressed out from working overtime," said Mark. "I should have put my foot down after Arthur died, but I felt sorry for Margo since she had no place to stay. Their house was repossessed, and she was bankrupt after the funeral. Corrine insisted that she move in with us."

"Grandpa Arthur died from a heart attack because he lost all their money and their house by gambling," said Sammy.

"Grandma Margo drinks too much wine," said Emily. "She's drunk when we come home from school. I get mad at her for pulling my hair!" cried Emily.

Mark reached into his shirt pocket and removed a pack of Marlboros. His hand quivered while lighting the cigarette.

"I thought you quit smoking, Mark," said Carl, coughing from the cloud of smoke, drifting toward him on the porch.

"I started smoking again when Margo moved in two years ago," he said.

"You shouldn't be smoking in front of the children," said Carl, annoyed by the smoke.

"I hate Grandma Margo! She smells because she only takes a shower once a week," said Emily.

"Why don't you kids go play on the swings in the back yard for a few minutes so that I can talk to your dad," said Carl.

"I'm going on the slide first," shouted Sammy, darting down the steps and heading toward the sidewalk leading to the back yard.

"Wait for me," shouted Emily, running after her brother.

"Dad, it's all my fault. I shouldn't have taken that job in

Philadelphia with Havlett Industries," said Mark, putting out his cigarette in an ashtray.

"You were adamantly opposed to working for your grandfather, Sam, because he was manufacturing lethal chemicals and shipping them to Iran and Iraq. What made you change your mind? You had a good job working in that lab in Skokie."

"Sam, told me that if I worked for him steadily for five years, I would inherit his business when he died," said Mark. "I…I couldn't stand living at home with Corrine and Margo anymore. I took the job because I hated Margo's constant nagging. Her interference was ruining our marriage.

"I really wanted her to leave by renting a condo, but Corrine wouldn't allow it. I've been coming home every other weekend for two years to spend time with my kids."

"Your children need you to be with them permanently and so does your wife. Mark, you swore you'd never work for Sam as long as you lived."

"The two women ganged up on me and told me to get out, if I didn't like living there with them. Frankly, I was miserable coming home to two angry women and naughty children every night.

"Finally, I called Sam long distance and took the job he offered me years ago. He was thrilled to have me working for him at his laboratory. Sam and I go out to lunch at least once a week. He's in good health in spite of his age."

"You did it to escape from Margo and Corrine," said Carl. "I feel sorry that your kids are being neglected and abused. Your wife's also been hospitalized several times since you left."

"Dad, I hope Sammy and Emily can live here for the rest of the summer. I have a girlfriend in Philadelphia who moved in with me a couple of months ago with her daughter.

They want me to bring Sammy and Emily to live with us. Clarissa is really nice and so is her daughter Laura, who's in the fifth grade. I want you and mom to meet them.

"Are you getting a divorce from Corrine?" asked Carl.

"I talked to Sam about it. He's hired a good lawyer for me. He'll see to it that I get full custody of my kids because of Margo's abusiveness and Corrine's health problems.

"Dad, would you please drive me to O' Hare after lunch? Sam's chauffeur will pick me up at the airport in Philadelphia."

"What about the children?" asked Carl. "Your mother will be back from church in a few minutes. She'll be even more stressed when she finds out your kids are living here. You know I'm leaving for Nepal the first week in August."

"Sam told me that Renee would help Mom with the kids while you're gone. They'll only be here for six weeks because school starts in Philadelphia after Labor Day. By then I'll have custody of Sammy and Emily and they'll be moved in with us in our new apartment," said Mark.

"My problem is that my flight doesn't leave until 4:00 o'clock. I'm so tense," he said, opening the front door and putting the luggage into the hallway. "Will you watch the kids while I take a walk?"

"Go right ahead," said Carl. "I'll keep an eye on them."

"I'll be back in an hour," said Mark, hurrying down the steps, and heading north toward town.

Chapter 4
"Barbara's Disturbing Dreams"

Carl returned to the kitchen and glanced through the sliding patio doors into the back yard. He noticed that the children were playing in the sand box, making a castle with water from the sprinkling can.

Deciding to send an email to Margaret Porter, he sat down at the computer and sent his condolence to her over the death of Krishna Manandhar.

A few minutes later, he heard his wife parking the car in the garage. Rising from the table, he opened the kitchen door, where he saw Barbara hurrying toward the house, oblivious to Sammy and Emily playing in the sandbox in the back yard.

"How was mass this morning?" asked Carl, holding the door open for her.

"It was fine, but I was late because of the traffic going south on Arlington Heights Road. When I turned right onto Biesterfield in Elk Grove Village, the cars were stalled due to a terrible accident.

"By the time I got to church, the offering basket was being passed as Father Lorenzo continued with the mass.

"After the service was over, I talked to him for nearly an hour about my dreams. He advised me to tell you how I feel about you going to Nepal and Mount Kailash with your colleagues from the university."

"First let me give you a hug. I really missed you not being in bed this morning. I know you were upset with me because of your dreams," he said, holding her tightly and kissing her tenderly on the lips.

"Oh, Carl," she gasped, as he kissed her again, pulling away from him to sit down. "I'm still angry with you because you always put your job first. Your career as an anthropologist has always been more important to you that being a husband and a father!"

"I'm sorry about that," said Carl, standing behind his wife and massaging her tense shoulders.

"You took off for six months to do research in Nepal on Shamanism after we were married, leaving me and the children behind," sighed Barbara.

"I know it wasn't easy for you raising the kids by yourself. I was so grateful that your mother, Renee, came all the way from Philadelphia to help you out. In those days it was either publish or perish at the university. This time I'll only be gone for month."

"I didn't want to tell you about my dreams, but Father Lorenzo said that I shouldn't keep any secrets from you. I have to admit that they are horrible," she said.

"Well, I dreamt that your airplane was bombed by the Taliban before you landed at the airport in Doha Qatar and everyone on the flight was killed!"

"What?" said Carl, pacing up and down in the kitchen.

"I read that the Qatari government recently allowed the Taliban to open an embassy in Doha," said Barbara. "I wish you would cancel that flight and go to Nepal on Indian Airlines like you've done in the past.

"I, also, had two dreams about you falling off the mountain while climbing Mt. Kailash," said Barbara, reaching into her purse for a tissue to wipe her eyes.

"In the second dream the tour guide, called me long distance and wanted to know whether they should cremate your body on Mt. Kailash or have your corpse sent to

Kathmandu by helicopter and then flown back to Chicago."

"Really!" said Carl bewildered "On Saturday I took out a traveler's life insurance policy, which covers accidents or death, including shipping my body home."

"Oh, my God," said Barbara. "Do you really want to hear about my third dream?"

"Of course, I do," said Carl, pacing the kitchen floor.

"I…I dreamt that you fell off the mountain but weren't killed. This time you broke your back and were flown by helicopter from Mt. Kailash to Kathmandu, where you were treated at Shanta Bhawan Hospital."

"That's a relief," said Carl, feeling tense.

"In the third dream I flew to Kathmandu with Kathy, Mark, and the grandchildren to visit you at the hospital.

"After two weeks in Nepal, we flew back to Chicago, where you were admitted to Loyola University Hospital. You stayed there three months in rehab before returning home with a cane"

"Wow, those are really disturbing dreams!" said Carl, glancing at the patio doors, where Sammy and Emily were standing with their faces pressed against the glass.

"What are they doing here?" asked Barbara, startled by their noses looking like pig snouts.

"Mark brought them here and then went for a walk," said Carl, rising from the chair and opening the patio doors.

"Hi Grandma," shouted Emily, rushing into the kitchen and throwing her arms around her.

"You look nice in that green dress, Grandma," said Sammy, giving her a hug. "We're thirsty!"

"How about some orange juice," said Barbara, getting up from her chair and going to the refrigerator. "First, you must wash your hands outside because you've been playing in the sand. I don't want it clogging the sink in our bathroom."

"Who's going to wash their hands first?" asked Carl, removing a towel from the drawer and leading the way through the patio doors to the spigot alongside the house.

"I'm going first," insisted Sammy, running past his sister to wash his hands.

"You always get to go first," said Emily, pouting as she rinsed her hands.

A few minutes later, they returned to the kitchen and sat down at the table to drink their orange juice.

"Grandma, we're hungry," said Sammy, gulping down his juice.

"How about some cereal?" asked Barbara. "Where's your father this morning?"

"He went for a walk," said Sammy. "I'm starving!"

"Mark said he'd be back in hour," added Carl, glancing at his watch. "He should be here in a little while.

Barbara reached for the box of Wheat Chex in the cupboard and filled two bowls.

"We didn't get any breakfast this morning," said Emily.

"Why not?" asked Barbara. "I thought your father and mother might be going out to lunch with us today."

"Corrine, didn't come here with Mark," said Carl, pouring the milk into the bowls.

"Grandma Barbara, I don't like that kind of cereal. I only like Frosted Flakes," said Emily.

"How about a bagel with cream cheese?" asked Carl, opening the refrigerator again.

"I like bagels," said Emily. "Mommy's angry with our daddy because he works in Philadelphia for Great Grandpa, Sam. She didn't want him going there to live."

"We only see dad every other weekend," said Sammy. "Our mom's been sick for a whole week."

"I hope your dad and mom weren't quarrelling again,"

said Barbara, putting the split bagel into the toaster.

"I'm afraid it's more serious this time," said Carl, opening the package of cream cheese.

"What do you mean?" gasped Barbara, worried about Corrine's illness.

"Emily, how about if you and Sammy eat at the picnic table on the patio?" asked Carl.

"No, I want to stay here in the kitchen with Grandma," said Sammy, gulping down his cereal.

"Do we have to go on the patio, Grandpa?" asked Emily, watching her grandma put a layer of cream cheese on her bagel and then handing it to her.

"Grandma, we're going to live here with you and grandpa for the rest of the summer. Our mom told us to get out and never to come back," said Sammy.

"What's going on?" asked Barbara, her eyes opening wide as she paced up and down.

"Mark told me that Corrine want's a divorce. That's why he brought two suitcases with the kid's clothes. He wants them to move in with us until he can find a new apartment in Philadelphia. Your father, Sam, already has hired a lawyer so that Mark will get custody of the children."

"Oh my God! Not a divorce," gasped Barbara. "Mark shouldn't have left his job in downtown Chicago. I still can't believe he actually took that job in my father's lab in Philadelphia. I was worried that something like this would happen!"

"Mark took the job so he wouldn't have to be around his mother-in-law, Margo. She hasn't been the same since the death of her husband, Arthur," said Carl.

"Grandma Margo's mean to us. When she's drunk, she beats me with a belt," sobbed Sammy. "I don't want to go back home ever again."

"She makes me stand in the corner," said Emily. "She doesn't want me to sing or make any noise."

"Where are your clothes?" asked Barbara, taking a deep breath and shaking her head.

"They're in the suitcases in the hallway," said Carl. "I wonder where Mark went. He said he'd be back in an hour."

"Carl!" shouted Barbara. "I can't quit my job at the museum to watch the kids. I have to give them a six week notice to get a leave of absence."

"Mark said that your mother, Renee, was willing to take care of the kids while you're at work," said Carl. "I'll help you with them for the next couple of weeks before leaving for Nepal. I'll only be gone a month."

"You always take off when I need you the most!" snapped Barbara.

"I'll call Renee on my cell phone!" said Carl, reaching for it on the desk.

"We like Great Grandma Renee," said Sammy. "She takes us to the park and the Brookfield Zoo. The last time she was here, we went to the Marriot Theater in Lincolnshire to see the 'The Wizard of Oz'."

"I liked Toto. He's such a nice dog, but he peed on the stage. I hate that old Wicked Witch of the West," said Emily. "She had an ugly, green face."

"Carl, my mother's never home. I have to leave a half-dozen messages on her cell phone before she ever returns my call. Renee's always chasing somewhere so that she doesn't have to be around Sam. She hangs out at the library, the country club, or her women's group."

"I'll try to reach her," said Carl, dialing Renee's cell phone. He paused when she answered the phone.

"Renee, I'm so glad your home. Yes, I'm still here. I won't be leaving for Nepal until the first week in August.

We've got a favor to ask of you.

"Yes, the grandchildren are fine. They're here right now. The problem is that Sammy and Emily have moved in with us. We were hoping that you could come here and help us baby sit for the month of August while I'm away. I'll be back home the first week in September.

"Barbara's still working at the museum. She also takes classes in yoga twice a week to maintain her health. Oh, you know all about Mark filing for a divorce and wanting custody of the children.

"The sooner you get here the better. Thanks so much. I'll let Barbara know that you'll be here tomorrow. Please say hello to Sam for me. Bye now," said Carl.

"Thank God my mother's coming to help. Carl, where's Mark?" asked Barbara, still pacing in the kitchen.

"Sammy! Emily. Go out and play on the swing. This time, please take turns. I've got to take Mark to the airport. He must be there an hour before his flight leaves," said Carl.

"That's the telephone ringing in the hallway," said Barbara, placing her hands over her face at the kitchen table.

Carl hurried to answer the phone, "Yes, Mark I'll pick you up from the bar in town. Of course, I'll put your gym bag in the car. I'll be there in a few minutes."

Upon entering the kitchen, Barbara stood frozen in front of the patio doors, watching Sammy push his sister on the swing tied to a branch, hanging from the maple tree.

"Oh Carl, I feel so depressed. I can't believe that Mark wants a divorce. I feel sorry for Corrine," she said, sitting down at the table and glancing at the newspaper.

Chapter 5
"Momentary Relief"

"What's this all about?" asked Barbara, gasping as she read the headline of the New York Times. "There's flooding in the Himalayas with pilgrims still stranded there because of the monsoon! Don't I have enough to worry about?"

"Barbara, the flooding is in Northern India not in Tibet where the altitude is higher," said Carl. "Mark just called me from the bar downtown. He wants me to pick him up and take him to the airport."

"What's he doing at the bar?" asked Barbara, biting her lower lip. "I hope he's not back to drinking."

"He's there watching a baseball game. He won't have time to unpack the children's suitcases. They're still in the hallway," said Carl. "I'll bring them up stairs before I leave."

"I'm already a nervous wreck," said Barbara, taking a deep breath. "I told Father Lorenzo that I was so proud of Mark being sober for several years now.

"I forgot to tell him that I hate Corrine's mother, Margo! She's a real bitch! Sammy and Emily are complaining about her all the time. What's wrong with that woman anyway?" shouted Barbara.

"She's an alcoholic," said Carl. "That's her problem. I'm worried that Mark will relapse due to the pressure of commuting to Philadelphia and working with Sam. He promised Mark that he would inherit his business if he stayed with him for five years."

"No!" gasped Barbara, pacing in the kitchen. "Sam threatened to disinherit me, if I married you. He promised to leave me his fortune and Havelett Laboratory if I didn't go to Nepal with you in the fall of 1976. I was miserable the whole time that you were gone.

"I finally realized that I sold my soul to the devil. My father was enraged when I told him that I didn't care about his inheritance or his business. That's when I decided to go to Nepal to be with you," she said.

"When you arrived in Nepal it was spring time. We sat in the garden of the Kathmandu Guest House under the pomelo tree and talked for hours," said Carl, approaching his wife with his arms outstretched.

"Just hold me for a few moments," sobbed Barbara, the tears flowing down her cheeks. "After we were married, I stayed with you for a whole year in Pokhara where you taught anthropology at Pritivi Narayan College."

Carl wrapped his arms around Barbara and kissed her on the back of the neck gently. "We returned to Chicago after Mark was born."

"Oh, Carl! What have I done to deserve all this stress! I'm worried about our grandchildren."

"You haven't done anything wrong," he whispered, kissing her. "I love you Barbara."

"Carl, I'm sorry that I was so abrupt with you this morning. I was blaming you for everything. Father Lorenzo told me that I need to pray and meditate daily, asking God to help me cope with the problems of life.

"Did you know that he was married for ten years before he decided to become a priest. He became a Jesuit after his wife died from breast cancer. They never had any children because of her medical issues."

"I like Father Lorenzo because he's so patient and tolerant. He reminds me of Father Moran, the Jesuit priest, from Kathmandu, who travelled with Nehru in India," said

Carl. "They went from village to village trying to stop the riots between the Hindus and Moslems after Gandhi's assassination."

"I remember him. He was a good friend of Father Kent, who married us in the chapel at St. Xavier's Boarding School. Oh, Carl, forgive me for being such an emotional wreck," she sobbed. "It really bothers me that Mark's getting a divorce from Corrine. She's always been so sweet and kind to me."

"She made a serious mistake by having her mother move in with her and Mark. I wouldn't be surprised if that's when he started drinking again," said Carl.

"I wonder if my father has also relapsed?" asked Barbara. "Sam was drinking heavily before you left for Nepal back in 2001 with Kathy."

"I'm sure you'll find out more about him when Renee arrives tomorrow," said Carl.

"Thanks for calling her," whispered Barbara, pausing while Carl kissed her again.

"Oh, Carl. I wish we were alone," she gasped, glancing at the clock. "Oh my God it's already 2:15 and you still have to pick up Mark at the bar."

"I wish we could go back to bed," he said, still holding her tightly in his arms."

"I can hear your heart beating," she whispered. "I should check on the kids in the back yard."

"And I have to get Mark's gym bag," he said releasing his hold on her. "I'll put the suitcases upstairs before I leave."

She hurried through the kitchen and opened the patio door. "Sammy! Emily! Come over here. I want you to help me unpack your clothes!"

Carl returned to the kitchen with the gym bag and was about to leave for the garage

"Emily and Sammy won't come into the house. They're being stubborn again. Will you help me with them?"

"Of course," said Carl, going out on the patio "Sammy! Emily! Your grandma's been calling you. Come over here right now."

"Grandma, my back hurts," said Sammy, running toward the patio with his sister following him.

"What's the matter with your back?" asked Barbara. "Did you fall down and hurt yourself?"

Sammy pulled up his shirt, showing her his wounds.

"Oh my God!" said Barbara. "Your back is black and blue from bruises and covered with welts."

"Grandma Margo held me down on the floor with her foot and beat me with a belt," sobbed Sammy.

"Why did she do such a horrible thing to you?" gasped Barbara, her eyes wide with alarm.

"It's because Sammy was chasing me around the dining room table with a rubber mouse," sobbed Emily. "It's all my fault she beat him!"

"Emily kept screaming while I was chased her. I forgot that Grandma Margo was watching 'Family Guy' on TV and drinking wine," said Sammy. "She tried to put us to bed, but we didn't listen to her."

"Mommy doesn't let us watch that show when she's home," said Emily. "She says it's not for children."

"I might have to take you to the Emergency Room," sighed Barbara.

"That won't be necessary," said Carl. "There's a tube of Neosporin and bandages in the medicine cabinet upstairs in the bathroom. Come on inside the house now!"

Carl took Sammy by the hand and led him into the kitchen. He was followed by his wife and Emily. While closing the patio door he heard the phone ringing again in the hallway.

"You kids go upstairs with Grandma while I answer the phone," he said.

"Hello Mark. I'm sorry I'm late. No, we haven't had time to unpack their suitcases yet. Yes, I have your gym bag with me. I know it's almost 2:30 and we should be on our way. I'll be right there. What's the name of the bar? OK I'll pick you up in front of DeMarco's Sports Bar in five minutes."

After Carl hung up the phone, he could hear Sammy yelling in the hallway bathroom.

"Grandma that hurts!" he screamed, as she washed his wounds with warm water before applying the Neosporin.

"I shouldn't have screamed when Sammy chased me with the mouse!" said Emily.

Carl peaked in the bathroom and said," I'm going now to pick up your dad at De Marco's Sports Bar."

"Can I come with you, Grandpa?" asked Emily. "I want to say goodbye to my daddy."

"Maybe another time," said Carl. "I'm running late. Your father should be at the airport at least an hour before his 4:00 o'clock flight. It will take 45 minutes to get there."

"Daddy told us that he was going to take us with him to Philadelphia before school starts," said Sammy.

"I want to go with him right now," said Emily, stamping her foot. "Mommy's mad at daddy because he's got a new girlfriend. Her name is Clarissa."

"Carl, we need to talk about this later," sighed Barbara

"I'll be home in about an hour and half," shouted Carl, leaving for the garage and driving the Toyota toward the bar.

Chapter 6
"Driving to the Airport"

When Carl pulled up in front of the bar, he noticed that Mark wasn't waiting for him outside. After a few minutes he parked the car and went into the dimly lighted bar. It was packed with customers watching the baseball game on large screens.

"Hi Dad," said Mark, slugging down his fourth martini, pushing his glass forward to get another drink.

"I thought you gave up drinking," said Carl, shaking his head. "Mark, you said you'd be waiting for me outside."

"I got distracted by the game," he said, sliding off the barstool. "Wait a minute, Dad, I have to take a piss."

"Mark! It's already 2:45," said Carl. "You're supposed to be at the airport an hour before your flight."

"I'll be right back, Dad," he said, staggering toward the men's room. A few minutes later he returned to the bar room, wiping his hands on his Levis.

"They're out of paper towels!" said Mark, following his father toward the exit. He glanced over his shoulder to get a final glimpse of the baseball game.

"Mark! We're going to be late!" insisted Carl.

"Did you bring my gym bag with you?" asked Mark, following his father to the car and sitting in the front seat.

"It's in the backseat," said Carl, starting the car and heading south.

"How's Mom do...doing these days?" asked Mark, slurring his words. "I didn't have time to talk to her."

"Give her a call when you get back to Philadelphia," said his father. "She's stressed because I'm leaving on the pilgrimage in August. I tried to console her after she got back from church this morning."

"I suppose she's mad about taking care of the kids for the rest of the summer," said Mark. "I slept on the couch on Friday night at Corrine's apartment. She invited me to stay overnight because her mother wasn't there.

"Corrine has high blood pressure and takes medication for depression. When she got home from work on Friday, she was too exhausted to even talk to me. After she put the kids to bed, she went straight to her room without even saying good night.

"On Saturday, Corrine had to work all day so I took my kids to the Brookfield Zoo. Sammy was complaining in the car that his back was hurting."

"Did you know that it was covered with welts and bruises?" asked his father.

"He told me that Margo beat him with a belt again! When Sammy showed me his back, I was furious!" said Mark.

"On the way to the zoo, I stopped at Walgreen's to get some Tylenol for him. Within a half hour he stopped complaining about his pain. We had a good time at the zoo.

"After wandering around looking at the animals for a couple of hours, I took them out to dinner at McDonald's."

"I'm pleased you spent the day with them," said Carl.

"After dinner I took the kids to see the movie, 'Frozen.' While waiting in line, Emily complained that Margo made her stand in the corner for two hours.

"I had an argument with Corrine when I took the kids back to her apartment because I bought them popcorn and soda at the theater. Corrine didn't tell me she wanted them home for dinner last night.

"I didn't know she had prepared a meal for them. Corrine made the kids sit down and eat even though they weren't hungry. Sammy played with his food, begging me to take him for a walk in the park, and Emily refused to eat anything, pouting at the table.

"Corrine exploded! That's when she told me to get out and take the kids with me. She pulled their suitcases out of the closet and packed their clothes within fifteen minutes, screaming that she wanted a divorce.

"I told her that I had already filed the papers, which only made matters worse. I shouldn't have opened my big mouth about it," said Mark.

"Later, Sammy told me she had pneumonia and stayed for two nights at the Alexian Brothers Hospital. Corrine was home the rest of the week with Margo before going back to work last Monday."

"It's been a very difficult weekend for you and the kids," said Carl, turning left onto Higgins Road." I hope you're not late for your flight."

"How is Kathy doing? I haven't seen her since Easter," asked Mark. "I was so busy I haven't had time to call her."

"You and Corinne came to her college graduation party with Sammy. He was three years old at that time," said Carl.

"After she graduated, Kathy worked for two years at a laboratory in Morton Grove before being accepted into Medical School at the University of Chicago."

"Dad, I'm so pleased that Kathy's now a doctor doing her residency at Rush," said Mark, lighting a cigarette.

"Mark, I'm worried that you're drinking and smoking again after quitting for years."

"I…I'm stressed out over the divorce. Sam's going to send me to rehab before we go to court," said Mark. "Corinne was in the hospital for weeks after Emily was born. It took her months to recover from the Caesarian."

"I remember how angry Sam got when you decided not to take any more money from him to finish graduate school," said Carl.

"Sam was furious when I refused to sign the contract to work for him at Kathy's graduation party from high school," recalled Mark.

"That was twelve years ago when Renee told us that Havelett Lab was manufacturing lethal chemicals and selling them to Iraq," said Carl.

"Is Kathy still dating that doctor, named Greg," asked Mark, changing the subject as they turned onto the exit, leading to the airport.

"Yes, they're engaged, but they haven't set a wedding date. Greg did his undergraduate work at the University of Michigan, where he played football.

"I never met Greg. It's been two years since I've been commuting to Philadelphia. Clarissa works for Sam in his office. He really likes her because she's so efficient. I met her about a year ago said Mark.

"Here we are at O'Hare," said Carl, pulling over to the curb of the terminal. "Have a good trip back to Philadelphia.

"Thanks a lot for the ride, Dad. I'll see you in two weeks," he said, leaving the car.

"Don't forget your gym bag in the backseat."

"Thanks for reminding," said Mark. "I'll call you to check up on the kids during the week."

"That's a good idea," said Carl. "You better hurry because your flight leaves in twenty minutes"

Carl watched his son enter Delta Airlines through the double doors. He sighed with relief as he departed from the airport, wondering if Sammy and Emily were behaving for Barbara.

Chapter 7
"Returning Home"

    Carl took a deep breath as he drove past Qatar Airways before departing from the crowded airport. The traffic was heavy as he drove back to Arlington Heights. He reflected on the standard package of travel insurance, which was reasonably priced. At the congested stop light on Manheim Road, he removed the insurance paper from his glove compartment. Glancing at the title, he read about the benefits.

    Coverages & Benefit Limits:
Accident, Sickness, Medical Expenses, $15,000
Baggage & Personal Effects, $750, Trip Delay, $500
Trip Cancellation or Interruption, 100% of Cost
Emergency Return due to Interruption, $500.00
Evacuation and Shipment of Remains, $1500

    For a few moments, Carl thought about Barbara's third dream. If it actually happened, his body would be flown home without her going into debt.

    When the taxi driver behind him began honking his horn because of the light change, Carl set the paper down on the passenger's seat and continued driving.

    On the way home, he stopped at Vali's to buy a dozen roses for Barbara, hoping to console her. Twenty minutes later, he arrived at their bungalow on Maple Street and parked in front of the garage. He hurried toward the back yard carrying the roses and the insurance paper.

    Carl was relieved to see Barbara sitting on the swing under the oak tree. Sammy was pushing her while Emily was making a sand castle.

"There's Grandpa," shouted Emily, rushing toward him with a small bucket full of sand. She set it down and gave him a hug. "Did you bring me a present?"

"No, Emily, I brought grandma some flowers," said Carl, giving her a hug.

"Grandma! Grandma!" shouted Emily, rushing toward Barbara, clinging to the ropes on the swing. "Grandpa brought you a present!"

Sammy stopped pushing her and hurried toward Carl. "Did you get me a present too, Grandpa?"

"Here is a candy bar for you and your sister," he said, removing them from his shirt pocket.

"I love chocolate," said Sammy, ripping off the wrapper and throwing it on the grass.

"Thank you for the candy," said Emily, delicately tearing the wrapper, not knowing where to put it.

Carl paused holding the flowers while his wife hurried toward him.

"That was quite a ride on the swing," said Barbara, out of breath. "Emily, Sammy, pick up that wrapper."

"Barbara, I brought you a present," said Carl, kissing her on the cheek and handing her the bouquet..

"Oh! You bought me red roses! They're just gorgeous. I'll put them in a vase," she said, pausing to kiss Carl. "What's that in your other hand?"

"It's the travel insurance policy that I took out for you in case your dreams should come true," said Carl. "The agent made two copies, one for you and one for me."

"That was very thoughtful of you," she said, frowning.

Noticing Barbara's crestfallen face, Carl realized that he shouldn't have mentioned the insurance policy.

"I suppose you'd like me to put these roses on your

casket after your body is shipped home," teased Barbara, glancing over the policy.

"I don't think those roses will last more than two weeks," said Carl, smiling.

"I'll change the water every couple of days so that they'll stay fresh for your funeral," said Barbara.

"What's the matter, Grandma? Is grandpa going to die?" asked Sammy, finishing his candy bar.

"I don't want grandpa to die," sobbed Emily, hugging Carl, and smearing chocolate on his Levis. "Grandma, I'm thirsty?"

"Don't worry about me dying," said Carl." Your grandmother has had some strange dreams."

"Grandma, please tell us about your dreams," begged Sammy. "You told us all about grandpa and Aunt Kathy being kidnapped and put in cave when they were in Nepal a long time ago."

"That's right! We were held hostage by terrorists. If it wasn't for Nigel Porter, we would have been killed," said Carl. "We better go inside so your grandma can put those flowers into a vase."

"May I please have a glass of milk, Grandma?" asked Emily.

"Who's Nigel Porter?" asked Sammy, following his grandparents into the kitchen from the patio.

Barbara reached for a vase under the sink and filled it with water. She said, "Nigel is Margaret Porter's son. He's a Buddhist monk, who saved your grandpa and Aunt Kathy, from being murdered.

"Carl, it's been a long time since we heard from Margaret. She invited us to her wedding at St. Paul's Cathedral in London, but we were too busy to make the trip there. I wonder if she's still married to that psychiatrist."

Sammy and Emily paused to watch Barbara cutting the stems of the roses at the sink and putting them into the vase while Carl poured them glasses of milk.

"Barbara, I…I got an email from Margaret, while you were in church this morning. She's no longer married to Doctor Krishna Manandhar. He died several months ago from a fatal car accident in London."

"That's terrible! I remember you telling me that Krishna helped Margaret recuperate from depression after Nigel's disappearance.

"I met him at the Kathmandu Guest House when Mark and I came to Nepal after you were released by the terrorists from that cave," said Barbara.

"That's when Margaret told us that she was engaged to Krishna," said Carl.

"How's Margaret dealing with the death of her husband?" asked Barbara.

"She's planning a trip to Nepal to visit Nigel," said Carl, pacing up and down the kitchen.

"Carl, there's more to the story than you're telling me," said Barbara, setting the vase of roses on the kitchen table. "When is she going back to Nepal?"

"Barbara, I swear I had nothing to do with this. I found out this morning that she's been studying Nepali on the internet with Samitra at the university and plans to join us on the pilgrimage to Mt. Kailash. After that she'll be travelling to Lhasa to visit Nigel before returning to London."

"It wouldn't surprise me if Margaret's looking for another husband," said Barbara.

"Excuse me please," said Carl. "My cellphone is ringing. "Namaste, Rama, tapailai sanchai hunuhuncha"

"Is grandpa speaking Chinese?" asked Sammy.

"He's speaking Nepali to his friend, Rama," she said.

"What did he say?" asked Emily, her hands covered with sticky chocolate.

"He said, 'Hello Rama, Are you well?'"

"Emily, you and Sammy go wash your hands in the bathroom in the hallway," said Barbara.

"I'll see that Emily washes her hands," said Sammy, leaving the kitchen with his sister.

"Rama, I didn't know Margaret is joining us on the trip until I opened my email this morning. I haven't been in contact with her for several years now," said Carl, noticing his wife was frowning.

"Yes, I'll meet you at O'Hare on August 4th at Qatar Airlines. Thanks for the call," said, Carl.

"Grandpa, Grandma Margo told us that you were too old to go to Tibet," said Sammy.

"She said you should be in a nursing home instead of going back to Nepal," said Emily, reaching for a chocolate chip cookie on the table.

"She told us that grandpa goes back to Kathmandu to meet his old girlfriend," said Sammy.

"Her name is Margaret Porter," said Barbara, placing her hands on her hips.

"Margaret was never my girlfriend. I felt sorry for her when she was running away from her husband, Jim, and Yorg Schmitt, the leader of the London Coven."

"Grandpa, what's a coven?" asked Sammy.

"It's a group of witches," said Barbara.

"When I first met Nigel, he was a spoiled brat. He was only eight years. His brother, Christopher, was five. They were sitting in front of me on the plane with their mother.

"I was shocked when Nigel stabbed his younger brother, Christopher, in the arm with a knitting needle and then ran down the aisle and locked himself in the bathroom."

"Nigel was a bad boy," said Emily. "He shouldn't have stabbed his brother.

"I used my handkerchief to stop the bleeding," said Carl. "The stewardess then cleaned his wound and bandaged it."

"Why did Nigel do that to his brother?" asked Sammy.

"He stabbed his brother because he was possessed by the devil!" interrupted Barbara. "Father Kent performed an exorcism on Nigel, but it didn't help."

"Grandma, what's an exorcism?" asked Sammy.

"It's when a priest drives out an evil spirit from a person, who's possessed by the devil," she said.

"That's creepy!" said Emily, shivering. She got up from her chair and hurried out the patio door. "Grandpa, Grandpa! Why is that bird making so much noise in the maple tree?"

"It's a crow," said Sammy. "Grandma Margo told us that crows bring bad luck!"

"I'm afraid to go outside with that crow making noise," said Emily, clinging to Barbara.

"I'll go scare him away," said Carl, hurrying through the patio door and across the lawn. He clapped his hands and shouted at the crow to leave the yard, watching it fly away.

Within a few minutes, he returned to the kitchen. "You kids can go outside and play now. I want to talk to your grandmother for a few minutes."

"What if that old crow comes back again?" asked Emily, hesitant to leave.

"He won't come back," said Sammy, hurrying through the patio door and heading toward the slide.

"I'm scared to go out there," said Emily.

Barbara took Emily by the hand, leading her to the sand box. "If that crow returns, come right back to the kitchen! If you behave yourselves, you can both have some vanilla ice-cream after I talk with grandpa," said Barbara.

Chapter 8
"An Unexpected Phone Call"

"Carl, I don't think we should talk about Nigel and the coven in front of the children. They're so young and impressionable.

"When Mark became engaged to Corrine, I told her all about your involvement with Margaret Porter, and her sons Nigel and Christopher," said Barbara.

"Barbara, I swear to God that my relationship with Margaret was platonic. She suffered from a nervous breakdown after the death of Christopher. Her husband, Jim, came all the way from London with his partner, Greg, to take Margaret and their son home. He was enraged when he found out that Nigel had been kidnapped by the London Coven."

"I forgot about Margaret's first husband. He had a terrible temper just like my father, Sam. I have to admit that I've always been jealous of Margaret because you told me she reminded you of Marilynn Monroe.

"What bothers me is that she was in Kathmandu when you went back again in 2001 with Kathy. Now Margaret's planning to go to Mount Kailash with you and your Hindu friends because she's in love with you!"

"Barbara, I feel sorry for her. She suffered terribly over the death of her son, Christopher, and then had to deal with the kidnapping of eight year old Nigel by Yorg."

"I know you still have strong feelings for Margaret."

"I feel compassion for her because she's grieving the loss of her second husband, Krishna, the psychiatrist. They were married for twelve years before his recent death."

"What's that noise?" asked Barbara.

"It's the kids playing in the yard," said Carl.

"It's also the telephone in the hallway," said Barbara. "Carl, you need to get hearing aids!"

"I'll go answer it while you check on the kids," said Carl, hurrying to pick up the phone.

"Why Kathy, I'm sorry I can't hear you very well. Will you please speak louder?"

"Dad, it's about time you invest in a pair of hearing aids," said Kathy. "Just press the auditory button on your telephone to increase the volume."

"Kathy, I spent a fortune on hearing aids when I was teaching full time at the university," said Carl, pressing the sound button.

"Are you able to hear me now?" asked Kathy.

"Yes, your voice is perfectly clear. I hated those hearing aids. When my students were taking their exams, I could hear their pens scratching on the paper. There was also screeching in my ears from the background noise!"

"Dad, that was fifteen years ago! The hearing aids today are much simpler and easier to adjust."

"I'll look into that once I get back from Nepal, I don't want to lose them in Tibet. They're terribly expensive!"

"Dad, I want to talk to you about the trip. Mom's been worried about you travelling on Qatar Airlines. She told me that last week the Taliban opened an embassy in Doha. She's worried that terrorists will blow up your plane before you land at the airport."

"Kathy, the Taliban had an office in Qatar for a whole year before opening an embassy there. I want you to know that my colleagues Rama and Samitra have travelled to Nepal several times on Qatar Airlines. They told me that the airport is modern and carefully guarded by the military even though runways are still under construction. They told me not to worry about the Taliban being there."

"I thought you might consider taking Indian Airlines," said Kathy. "It would relieve mom of her stress."

"I've already paid for my tickets. I don't intend to turn them in for a refund because I'll lose a large sum of money. Kathy, did mom talk to you about her dreams?"

"She told me all about them this morning when she got stuck in traffic on her way to church. Mom's stressed out about you going to Tibet!"

"Your mother told me about her dreams when she got home from church. I was relieved because she spoke to Father Lorenzo about them after mass. He calmed her down quite a bit. Did you know he was a good friend of Pope Francis? They studied together for the priesthood in Argentina," said Carl.

"Everyone on the faculty at Rush likes the new pope," said Kathy. "I'm so grateful that I'm doing my residency here. It's a wonderful hospital."

"We enjoyed your graduation ceremony last spring. It was memorable. Your mom and I are so proud of you and Greg, because you're now doctors."

"Dad, you won't believe this. I filled out the papers to do an International Rotation in several places. Guess what? I've been accepted to do a month's rotation at Shanta Bhawan Hospital in Nepal."

"You're kidding. That hospital's located in Patan, only a few miles from Kathmandu," said her father.

"I remember going with you to the zoo in Patan, where we saw two female rhinoceros. The zookeeper told us the mother rhinos were angry in captivity because their babies had been taken from them and sent to a zoo in Europe."

"The mother rhinos were tranquilized by using dart guns and then transported from the Chitwaun National Park to a zoo in Patan," said Carl.

"Dad, I just finished reading, 'The Soul of the Rhino' by Hemanta Mishra that he wrote in 1987 and finally got published. He said that King Birendra donated two baby rhinos to our National Zoo in Washington D.C.," said Kathy.

"At that time in order to capture the baby rhinos in Nepal, the mother rhinos were killed because they were dangerous and highly protective of their young," said Carl.

"Gyanendra, the king's older brother, put an end to the practice of killing the mother rhinos when he was managing the national park," continued Carl.

"During the Maoist revolution in Nepal, the rhinoceros and tigers inhabiting the park were no longer protected from poachers," said Kathy. "They killed numerous rhinos, elephants, and tigers and shipped their body parts to China to be used for decorative rugs, ivory figures, or medicinal purposes.

"Hemanta wrote that the Chinese now have farms, where they raise tigers for their body parts like we raise beef cattle. They've also been buying pig farms in the Midwest here and shipping the pork back to China," said Kathy.

"I'll never forget how you and I were kidnapped by those terrorists from India and held for ransom in a medicine cave north of the Tyangboche Monastery. We were treated like captured animals."

"It was Nigel who saved us from being killed by the terrorists," said Carl. "We managed to escape just before the mountain collapsed due to an earthquake."

"I emailed Shanta Bhawan Hospital and received noticed that they switched my rotation to August. I asked them to do it because I knew you were going back to Nepal at that time.

"My only problem is I have to pay for my own flight. Can you lend me the money, Dad? I'd be glad to pay you back once I finish my residency. I'm short on cash this month because I'm having my car fixed."

"I would be glad to pay for your flight. What airline are you taking to Nepal?"

"Mom, told me to take Indian Airlines, but I'd prefer to go with you if there's space on Qatar Airlines," said Kathy. "Mom said you're departing on August 4th and will return on September 2nd."

"Kathy, I'll book your flight right away," said Carl.

"Dad, thank you so much. I can't wait to tell Greg that I'm going back to Nepal with you. He also applied to go with me, but they're sending him to Quito, Ecuador because he speaks Spanish."

"Say hello to Greg for me," said Carl.

"Thanks Dad. I can't wait to go back to Nepal with you. Mom will be pleased because she told me to keep an eye on you so you won't get into trouble."

"I'll talk with you again soon. Bye now," said Carl, hanging up the phone. He took a deep breath before returning to the kitchen where Sammy and Emily were sitting at the table, eating ice cream.

"Who was that on the phone? I hope it wasn't Margaret Porter," said Barbara.

"That's grandpa's old girlfriend," said Emily.

"It wasn't Margaret on the phone, and she's not my old girlfriend. I'm married to your grandma, and I don't fool around with other women," said Carl.

"I wonder if Margaret still looks like Marilyn Monroe?" asked Barbara. "She was grandpa's favorite movie star."

"No she wasn't. "I still tell your Grandma Barbara that

she reminds me of Audrey Hepburn," said Carl

"I don't have a pixie hair style anymore," said, Barbara, running her hand through her hair.

"You're right! Grandma looks like Audrey Hepburn in the movie 'My Fair Lady," said Sammy. "Great Grandma Renee took me and Emily to see the play at Lincolnshire."

"There was a lot of singing and dancing in that play," said Emily. "Grandma Barbara's too old to be singing and dancing. She has to work all week at the museum downtown."

"Carl, you still haven't told us about the telephone call. Are you trying to keep it secret?" asked Barbara, irritated by Emily's comment about her age.

"It was Kathy. She called during her break at Rush to tell me she was accepted to do an international rotation. Guess where she's going?"

"I hope she's not going back to Malawi. I was so worried when she and Greg were in Africa before her graduation last year," said Barbara. "They flew into Nairobi a week before the Islamic terrorists attacked and shut down the airport.

"From Nairobi they went to Tanzania to trek up Mount Kilimanjaro before flying back to Malalwi, where they worked at a primitive hospital for a month. I was worried about their safety due to malaria and Aides," said Barbara.

"They got home a few days before graduating from medical school," said Carl.

"Where is Kathy doing her international rotation?" asked Barbara.

"She'll be doing it in Nepal at Shanta Bhawan Hospital and will go with me to Nepal on Qatar Airlines. She asked me to book a flight for her today," said Carl.

"Oh my God!" shouted Barbara. "What on earth is going on with this crazy family!"

Chapter 9
"Preparing to Leave for Nepal"

On August 4th Carl and Barbara were up early. After breakfast he took Sammy and Emily to the park where they played for a couple of hours while Barbara and Renee went to the morning church service in Elk Grove Village.

After lunch he played checkers with the children on the front porch. He was so pleased when Renee agreed to take them to a movie so that he could have time to change the oil in the car and pack his clothes. He was also hoping to spend some time with Barbara before he left for the airport.

Carl glanced at the clock on the dresser in their bedroom, where he had been packing his suitcase. It was 3:30 when Barbara finally joined him. After putting on her pink night gown, she curled up under the sheet. He quickly removed his clothes and stood naked on the right side of the bed.

"What's wrong?" he asked, scratching his hairy chest before sliding into bed and covering himself with the sheet.

"I didn't sleep very well last night," sighed Barbara, waiting for him to move closer to her.

"Barbara, I love you," he said, kissing her tenderly on the lips. "I'm mesmerized by your Este Lauder perfume."

"You bought it for me last Christmas," she whispered, clinging to him as he stroked the back of her neck.

"You always have that magic touch," he whispered as her fingers caressed his chest and moved down to his navel.

Feeling aroused, Carl kissed her passionately on the lips while his hand touched her breasts and moved down her stomach.

She gasped for breath when he entered her, feeling as if she had been lying in the sunshine under a palm tree before thrust into a waterfall.

After making love, Carl continued kissing Barbara gently on the lips. They both rested for several minutes, before becoming aroused once again, not expecting to hear footsteps in the hallway.

"Did you lock the door?" asked Barbara, alarmed by the voices in the hallway.

"No," said Carl, startled by the knocking on the door. He leapt from the bed and put on his robe while Barbara pulled a blanket over herself.

"Grandpa! Grandma! Are you guys in your bedroom?" yelled Sammy, pushing open the door and entering. He was followed by Emily.

"We just got back from the park," sobbed Emily, rushing toward Barbara's side of the bed. "Grandma, why is your night gown on the floor?"

"I'm going to put it in the laundry in a few minutes," she said. "Emily, tell me why you're crying."

"I'm not going back to Grandma Renee's room!" she pouted. "She likes Sammy because he's a boy, but she doesn't like me because I'm a girl!"

"That's not true! Grandma Renee was reading us a story called 'The Adventures of Tom Sawyer'," said Sammy. "It's kind of like a big comic book for kids."

"It's a condensed book for children," said Carl. "They're very popular these days."

"Emily got mad because she wanted Grandma Renee to read 'The Cat in the Hat' by Dr. Seuss. She started crying, so I brought her to stay with you to calm her down."

"Carl, please see if Renee is all right. It's really time for us to be getting up. Oh my God, it's already 5:30 pm and your grandpa must be at the airport, two hours before his departure. His flight leaves at 8:55 p.m."

"Isn't it kind of late for you and grandpa to be taking a nap," said Sammy, pulling up the shade and glancing out the window. "That crow's still there in the back yard."

"Barbara, I'll check on Renee and then go take my shower," said Carl, heading down the hallway.

He knocked on the bedroom door, where his mother-in-law was staying. She had already been with them for over two weeks.

"I'm coming," said Renee, opening the door. "I'm sorry Emily was so upset. I tried to calm her down. I think she's overtired from going to the movie and then playing on swings in the park."

"Renee, were you planning to come to the airport with the kids in your limousine?" asked Carl.

"No, I'm staying here with them," she said.

"I want to go to the airport to say goodbye to grandpa," said Sammy, entering her bedroom.

"I don't think there's room for you in the Toyota," said Carl. "Sammy, you and Emily are going to stay here with Grandma Renee."

"What's going on here?" asked Barbara, coming into the room wearing a maroon bathrobe and holding Emily's hand.

"I want to go to the airport to say goodbye to grandpa! We might never see him again," said Emily.

"Who told you that?" asked Barbara.

"Grandma Margo told us that grandpa's too old; he'll probably have a heart attack on the mountain and die there," said Emily.

"I hope Grandma Margo's wrong about me dying on Mount Kailash. Please excuse me. I've got to shave and take a shower" said Carl, heading toward the bathroom..

Twenty minutes later Carl returned to the kitchen wearing a corduroy sport coat with a blue shirt and red tie. He was carrying his suitcase and a back pack, which he set down in front of his desk.

Carl poured himself a cup of coffee and sat down at the table to read the "Chicago Tribune." He paused when Barbara entered the kitchen and set down the newspaper.

"Barbara, you look gorgeous in that low cut dress."

"I wore it purposely since I might never see you again," she said. "I hope to God none of my dreams come true!"

"That red silk dress will get attention at my funeral," said Carl, giving her a hug. "We were having a great time in bed this afternoon until we were interrupted."

"Oh Carl, please be careful," she pleaded. "I'll miss you terribly while you're gone. I talked to Father Lorenzo again about those dreams. He told me to ignore them and to pray for your safety while you're travelling."

"Dreams are either wishes or predictions and should be treated with respect," said Carl, "Remember the Biblical story about Joseph being sold into slavery by his brothers. Eventually he became a prominent figure in Egypt because he interpreted the Pharaoh's dreams about the famine."

"Of course I remember the story," said Barbara. "Joseph's whole family moved to Egypt from Israel because of the ten plagues due to climate change."

"Will Kathy's boyfriend, Greg, be bringing her to the airport this evening?" asked Barbara.

"Yes, I believe so. I promise you, I'll be extra careful on the long road to Mount Kailash," said Carl, kissing her tenderly on the lips. "The guides always bring oxygen tanks along in case of problems at high altitude."

"I'll be going to mass every day and praying for your safety," said Barbara.

"I'm very jealous that you'll be seeing Father Lorenzo while I'm gone," said Carl.

"Carl, he's almost 80 years old," sighed Barbara. "I'm still jealous because you'll be travelling with Margaret Porter all the way to Tibet. I suppose she'll be on the flight from Chicago with you along with your Hindu colleagues."

"No, she's coming to Nepal on Indian Airlines from London. We better get going. It's getting late" said Carl, pausing to listen to the footsteps coming down the stairs.

"Here come the kids!" said Barbara.

"Grandpa! Grandpa! We came to say goodbye," said Sammy, giving Carl a hug.

"Good bye Grandpa! I'm hungry," said Emily. "I want to play in the back yard after we eat."

"I'm taking the kids to Mc Donald's for dinner," said Renee, entering the kitchen. "Carl, I hope you have a safe trip to Nepal and Tibet."

"Thanks, Renee. I'll be travelling to Tibet with thirty-three Hindus. Most of them are followers of Shiva," said Carl. "They believe that Shiva is the Creator, Preserver, and Destroyer."

"Some of my Hindu friends believe Brahma's the Creator, Vishnu's the Sustainer, and Shiva's the Destroyer," said Renee "Hinduism is too complicated for me."

"We're leaving now for McDonald's. It's only a couple of blocks from here and we're going to walk there," said Renee. "Come on kids. Let's go."

Carl gave Renee and the grandchildren hugs before picking up his suitcase and back pack. He left the kitchen with Barbara and went directly to the Honda, parked in front of the garage.

A few minutes later they were heading down Arlington Heights Road toward the airport with Carl driving.

"I'm worried about Renee watching the kids while I'm at the museum," said Barbara. "She told me that my father, Sam, wants to bulldoze our house and build a new one while you're gone. He's so annoying these days even though he's been sober for several years."

"Mark told me that he and Sam get along quite well. Did he tell you about his new girlfriend?"

"No, I didn't even know Mark had a new girlfriend," said Barbara, removing her rosary from her purse and making the sign of the cross.

"What's her name?" asked Barbara.

"Her name is Clarissa, and she has a daughter in the fifth grade. Mark moved in with her after living with Sam and Renee for over a year."

"Oh, my God! We might have them living with us for a year if Mark's divorce is finalized," she said.

"Mark told me he wanted the kids to move in with him and Clarissa before school starts in Philadelphia."

"I guess Corrine's in bad shape. She's always been fragile. I'm worried about Mark's drinking. He told me not to worry because he was planning to go to rehab for a week before going to the divorce court."

Chapter 10
"Departure from O'Hare"

"The airport's really crowded," said Carl, pulling behind a limousine at Qatar Airlines and parking. He handed the car keys to Barbara. It's already almost seven o'clock. The plane leaves at 8:50 p.m.

"We're only allowed to park long enough to get the luggage," said Barbara. "The traffic's awful at this time!"

After Carl removed his suitcase and backpack from the trunk, he set them down and gave Barbara a hug.

While kissing her, he paused as a taxi pulled up behind the Toyota with the driver beeping the horn. The door of the taxi flung open and Kathy came running toward them.

"Mom, Dad, it's so good to see you" she said, giving them each a hug while her boyfriend approached them, with her luggage.

"Greg, don't tell me you're going with Kathy to Nepal?" asked Barbara.

"I may come to Nepal later if I can switch my rotation from Quito, Ecuador. I better get going or I'll be late for work. I'm on the evening shift at the hospital this week," said Greg, heading toward the taxi.

"Please move along," interrupted a stout female guard in a uniform. "You're not allowed to park here and talk!"

Greg rolled down the window and shouted, "Carl, have a great trip to Mount Kailash! Kathy, be sure to send me an email every day like you promised."

"I love you Greg!" shouted Kathy, rushing toward the

open window of the taxi to give him a final kiss.

"Move along or I'll give you a ticket!" snapped the female guard.

"Carl, you better get going before I get a ticket," said Barbara, wiping the tears from her eyes. Her hands were trembling as she held the keys to the car.

Kathy frowned at the guard as the taxi pulled away. She hurried toward Barbara and said, "Don't worry Mom about those dreams. I'm sure dad will be careful when he climbs Mount Kailash."

"Father Lorenzo told me to ignore my dreams," said Barbara, giving Carl a farewell kiss.

"Hey! You there in the red dress! I asked you to move your car five minutes ago! And you're still here talking. Move it right now or I'll give you a ticket!"

"Stella, what's going on here?" asked a police officer, patrolling the entrance of Qatar Airlines.

"These people have been parked here too long!" she shouted, scowling at them.

Barbara hurried toward the Toyota and rolled down the window shouting, "Carl, be careful trekking in Tibet!" "Kathy, have a wonderful trip working in Nepal."

Carl waved to Barbara as she entered the stream of traffic. He turned his head toward Stella who was talking loudly to the police officer.

"Who does that woman think she is wearing a low cut dress?" said Stella.

"That woman's my mother," said Kathy. "She wears that red dress because she likes playing the role of Scarlett O'Hare from 'Gone with the Wind'. She purposely comes to the airport and holds up traffic because the airport was named after her Irish ancestors!"

"That's ridiculous!" snapped Stella. "Vivian Leigh has

been dead for years. "She was already washed out when she played Blanche in 'Street Car Named Desire'."

"Your name, Stella, reminds me of Marlon Brando's wife," said Kathy. "She was pregnant when her husband raped Blanche."

"I'm going to write you a ticket for loitering and insulting me because of my weight!" snapped Stella, reaching for her pen from behind her ear and a ticket pad from her hip pocket.

"Don't waste your time arguing, Stella," said the police officer. "She's only teasing you. Please go over to that limousine and tell the driver to move along."

"He's been parked there seven minutes," said Stella, glancing at her watch. She bolted toward the limousine, waving the ticket pad at the driver, determined to write a ticket this time.

Carl and Kathy entered the terminal through the double doors into a crowded room where long lines of passengers were moving slowly in the roped areas toward several check in-counters. Removing his passport and their tickets from his coat pocket, Carl, gave Kathy her ticket. "Rama and Samitra are checking in at the other counter," said Carl, waving to them.

"I can't wait to meet them, Dad. You talk about them all the time."

"We've been planning this trip for twelve years."

"Mom talked to me on the phone for an hour when Sammy and Emily moved in with you guys a few weeks ago," said Kathy.

"I'm concerned about your mother's health and the future of the kids," said Carl.

"Dad, I don't blame you for being concerned. I've been worried about mom and her dreams. She's finally calmed down after talking with Father Lorenzo. He's the priest that married Mark and Corrine and baptized Sammy and Emily."

"Kathy, how do you deal with stress when you feel overwhelmed during your residency?"

"When I get stressed out from working with patients, I go to the chapel to meditate during my lunch hour. I calm down after fifteen or twenty minutes.

"After the death of a patient, I leave the building and go for a long walk. The exercise helps me to relax," said Kathy, handing her passport and ticket to the clerk at the desk.

"Good evening," said the clerk. "You'll be on the plane for 12 hours before landing at Doha Qatar. A bus will take you to the air conditioned terminal. The airport is under construction and is a half hour ride before you disembark."

"I would like to sit near my father, Carl Brecht, and his friends, Rama and Samitra Narayan," said Kathy, watching the clerk put a tag on her luggage and stamp her passport.

"Your father and his friends are seated on the left side of the 747-Jumbo Jet. There are a few seats available in the back of the plane across from your father."

"Thank you so much," said Kathy, sighing with relief.

"I've read about you in the Chicago Tribune," said the clerk to Carl. "You're an anthropologist from the University of Chicago. There was an article in the paper about you and your daughter, being kidnapped by terrorists in Nepal some years ago after the assassination of the Royal Family."

"We were held hostage in the Himalayas but managed to escape. We hurried down the mountain pass and boarded a plane that took off just before an earthquake struck the area," said Kathy.

"While looking out the window of our plane we saw hundreds of villagers fleeing from the debris coming toward them from the collapse of the mountains," said Carl.

"The monastery in that area was spared in spite of the earthquake," said the clerk.

"You certainly have a good memory," said Carl, glancing at her name tag. "Joshi Shah, do you happen to be a relative of the royal family of Nepal?"

"No, Dr. Brecht. My husband and I are members of the Hindu Temple of Greater Chicago. That's where we met Rama and Samitra Narayan. We see them every Sunday there and during the Hindu holidays," said Joshi.

"I often go there to celebrate the holidays with them." said Carl.

"I hope you will have a wonderful flight. Rama and Samitra told me that you were going on a pilgrimage in Tibet with them at the temple last week. Will you be going with them, Kathy?"

"No, I'll be doing an international rotation at Shanta Bhawan Hospital for a month in Patan, Nepal."

"Have a great trip," said Joshi, handing them their passports and boarding passes.

"Thanks so much," said Carl, hurrying down the hallway with Kathy toward the security check point.

After walking through an electronic scanner, they retrieved their belongings, continuing down the crowded corridor past restaurants and shops until they reached the gate where Carl introduced Kathy to his friends.

"Once again we get to meet your beautiful daughter, Kathy," said Rama Narayan. "Your father showed me your graduation picture from medical school. We haven't seen you since you graduated from high school."

"How did you get excused from your residency at Rush?" asked Samitra.

"I filled out papers for an international rotation several months ago for Shanta Bhawan Hospital," said Kathy.

"I was admitted there when I came down with bronchitis after returning to Katmandu with Rama in 2006," said Samitra. "It was a difficult time to be in Nepal because of the Maoist Revolution."

"That hospital was founded by Lutheran missionaries in the 1950's" said Rama. "I'm sure you'll enjoy working there, Kathy. It's the best hospital in the Kathmandu Valley."

Carl mentioned that his son, Mark, was born at Shining Hospital in Pokhara, which was staffed by missionary doctors and nurses from Scotland.

Everyone paused due to an announcement over the loud speaker.

"Will all passengers on Qatar Airlines 0992 begin boarding at this time," announced the attendant on the microphone. "Please have your boarding passes and passports ready. We will be departing at 8:55 p.m."

Chapter 11
"The Flight to Doha Qatar"

Within a few minutes, Carl and Kathy were following Rama and Samitra down the ramp to the entrance of the plane.

Most of the passengers on the flight were Qatari citizens heading home after vacationing with their families in Chicago or university students leaving for the summer.

Upon entering the jumbo jet, Rama and Samitra paused in the aisle, waiting for the passengers ahead of them to place their belonging into the compartments above the seats.

They were finally seated on the left side of the plane a few rows from the back. Carl arrived, taking his seat next to his friends while Kathy sat across the aisle from him.

As the passengers moved down the aisle to their seats in the rear of the plane, Carl chatted with Rama while Samitra glanced out the window at the luggage being loaded.

"Carl, since we're arriving in Nepal a few days before we leave for Mt. Kailash, we should visit the temples and shrines because August is the month of Hindu and Buddhist holidays," said Rama.

"I would like to see the Royal Palace because it's now an enormous museum," said Carl.

"The entrance fee is 500 rupees for international tourist but only 250 rupees for Chinese visitors, and 125 for Nepalese," said Rama.

"What's the exchange rate for the rupee?" asked Carl.

"Right now it is 95 rupees to a dollar," said Rama.
"I'd like to visit the Buddhist Shrine, Swayambunath, because a friend of mine, Dorothy Mierrow, built a museum on the university campus in Pokhara, where she taught geography and geology for many years.

"Dorothy died in Colorado Springs in 2000, where she was cremated. Her ashes were flown to Nepal and taken to Swayambunath, where Peace Corps volunteers, returning to Nepal for a reunion, held a memorial service at that shrine to express their condolences.

"After chanting prayers by Buddhist monks, Dorothy's ashes were scattered into the nearby Vishnu Mati River," said Carl.

"It was must have been quite a ceremony," said Samitra. "I wish we had time to visit her museum, but for now I'd be pleased to see the Royal Palace."

"I've always wanted to see the interior of the Royal Palace," said Rama. "It was built by the Shah Dynasty on 35 acres of land in the center of Kathmandu.

"A high fence surrounds the property where fruit bats hang from the palm trees like black umbrellas. The bats sleep during the day and come out at night before leaving the palace grounds," added Rama.

"The Shahs hired European architects to design their palace and the other buildings on the grounds, but I believe Newari craftsmen built them," continued Rama.

"Will all passengers please fasten your seat belts as we prepare for takeoff," announced the hostess, going over the flight rules about the location of oxygen masks, flotation devices and exits.

"Every seat is equipped with a TV set, and a map to follow as we travel from Chicago to Qatar. There are also classic and current films to entertain you during the flight.

"While travelling, all passengers will be served three meals in addition to drinks and snacks. You have signed up for vegan, semi-vegetarian, or meals with meat.

"Please note the locations of rest rooms in the back, middle, and front of the plane. If you need a blanket or assistance contact a flight attendant. We are now ready to depart. I hope you'll have a wonderful trip to Doha Qatar."

"Dad, I never expected to be travelling with you to Nepal again," said Kathy from across the aisle. "I wish I could go with you and your friends to Tibet."

"I'm sure you'll enjoy your rotation at Shanta Bhawan Hospital in Patan. You'll be dealing with patients who have high altitude illnesses and tropical diseases."

"I'll love being back in Nepal. I called Grandpa and Grandma Brecht to say goodbye.

"How are they doing?" asked Carl.

"They were both surprised that I was travelling with you. They're also worried about Mark and Corrine getting a divorce," said Kathy.

"I took Sammy and Emily to visit them last week," said Carl. "We enjoyed spending the afternoon on the farm."

"They don't have farm animals anymore, but their barn is still there. Mark and I worked the whole weekend painting it about ten years ago," said Kathy.

"I took Sammy and Emily up the ladder into the hayloft last week. They were startled by the pigeons cooing in the rafters," said Carl.

"I'll never forget playing with the kittens in the hayloft," said Kathy. "I was scared to death when the mother cat returned with a mouse dangling from her mouth."

"We should send them an email when we get to Kathmandu," said Carl.

"I had a rough day working in the Emergency Room

nonstop for 12 hours and then going home to pack for the trip. I'd like to take a nap because I'm exhausted."

"Go right ahead," said Carl, reaching into his satchel and removing a printout. "Rama, I need to get caught up with the history of the Maoist revolution."

"My wife and I were in Nepal during the peak of the revolution when there was marching and protesting against the monarchy and the Congress Party.

"The Maoists followed the philosophy of Mao Tse-tung, whose slogan was that political power is in the barrel of a gun," said Rama.

"It says here that Prachanda was the Chairman of the Communist Party, founded back in 1994," said Carl. "His real name is Pushpa Kamal Dahal"

"I remember when he launched the revolution known as 'The Nepalese People's War' in 1996. His army steadily gained control of the rural areas in the mountains," said Rama. "The Civil War escalated when the Maoists attacked the Nepalese Army for the first time after the massacre of the royal family in 2001 by Prince Dipendra.

"The people didn't like King Gyanendra ruling the country. He summoned the Nepalese Army to attack Maoist troops in the rural areas.

"Numerous Gurkha soldiers deserted the Royal Nepalese Army and joined the Maoists to train soldiers to fight against the monarchy," said Rama.

"Women and children were also conscripted into the 'Communist Party. Some were trained as combatants while others became couriers, travelling with messages to the districts, controlled by the Maoists.

"They blamed the Shah Dynasty and the wealthy landlords for poverty in the rural area. Their goal was to get rid of the monarchy and establish a new constitution.

"Maoists went to the schools and villages in the mountains and signed up students to join them, which eventually led to massive protests and uprisings, involving a million demonstrators in Kathmandu," said Rama.

"This general strike caused the shutdown of schools and business in the three cities of the valley. The violent clash of the protestors against the Nepalese Army eventually led to the surrender of the monarchy," said Rama.

"Carl, a lot has happened since Prachandra, the Maoist Leader, signed the peace agreement in September 2006," said Rama, reaching into his satchel and removing his copy of "The Predictable Rise of a Red Bourgeoisie: The End of a Mythical Nepalese Maoist Revolution."

"What refreshments would you like?" interrupted a flight attendant, pausing in the aisle with her cart.

"I'll have orange juice and peanuts," said Samitra, yawning and stretching her arms. "If you guys want to continue the discussion that's OK, but I'm going to watch a movie on my screen."

Chapter 12
"An Emergency on the Flight"

"Rama, how's your family doing in Kathmandu? It's been a few years since you've been back," asked Carl, as the flight attendant set down tomato juice and a bag of peanuts on his tray.

"My brother, Prasan, has been teaching English at Tribuwan University. He complains about tension among his students due to the unstable economy in Nepal. Most of them want to leave the country after they complete their bachelors' degrees. They usually go to India or China for further education. Some travel to Moscow, while others to London. Very few will get visas to come to the United States unless they are engineers or medical doctors.

"I have a nephew named Shankar who has been studying at the University of Beijing. He's been there three years and will graduate as a doctor in May."

"How does he like living in China?" asked Carl. "It must be quite a change for him."

"He's speaks fluent English and has been studying Chinese with a tutor," said Rama.

"You must be proud of him," said Carl, noticing that Kathy was asleep across the aisle.

"Beijing is a terribly polluted city," said Rama. "The Chinese government made an effort to clean it up for the Olympic Games some years ago."

"I was amazed by the grand opening of the Olympics in

China," said Carl. "My wife, Barbara, and I watched the performances with awe. The music, dancing, and the costumes were amazing."

"The Chinese went out of their way to impress the entire world with their thriving economy and talented culture," said Rama.

"Prior to the games in 2008 the Olympic Torch was lighted and the 85,000 mile worldwide torch relay began. When the torch bearers reached California, there was violent protesting by Tibetans.

"The Chinese government was angry with President George Bush for giving the Dalai Lama 'The Congressional Gold Medal for World Peace,' two weeks before the relays," said Rama.

"The Dalai Lama came to Washington to receive that award stating that violence breeds violence," said Carl. "He didn't approve of the bloody revolts taking place in Chinese occupied Tibet."

"The Tibetans were enraged due to the immigration of thousands of Han Chinese to Lhasa, who opened numerous shops and were living in new apartment buildings built for them by the government," said Rama.

"A week after the Dalai Lama received his award, thousands of Tibetans rioted in Lhasa, setting fire to 1000 Chinese shops and businesses according to Radio Free Asia, Voice of Tibet."

"This was a reaction not only to the immigration of the Han Chinese but to the One Child-Rule involving compulsory sterilization and abortions performed on Tibetan women, who didn't conform to the law imposed upon them," said Carl.

"During the riot armed guards killed 80 Tibetans and arrested 5000 protestors, which led to the government suspending tourism to Tibet indefinitely.

"If you want to take a leap back into history, the violence at Tiananmen Square in 1989 was even worse," said Carl, pausing. "Do you hear that noise?"

"Help me! Help me!" screamed a woman, startling the passengers, who had been watching their TV screens.

"Something's wrong with her," said Samitra. "I can hear children crying."

All heads turned toward the woman from India with long black hair. She was trembling in the aisle, wearing a purple silk sari that was wet and clinging to her body.

"Help me! Someone please help me?" she screamed, as a flight attendant approached her.

"May I have your attention please. If there is a doctor aboard this flight, will he please stand up in the aisle. There's a woman in need of your assistance!

"Will all other passengers remain seated except for those sitting in the last two rows of the plane in front of the kitchen and the rear restrooms. We would like you to come to the front of the plane with your belongings. You'll have seats in the first class section of the plane for the rest of the flight."

"Kathy! Kathy! Wake up!" shouted Carl, reaching for his daughter's arm and shaking it.

"What's the matter?" she asked yawning, puzzled by the grumbling passengers from the rear of the plane, going up the aisle with their belongings.

"This is an emergency! If there is a doctor aboard this flight, please step into the aisle," requested the hostess.

Kathy unfastened her seat belt and stepped into the aisle, removing her medical bag from the compartment above her seat as a flight attendant approached her.

"You must be Doctor Kathy Brecht. I saw your name on the passenger list. That hysterical Indian woman won't tell me what's wrong with her," said the flight attendant.

"Come with me please" she said, leading Kathy up the aisle toward the screaming woman.

"Are you a doctor?" gasped the woman, introducing herself as Shanti Sharma.

"Yes, I'm a doctor," said Kathy. "Please tell me what I can do to help you," she said, reaching for the stethoscope from her kit to listen to Shanti's heartbeat.

"Our mommy's not feeling well," cried six year old Lakshmi. "I want my daddy."

"She's been having morning sickness every day." said her ten year old son, Ganapati.

"Please Mrs. Sharma, tell the Doctor Brecht what's wrong!" pleaded the attendant.

"Just call me Kathy," she insisted.

"Kathy, I'm…I'm going to have a baby," whispered Shanti. "I'm seven months pregnant and my water just broke. I'm having labor pains!."

"Is there a place where Shanti can lie down on the plane?" asked Kathy, glancing at her watch, noticing it was already past 10:30 pm. "She needs clean clothing, sheets, and a blanket."

"We've already vacated the last two rows in the rear of the plane. The arm rests from the seats have been removed so that Mrs. Sharma can lie down. There's an attendant making up a bed for her right now. I'm so relieved that she's a small woman because the seats are so narrow," said the flight attendant. "I'll take Shanti to the rear of the plane."

"Please ask my father to come here to watch Shanti's children. He's sitting across the aisle from where I was seated, reading a book."

Within a few minutes Carl came up the aisle carrying the book, "Bones of the Tiger" with him. He paused while

Kathy introduced him to Shanti's children.

"My father's name is Carl Brecht. He'll tell you stories about tigers in the jungles of Nepal, while I take care of your mother in the back of the plane."

"I want to see my mommy," cried Lakshmi.

"We want to be with her!" shouted Ganapati.

"Your mother's having a baby," said Kathy. "She's at the back of the plane, where I'll help deliver her baby."

"What does deliver mean?" asked Lakshmi.

"It means helping your Mommy so that the baby can come out of her tummy," said Kathy. "After the baby is born, my father will take you to them!"

"Oh…Oh...here come's more pain," screamed Shanti.

Kathy rushed down the aisle to the back of the plane where Shanti was moaning from the contractions.

The flight attendant held up a blanket while Kathy helped Shanti remove her wet sari, replacing it with a loose white gown. After injecting her with a sedative, she helped her to lie down in the middle row, made into a bed with sheets and pillows.

"Take deep breaths when you are having contractions," said Kathy, holding her hand.

"What can I do to help?" asked the flight attendant.

"You could bring my father and Shanti's kids a children's book and some refreshments," said Kathy, observing that Shanti's labor was intense.

"Keep taking deep breathes and try to relax between contractions," she said, holding Shanti's hand, trying to calm her down. Within five minutes the sedative was working, and she stopped screaming.

After staying with Shanti for a half hour, Kathy saw the head of the baby emerging. She encouraged Shanti to keep pushing as much as possible while she pulled the infant from the womb with a forceps, placing the crying baby on the mother's stomach.

The umbilical cord continued to pulsate, supplying the new born infant with oxygen until she began breathing normally. Kathy clamped the cord on the belly before cutting it.

"How is my baby doing?" asked Shanti, feeling exhausted and breathing heavily.

"Your daughter's doing just fine," said Kathy, clearing the infant's nose, mouth, and then drying the baby. "Have you decided on a name?"

"My husband and I agreed to call her Parvati," said Shanti. "How much does she weigh?"

"I'm estimating that she's about five pounds," said Kathy. "I'll hand Parvati to you in a few minutes, but first I want to give her antiseptic eye drops to prevent an infection because of bacteria in the birth canal."

"Please hold her for about a half hour until she gets used to you before trying to breast feed," said Kathy, wrapping the baby in a blanket and handing her to the mother.

"Thank you," sighed Shanti. "She's so tiny and delicate."

"Parvati's a beautiful name," said Kathy. "What part of India are you from?"

"I was born and raised in New Delhi. I was working as a secretary in the embassy where I met my husband. After we were married we moved to Nepal where he was stationed at the Indian Embassy."

Shanti calmed down as she began talking about raising her family in Kathmandu. Within thirty minutes, she was nursing her baby before falling asleep from exhaustion.

Kathy reached for the infant and wrapped her in another blanket taking Parvati down the aisle to show to Shanti's children. They were delighted to see the new born baby while the passengers applauded.

Lakshmi and Ganapati followed Kathy with the baby back down the aisle to see their mother. However, Shanti was sound asleep. The children whispered quietly to each other for a few minutes and then said a prayer in Hindi before returning to their seats where Carl was waiting to read them another story.

He listened to them talk about their baby sister for quite a while before reading them, "Peter Rabbit and Benjamin Bunny".

Kathy sat in the vacant seat across from Shanti, finally handing the sleeping baby to a flight attendant, who arrived with refreshments.

Taking a deep breath, Kathy sat down and turned on the TV to watch the black and white film, "Night of the Iguana" staring Ava Gardener, Deborah Kerr, and Richard Burton. After gulping down a glass of lemonade and munching on salted peanuts, she fell asleep, weary from the stress of delivering the baby on the plane.

Chapter 13
"Continuing with the Flight"

Early the next morning around 6:30 a.m., Carl woke up after a restless night. He patiently read "Horton Hatches the Egg," a second time to Lakshmi and Ganapati while the flight attended handed the children their breakfast trays.

"Mayzie isn't a very nice bird. She's mean to Horton. She told him to 'Get out of my nest and get out of my tree'," said Lakshmi, sipping her orange juice.

"Who ever heard of an elephant bird," said Ganapati, finishing his cereal. "That's not a true story. May we go see our Mom and baby sister now? I want to talk to her this time."

"What's the baby's name? I forgot," said Lakshmi.

"Mom told me if she had a boy she would name him Jaya, but if she had a girl she'd call her Parvati."

"Those are good names," said Carl, rising from his seat to stretch. "By the way what is your dad's name?"

"His name is Govinda Sharma. He works at the Indian Embassy in Kathmandu," said Ganapati.

"Timi Nepali bhasa bolnu sakcha?" Do you speak Nepali?" asked Carl.

"Hami dui jana Nepali bhasha bolnu sakchau, We both speak the Nepali language," said Ganapati.

"Where do you go school?" asked Carl.

"I go to St. Xavier's and my sister goes to St. Mary's," said Ganapati. "We both get very good grades."

"Let's check on your mother," said Carl, leading the way

down the aisle. He spoke softly to the children. "If she's still asleep we won't wake her up. We'll take a peek at the baby and then go back to our seats."

When Carl came down the aisle with the children, he paused to speak with his friends.

"I'll help you with them," said Samitra, coming into the aisle from her seat next to Rama.

"You've been with them all night," said Rama. "Carl, you need to take a break."

After the children were introduced to Samitra, she took them to the rear of the plane while Carl sat down in her vacant seat.

"I'm so grateful that Kathy's travelling with us. She's the only doctor on this flight," said Carl.

"Kathy told us that Shanti will be taken to a hospital after we land in Qatar. Her husband Govinda Sharma has been contacted at the Indian Embassy in Nepal and will arrive on a private jet to meet his wife and children. He'll be waiting for them when our flight arrives at Doha."

"That will be a great relief for Kathy," said Carl, taking a deep breath. "Where were we? Tell me little more about the revolution."

"Carl, 'The Communist Party of Nepal (Maoist)' was only in power for a brief period of time before Prachanda resigned as Prime Minister in 2009. After a few more years of negotiations with the armies, Prachandra and the Maoists reentered the government and resolved the conflict.

"The Maoists soldiers were given resettlement grants so that they could return to civilian life after being inactive in barrack camps for two years," said Rama.

"The soldiers claimed that 500 rupees were taken out of each month's salary and put into their saving accounts by the Maoists, although the party didn't give them back their money," said Carl.

"The Maoist leaders were criticized for living in mansions and sending their children to the best boarding schools in Kathmandu." said Rama, interrupted by the stewardess arriving with her cart.

"Here are your vegetarian meals," she said, handing them their trays. "I hope you enjoy the fruit salad, rice and lentils. What would you like to drink?"

After giving them each a bottle of water, she departed while they continued talking and eating.

"Why was King Gyanendra so unpopular? I read that he had done a lot to preserve the wildlife in the Chitwaun National Park before taking office," said Carl.

"Gyanendra was unpopular because of his son, Paras, who was involved in two hit-and-run car accidents that caused the death of a child and a Nepalese singer. Paras was never arrested or punished for the crimes," said Rama, noticing his wife walking past them with Shanti's children as they returned to their seats.

"When the Maoists gained controlled of the parliament, the king's status was reduced to a figure head. After he was removed from the palace, the 200 year Shah Dynasty came to an end," said Rama.

"Have the Nepalese people recovered from the chaos of the revolution?" asked Carl.

"In spite of the revolution, the people and their culture are basically intact. The foundation of our society is rooted in the importance of the family and our ethnic heritage, including tolerance of different religions. Most of our citizens are Hindu or Buddhist. We also have a large number of Nepalese Christians, Moslems and Jews," said Rama.

"Please excuse me for a few minutes. I want to check on Kathy in the rear of the plane," said Carl leaving.

"Kathy, how are you doing?" he asked sitting down next to her.

"I fell asleep while watching 'Hunger Games, Catching Fire,' with Jennifer Lawrence, playing Katniss. I was impressed by the special effects, especially her red dress bursting into flames while she was driving the chariot."

"How are your patients doing across the aisle?" he asked.

"Shanti's sound asleep with the baby in her arms," said Kathy. "I'm still worried about mom."

"Barbara's a lot better now that your grandmother's helping her with the children. She and Renee are planning to take the children to Springfield to tour the Lincoln Museum," said Carl. "They also will be visiting Lincoln's house before driving to New Salem to see the long cabins.

"Mom said they'd be leaving as soon as Renee's valet arrives with her limousine from Philadelphia," said Carl.

"Barbara's not so uptight about her dreams anymore," said Carl.

"She's calmed down quite a bit since she's been attending mass regularly and talking her problems over with Father Lorenzo," said Kathy.

"Dad, please sit down and watch 'The Great Gatsby' staring, Leonardo DiCaprio. Even though the reviews weren't that great, I wanted to see the movie when it first came out but I was too busy working at the hospital."

"Sure, I'll join you," said Carl, sitting down next to her.

While Kathy was searching the screen for the film, she said, "Dad, please tell me a little bit about the plot."

"In the opening scene Nick Caraway is being treated for alcoholism in a psychiatric hospital during the Roaring Twenties when boot legging was so common. His doctor encourages him to write about how he became addicted to alcohol. Nick informs him that he began to drink heavily after moving from the Midwest to New York where he met Jay Gatsby on Long Island during the Roaring Twenties."

"Dad you go ahead and watch the movie," said Kathy. "Please excuse me. Here comes the hostess with a tray that I ordered for Shanti. I need to hold the baby while she eats."

"We'll talk again later," said Carl. He continued to watch the film. Twenty minutes later he glanced across the aisle at his daughter, who was busy changing a diaper, while Shanti was finishing her meal.

Fifteen minutes later, Carl noticed that Shanti was having trouble breathing. A few minutes later a flight attendant came down the aisle with an oxygen tank.

Carl continued watching the film. Eventually Tom Buchanan was outraged when he discovered that his wife, Daisy, was having a love affair with Jay Gatsby, ignoring the fact that he was having a love affair with Myrtle, a married woman living in the Valley of Ashes.

This time the film was interrupted by the arrival of the stewardess with refreshments. He paused noticing that Shanti and the baby were now on oxygen and that Kathy was taking her blood pressure.

Carl paused to listen to the announcement over the loud speaker by the cabin stewardess. "Will all passengers please fasten their seat belts because we'll be landing at Doha Qatar in twenty minutes. Please remain seated until the fight comes to a halt.

"After landing we are asking everyone to remain seated because of our medical emergency. Our pilots and staff want to congratulate Doctor Kathy Brecht for delivering a baby girl on this flight. We also wish to congratulate Parvati's mother, Shanti Sharma, for her bravery.

"Upon arrival at Doha Qatar, please set your watches for 6:25 p.m. Remember the date will be August 5th. A team of medical assistants will come aboard to take Mrs. Sharma and her three children off the plane to an ambulance, waiting to take them to a hospital in Doha.

"After departing from the plane, three buses will be waiting to take you to the terminal," said the hostess. "I hope you'll enjoy your stay in Doha Qatar. For those in transit, have a wonderful flight to Kathmandu."

Carl glanced over his shoulder across the aisle at his daughter, disconnecting the oxygen tank from Shanti while a stewardess was holding her baby.

Turning back to the movie, Carl watched Daisy driving Jay Gatsby's yellow convertible late at night. They had both been drinking heavily at the hotel in New York. While speeding past the filling station in The Valley of Ashes, Daisy accidently struck down Myrtle waiting on the side of the road and killed her. After arriving at the mansion, Jay called the police assuming responsibility for the accident.

As the plane landed at Doha's airport, Carl finished the film, disturbed by Gatsby's funeral. After turning off the TV, he glanced across the aisle at his daughter, waiting for the paramedics to arrive with a stretcher.

"Dad, please bring my suitcase to the bus," said Kathy. "I'm going with Shanti and her baby to the hospital in the ambulance. I'll come back to the terminal once they get settled down."

Carl watched the medical assistants coming down the aisle with a stretcher. Within minutes, they were carrying Shanti, followed by Kathy carrying the baby in her arms.

Passengers crowded the aisles, gathering their hand bags and possessions from the upper compartments and then slowly moving toward the exit.

Chapter 14
"A Crisis upon Landing"

Carl was eager to leave the plane after the twelve hour flight from O'Hare. He inched his way up the congested aisle with a suitcase in each hand. Upon reaching the exit everyone was complaining about the 95 degree heat and the heavy humidity.

While following them down a flight of metal stairs, Carl was overwhelmed by the change in temperature and the fact that it was dark outside.

In the distance he could see Kathy standing behind the ambulance, wiping her forehead with a handkerchief. Her whole body was illuminated by the lights of a limousine arriving and parking behind the ambulance.

"Dad, I'm just exhausted," said Kathy, sighing as he approached her with their luggage. She glanced at the stream of passengers, murmuring about the heat as they boarded the three air-conditioned buses.

"How's Shanti doing with her baby?" asked Carl.

"They both needed oxygen as soon they got settled in the ambulance because of the heat. Her children were crying because their mother was gasping for breath on the stretcher while coming down the metal stairs.

"I was right behind them carrying the baby. Shanti begged me to go with her in the ambulance to Women's Hospital," said Kathy. "Here comes Shanti's husband. He's going to follow us to the hospital in the limousine."

"Hello Doctor Brecht," said Govinda Sharma, hurrying

toward them with his children. "I want to thank you for reading to Ganapati and Lakshmi on the plane. They asked me to order a copy of 'Horton Hatches the Egg,' from Amazon as soon as we get back to Kathmandu."

"Just call me Carl," he said shaking Govinda's hand.

"I'm so grateful that Kathy was on the plane and agreed to accompany my wife and our baby to the hospital."

"Carl, I hope that you and Kathy will come to visit us when we return to Kathmandu. I already gave her my telephone number at the Indian Embassy and our home address."

"I looked up Women's Hospital in Doha on my cell phone. The Neonatal Intensive Care Unit is highly rated," said Kathy.

"Carl, here's my cell phone number and the hospital's if you need to contact us," said Govinda, handing it to him..

"Excuse me," interrupted the Qatari driver of the ambulance. "Doctor Kathy, we must leave now for the hospital. It's about a half hour drive from here."

"Dad, I'll see you later," said Kathy, giving him a kiss on the cheek and entering the ambulance.

"It was a pleasure meeting you Carl," said Govinda, hurrying with his two children toward the limousine.

After watching the vehicles depart, Carl headed toward the first bus with the luggage and tried to enter, but every seat and the aisle were bulging with passengers. He headed towards the second bus, which was filled. He finally stood in line for a few minutes before boarding the third bus.

By the time he got inside, all the seats were taken. Carl stood in the aisle, holding a hand grip. At the opposite end of the bus, he saw Rama and Samitra, standing with their luggage on the floor next to them.

The passengers were still murmuring about the heat as

the air conditioned bus departed. As they drove, there was a great deal of vacant space because the airport was under construction for miles.

As they sped along the rugged dirt road, Carl glanced out the window, noticing a brick wall enclosed the airport. On the opposite side of the wall there were glowing lights from the city and palm trees wavering in the breeze.

He was amazed at the number of buses whizzing past them, loaded with departing passengers. There were also huge oil tankers passing them at a slower pace.

"Is this your first trip to Qatar?" asked a young man standing next to Carl. "My name is Yahwah. It's Arabic for Jehovah."

"I'm Carl Brecht and it's my first trip to Qatar. I'm travelling with Hindu friends to Nepal. We have a six hour wait at the terminal before departure."

"It's only a half hour ride to the international terminal," said Yahwah. "We have a lot of Nepalese laborers here in Qatar. Several of them work as janitors in the airport."

"Where is Qatar on the map and what is the current population?" asked Carl.

"Qatar is a peninsula south of Saudi Arabia, surrounded by the Persian Gulf. It's a sovereign Arab country with 1.8 million people," said Yahwah.

"Where are those oil tankers going?" asked Carl.

"Those oil trucks that you see passing the bus are heading toward the gulf for shipment to other countries. Our little country has the third largest natural gas and oil reserves. It's the richest country per capita in the Arab World. We have 278,000 Qatari citizens living here, the rest are foreign workers. By the way I'm a business man working for the petroleum company. What do you do for a living?"

"I'm a retired anthropologist working part-time at the

University of Chicago," said Carl, noticing an oil truck whizzing past the bus. "I understand that Qatar has an absolute monarchy," said Carl. "Tell me a little about your country's history."

"During World War I, Qataris participated in the Arab revolt against the Ottoman Empire. Thanks to the British influence, the Ottoman Turks were forced to leave our country," said Yahwah.

"The film, 'Lawrence of Arabia', deals with the Ottoman occupation of Arabia," said Carl. "It's listed as one of the greatest films ever produced."

"I've watched it several times while travelling to other countries. Peter O'Toole played the role of Lawrence, the misfit British soldier. He blended into our culture and society in spite of his blue eyes and blonde hair. What impressed me the most was that he spoke Arabic and could read the Quran.

"That film got seven Academy Awards and had many famous actors including, Alex Guinness, Anthony Quinn, and Omar Sharif," said Yahwah.

"The ending of the film was tragic when Lawrence returned to Britain and died after being struck down due to motorcycle accident," said Carl.

"It was a rather tragic ending," said Yahwah pausing. "With the decline of the British Empire after World War II and the independence of India and Pakistan, there was pressure for the British to withdraw from the Persian Gulf," said Yahwah.

" Unfortunately Qatar didn't became a sovereign state until 1971 when Khalifa bin Hamad seized control and annexed all foreign oil companies. This led to economic progress for our independent country."

"That accounts for those oil trucks whizzing past the bus

every few minutes," said Carl.

"That's right. Emir Hamad took control of the country with the army's help in 1995. Under his rule major changes took place, including the building of a modern TV station, support of women's right to vote, drafting a constitution, and building a Roman Catholic Church for tourists and businessmen," said Yahwah.

"That's quite a list of accomplishments," said Carl, pausing as the bus suddenly slowed down and came to a screeching halt due to a violent explosion of an oil truck about half the length of a football field from the bus.

The bus was shaking due to the vibrations causing several passengers to fall to the floor, where they were moaning and groaning.

The driver immediately started the motor of the bus and swerved off the road away from the volcanic eruption of the flaming oil truck, which was spewing clouds of heavy black smoke toward the bus.

The passengers were coughing and rubbing their eyes from the smoke, which drifted into the bus through the air conditioner even though the windows were closed.

Carl was swaying back and forth but still standing in the aisle next to Yahwah. They both hung onto their leather handgrips as the bus headed down the rugged open field some distance from the road and the explosion.

"What's happening out there?" asked Carl, concerned about the moaning passengers, struggling to get up from the floor while the bus was moving along.

"I'm not sure," said Yahwah. "It must have been a careless driver who smashed into the walled fence. I hope the oil truck wasn't blown up by terrorists."

"I heard that the Taliban recently opened an embassy in Doha," said Carl, recalling Barbara's dream about his plane being blown up before landing in Qatar."

"Yes, it's ironic that the explosion happened at this time of the day. It's been only a few weeks since the Taliban was granted permission to open an embassy here," said Yahwah. "They had a temporary office in Doha for about a year but it wasn't official.

"Our country had a terrorist attack eight years ago, when a suicide bomber murdered a British teacher at the Doha Players Theater during a performance. The bombing was done by an Egyptian, who had ties with Al-Qaeda."

Their conversation was interrupted by announcement on the loud speaker. "I'm your driver, Hamid, and I want to apologize for having to suddenly stop the bus because of the oil tanker's explosion. I'm very sorry that some passengers have been injured after falling onto the floor. I've turned on the overhead fans to clear out the smoke.

"I've also contacted the terminal and want you to know that the other two buses with passengers from your flight arrived there safely. Armed guards have been stationed there for your safety as well.

"There have been no other explosions at our airport. Our bus is now quite a distance from the smoke and the fire. Will the standing passengers please help those who are lying on the floor to get up. Thank you for your cooperation."

"Let me help you," said Carl, reaching for the hand of an elderly man, who was sprawled on the floor. He continued down the aisle, assisting the alarmed passengers while Yahwah reassured them in Arabic

"What's that noise?" asked a woman, shrouded in her burqa. "I hope it's not another oil truck exploding!"

Momentarily there was a murmuring throughout the bus as the sirens became louder.

"This is your driver, Hamid. Please do not panic! The

noise you are hearing is from fire trucks approaching the exploded oil tanker. If anyone aboard has been injured due to the explosion please let me know, and I will call ambulances to meet us at the terminal. We should be there in about fifteen minutes.

"I have a bump on my head from falling down on to the floor," said a middle-aged woman.

"My back is sore and so is my right knee," said her husband, getting up from the floor and taking his seat with Carl's assistance.

"It was such a pleasant flight until we landed at this airport that's under construction," shouted a man. "My shoulder really hurts from the fall."

Carl continued to help injured passengers get up from the floor, while others offered them their seats. Several people were seriously injured and others had minor bruises.

As they approached the airport, the driver announced, "I want to inform you that we have a modern terminal here in Doha Qatar with a beautiful lounge. For a reasonable fee you can stay in the lounge where you may take a private shower. There's also a fine restaurant and gift shop in the terminal. Even though it's terribly hot outside, the terminal is air conditioned. Ambulances will be available to take the injured to the hospital for further treatment."

Chapter 15
"The Doha Qatar Terminal"

Upon arrival at the terminal, Hamid departed from the bus while the passengers waited for his permission to disembark. He was approached by eight paramedics, who had been standing in front of four ambulances, guarded by a half a dozen armed soldiers.

Within fifteen minutes the paramedics boarded the bus and placed the severely injured passengers on stretchers. After returning to the bus, Hamid announced that the passengers suffering from minor wounds should come forward. Twelve people left the bus and were escorted by armed guards to the First Aid Station inside the terminal.

A few minutes later Carl followed the other passengers with their back packs and suitcases toward the guarded entrance. Most of them were complaining about the heat.

Upon entering the modern terminal, the passengers were amazed that the Doha International Airport was spotless and the air conditioning was a relief from the heat. They were encouraged by neatly dressed guards to go directly to the check-in counters where their passports would be inspected. There was a long line of passengers from several flights waiting to be processed.

"The last time we came here, the pilot told us that they served about 12 million passengers per year," said Rama, standing in line next to Carl, waiting to check-in.

"At that time the passengers were Qatari students, businessmen and family members, returning home after travelling, working or for a summer vacation," said Samitra.

"This year 21 million passengers have come through this terminal and it's only August. We're expecting about another 10 million before the New Year," said Yahwah.

"That's quite a number," said Carl, wondering how Kathy was doing at the hospital.

"Qatar served as the United States headquarters and launching site for the invasion of Iraq. Of course that was two years after the bombing of your Twin Towers when Mr. George Bush, was your President," said Yahwah.

"President Obama shouldn't have sent troops to Pakistan to assassinate Osama bin Laden. It happened only two years ago in May. That violent attack took place in Bin Laden's compound in Pakistan," said Yahwah.

"Bin Laden should have been captured by the military and brought to trial because he was unarmed at the time of the invasion of his compound," insisted Yahwah.

"What bothers me is that Pakistan's Central Intelligence Chief knew that Bin Laden was hiding in an urban setting, although our soldiers searched for him in the rugged mountains and foothills of Afghanistan," said Carl.

"The legal and ethical aspects of the assassination were questioned by Amnesty International," said Yahwah.

A majority of Americans supported the assassination, including NATO, the European Union, and the United Nations," continued Rama.

"In spite of the majority approval, I questioned whether it was ethical to kill an unarmed enemy, who could have surrendered and been brought to trial," said Yahwah. "I also believe it was immoral to bury his corpse at sea."

"That invasion was conducted by U.S, Navy Seals and led by the CIA," said Carl. "What concerns me is that every action has a reaction - violence breeds violence!"

"After Bin Laden's assassination several terrorist

groups threatened revenge, which materialized during the Boston Marathon."

"I remember three people being killed immediately and 264 people were injured when two pressure cooker bombs exploded during the marathon in Cambridge.

"Two Chechen brothers were responsible for the bombings. While being tracked down by the police, one was killed and the other wounded. When Dzhokhar was taken to the hospital, he confessed that Islamic groups from Iraq and Afghanistan encouraged him to seek revenge for the killing of Osama bin Laden," said Rama.

"You, Americans, have more people in your prisons than any other country in the world! I've read that students at your universities have been known to murder professors, and school children by entering classrooms with guns and shooting their teachers and classmates," said Yahwah.

"Do you know what was responsible for the explosion of the oil tanker?" interrupted Carl.

"Our whole country has been alerted about the incident. That's why there are soldiers guarding the entrance of the terminal. We're very concerned about terrorists attacking Doha. Our country has been supporting NATO's operations in Libya by arming the opposition. We also fund weapons for opposition groups in the Syrian Civil War."

"May I see you your passport," asked the clerk.

"Of course," said Carl, handing it to her.

"Oh, you're a citizen of the United States in transit to Kathmandu, Nepal."

"That's right," said Carl. "The flight was very pleasant, but the trip to the terminal was rough due to the explosion of the oil tanker."

"I'm sorry about the delay," said the clerk. "Are you aware that it's illegal to bring alcohol, pork, narcotics, pornography, or religious books with the intension of converting our citizens into the country?"

"I didn't know that," said Carl. "But I don't have the things that you mentioned in my luggage."

"All hand luggage and back packs will be scanned for DVDs and videos. We always confiscate forbidden objects," said the clerk.

"You don't have to worry about Carl and his friends," interrupted Yahwah. "They are university professors going on a pilgrimage to Mount Kailash in Tibet."

"Thank you for the information, but it's my duty to inform them that the penalty for possession or selling drugs is imprisonment. It's also against the law to drink alcohol in public in Qatar," said the clerk, stamping their passports.

After their hand luggage was inspected and they had gone through security, Carl and his friends strolled into the spacious lobby, with rows of metallic chairs.

"I'd like to go shopping at the duty free gift shop," said Samitra.

"I'll show you where it's located before I check into the lounge, where I can take a shower and then order a decent meal. We have a long wait before departing for Kathmandu," said Yahwah.

"I've been to the gift shop during my last trip. You don't have to take me there," said Samitra.

"Here we are at the Oryx Lounge, where I reserved a private room," said Yahwah. "I'm anxious to change my clothes because they still smell from smoke."

"We'll see you later when we leave on the bus, before boarding the flight to Nepal," said Carl, continuing through the lobby with Rama and Samitra.

"We need to exchange some cash into Qatari currency. There's a bank next to a restaurant, where we can get snacks and a cup of coffee," said Rama.

After exchanging currency, Samitra asked her husband if he'd like to go shopping with her at the gift shop.

Rama informed her that he'd prefer to continue his conversation with Carl at the nearby restaurant.

"Have fun shopping, Samitra," said Carl, entering the dining room with Rama. It had dozens of empty tables in a spacious area, stretching to an indoor park, where children were screaming and shouting while playing on the swings and slides.

The men went to the food counter where only a few people were placing orders with the cashier at the register.

"The coffee here is expensive," said Rama. "It's $8.00 for a large cup."

"That's a terrible price for a cup of coffee," said Carl.

"I'll treat you this time. You can pay me back when we stop here on our way home in September," said Rama.

After purchasing the coffee, they sat down at a vacant table to continue their conversation about the Maoist Revolution.

Chapter 16
"Where is Kathy?"

Carl glanced at his watch, noticing that in two hours; they were scheduled to depart from the terminal by bus to the plane destined for Kathmandu.

"Rama, I'm worried about Kathy because she didn't return my call. She said she'd be back from the hospital in couple of hours."

"Govinda Sharma gave you the telephone number of the hospital and his cell phone. Try calling them."

"I'll call Women's Hospital," said Carl, concerned about his daughter's safety. He dialed his cell phone, waiting for an operator to answer

"My name is Carl Brecht. My daughter, Kathy, arrived at the hospital several hours ago. She came from the airport in an ambulance with Mrs. Shanti Sharma, who gave birth to a baby girl during the flight from Chicago," he said. "Yes, I can wait until you connect me with obstetrics."

"Here comes Samitra. It looks like she bought out the store," said Rama.

"Rama, would you mind getting me a cup of coffee?" asked Samitra, putting her shopping bags down on floor.

"I'll be back in a few minutes with your coffee," he said.

"How are you doing?" asked Carl, still waiting to be connected to obstetrics on his cell phone.

"I'm exhausted from shopping," she said, glancing at her watch. "In less than two hours, we'll be leaving for Nepal."

"Please excuse me. Yes, this is Carl Brecht. I'm

enquiring about my daughter, Dr. Kathy Brecht, who delivered Shanti Sharma's baby on the airplane. May I please speak to her or the husband, Govinda Sharma…What time did they leave? Thanks so much."

"What's wrong?" asked Samitra.

"I'm worried about Kathy. She left the hospital an hour ago," said Carl, dialing Govinda's cell phone.

"Here's your coffee," said Rama, setting the cup down on the table in front of his wife. "You certainly did a lot of shopping."

"Rama, I didn't have time to shop before leaving Chicago. I wanted to bring gifts to my relatives since we'll be staying with them for a few days before we leave on the pilgrimage to Mount Kailash, and again when we return to Kathmandu," she said.

Carl walked away from the table, holding his phone. "Govinda! I'm worried about Kathy. I was told that she left the hospital over an hour ago. I hope she gets here soon. Thanks a lot," said Carl, returning to the table.

"Where is Kathy? I'm worried about her," said Samitra, sipping her coffee. "It won't be long now before we board the busses. I've been nervous about terrorists attacking ever since that oil tanker exploded."

"It takes at least a half hour to get to the plane," said Rama. "I wonder if something has happened to Kathy because of Qatari regulations."

"Do you know anything about how the law works here?" asked Carl, glancing at his watch again.

"Qatari Civil Law is strict and private. The Prime Minister and cabinet members draft the legislation and submit it to the Emir, for ratification. He's an absolute monarch and has the final say in all matters.

"For example, the size of Qatar's national debt, income

and business investments are not published or released to the public," said Rama greeting, Yahwah as he sat down with them at the table.

"We were talking about Qatar's Civil Law," said Carl.

"Tell us about Sharia Law. I understand it applies to the personal conduct of the citizens," said Rama.

"Sharia Law deals with family inheritance and criminal acts involving adultery, robbery, and murder. That law wasn't introduced here until 2006. However a female's testimony in court is not given as much credibility as a male's. Usually a woman testifying against a male is dismissed," said Yahwah.

"Is it true that if a Moslem woman in Qatar commits adultery with a foreigner, she'll be put to death?" asked Carl.

"Yes, that's right. However if a Moslem male commits adultery with a Moslem female, they'll both be flogged with 100 lashes.

"Illicit sexual relations and alcohol consumption are crimes. Most Qatari citizens don't drink because it's forbidden by our religion. Other Moslems who are caught consuming alcohol are flogged and deported. The majority of the crimes here are committed by foreign nationals," said Yahwah.

"Stoning criminals to death is still legal in Qatar. It occurs when Moslems are caught, engaging in homosexual acts," continued Yahwah.

"Even though Doha has a Catholic Church for foreign workers and tourists, proselytizing leads to imprisonment. Qataris are not allowed to convert to other religions."

"There's, also, a dress code here for tourists. Female tourists are not to wear leggings, sleeveless dresses or miniskirts. Men also are not to wear shorts or sleeveless shirts in public," said Yahwah.

"Who's that Moslem woman coming this way with a black handbag?" asked Carl.

"A Moslem woman must wear a burqa in public. Her whole body's covered, including her face with a net so she can breathe," said Samitra.

"That woman's carrying a black bag, which is just like my daughter's," said Carl, rising from his chair.

"Are you friends of Doctor Kathleen Brecht," asked the woman with high pitched voice."

"I'm her father," said Carl. "I hope Kathy's all right."

"I wanted to let you know Kathy was arrested for wearing tight slacks at the hospital. She wanted you to have her medical kit and her handbag," said the woman, setting it on the table.

"What!" gasped Carl, frowning at the stranger.

"Don't worry about her? She told me that Govinda Sharma agreed to get her out of jail within a day or two."

"A day or two!" snapped Carl. "We'll be leaving this terminal in about a half hour."

The stranger began laughing hysterically as she lifted the veil of her burqa.

"It's me, Dad," said Kathy, removing the veil.

"Kathy! You scared the hell out of me!" said Carl.

"We're pleased to see you! We've been waiting for you to arrive for several hours," said Samitra, helping Kathy remove the burka and put it into her suitcase.

Everyone paused to listen to the announcement on the loud speaker. "Will all passengers destined for the next flight to Katmandu come to the exit across from the restaurant on the ground floor to board the buses."

"Why were you wearing that burka?" asked Rama.

"I got here just in time. You'll never believe what happened at the hospital," said Kathy, wearing the same clothes she had on before leaving the airport. She paused to pick up her suitcase.

"Kathy, I tried to call you, but you didn't answer your phone. When I finally reached Govinda, he said you had left the hospital and were on your way to the airport in a taxi!"

"Dad, I was about to enter the taxi when two armed guards arrested the drunk driver. They asked to see my passport. I told them that I'm a doctor, who delivered a baby on the plane before coming to the hospital with Shanti in an ambulance and was heading back to the airport to continue my flight to Nepal with my father."

"When they said I was under arrest for wearing slacks in public, I told them I didn't have time to change into a dress on the plane. I also told them to contact, Govinda Sharma, who was with his wife in the hospital with their children, and that he worked for the Indian Embassy in Kathmandu.

"One of the armed guards took the drunken taxi driver away and the other took me back into the hospital. When we finally got to Shanti's room, she told us that her husband and the children were in the cafeteria having dinner.

"The guard talked with Govinda for ten minutes before asking a nurse to bring me a burqa to wear to the airport.

"Once I put it on the guard escorted me to the front of the hospital where an officer was waiting in his police car to bring me to the terminal.

"I'll tell you, I was scared to death that I would have to spend the night in jail for wearing slacks," said Kathy.

"We're all grateful you got here just in time. Let's get going to the exit to board the bus," said Rama, leading the way out of the cafeteria through the waiting area with rows of chrome chairs being polished by Nepalese workers.

"Most of those workers are stranded here because they can't afford to fly to Nepal," said Yahwah.

"It's a real dilemma," agreed Samitra. "Our Nepali citizens come here to work because of the high rate of unemployment in Nepal due to the Maoist Revolution."

"We're going to be the last passengers to board the bus," said Kathy. "I'm sorry for the delay. I was shocked when I smelled the breath of the taxi driver as soon as I opened the door to the back seat of the cab. I didn't expect those armed guards to be there waiting to arrest him.

"I was, also, surprised to see so many armed guards at the terminal, checking everybody's passports before allowing them to enter. I'm sure it was because the Qatari government suspected that terrorists had sabotaged that oil tanker. I was horrified when I heard about your bus being delayed because of the explosion."

"May I see your boarding passes?" asked the hostess at the upper exit. "Please take the stairs or the elevator to the lower level and wait there.

"Your three buses have arrived and the passengers are now boarding. You will be travelling for a half hour on your bus before boarding the 747 Jumbo Jet. It will reach Kathmandu at 8:35 a.m. on August 6th, depending on the weather."

Chapter 17
"Flying to Kathmandu"

After heading down the stairs to the lower exit, the passengers waited in line to board the buses, which were guarded by Qatari soldiers. Once the buses were filled, they departed accompanied by jeeps with armed guards.

Twenty minutes later they reached the plane. While the passengers were boarding, they complained again about the stifling heat. After locating their seats and getting settled, everyone was relieved when the plane departed.

Most of the passengers turned on their TV sets, choosing films to entertain them during the flight.

Kathy, who was sitting across the aisle from her father, said "Dad, I'm going to watch, 'Frozen'."

"Mark took Sammy and Emily to see that movie at the Elk Grove Theater," said Carl.

"I love Disney movies. They're a relief after working all day at the hospital," said Kathy.

"You deserve a reward because you were almost put in jail for wearing slacks," said Carl.

"'Frozen', is based upon Hans Christian Anderson's children's book, 'The Snow Queen'," said Kathy. "I remember you reading it to me when I was little girl."

"I vaguely remember the story," said Carl.

"It's about two sisters who are princesses. Elsa has magical powers and accidently injures her younger sister, Anna while playing. After that Elsa is forbidden by her parents to have any contact with her sister.

"Are you sure you don't want to watch it on your screen

so that we can discuss it later?"

"No, Kathy," said Carl. "Enjoy the film. You can tell me more about it later on. I want to talk to Rama about the holidays being celebrated in Nepal in August."

"We certainly have a lot of them during the monsoon season," said Rama, noticing that Samitra was sound asleep next to him.

"Upon returning to Nepal everyone will celebrate, 'Gunla', the most sacred month of the year for Buddhists," said Rama. "The celebration reminds me of Lent for Christians or Ramadan for Moslems.

"The Buddhists get up early in the morning and go to the two largest Tibetan Buddhist Shrines in the Kathmandu Valley," said Rama.

" Swayambunath means the 'Self Existent Lord'. The only obstacle is we must climb 365 cement steps before reaching the shrine. Along the way we'll be approached by monkeys swinging from the trees on the hill. They're notorious for stealing purses, umbrellas and cameras from the tourists," said Carl.

"At the top of the hill, there's a monastery with a 12 foot golden statue of the Buddha, where devotees offer flowers, incense, and oil lamps. Upon leaving the shrine, we'll visit the Hindu temple to Ajima, the Goddess of Small Pox," said Rama.

"That name reminds me of Ajima Shakti Dev from the film, 'Indian Jones And The Temple of Doom'," said Carl.

"That film was produced by Steven Spielberg and George Lucas back in 1984," said Rama.

"When Indiana Jones arrived in North India, he was approached by a villager, who asked him to go on a quest for three mystical stones. While searching for the gems, they stumble upon a black magic cult that enslaved children and performed human sacrifice to the Goddess, Kali," said Carl.

"Kali is the fierce aspect of the Mother Goddess," said Rama." In the film she's called Ajima Shakti Dev, a blood thirsty goddess."

"The ancient texts, 'The Puranas', depict the gods and goddesses as either honest and loving or vulgar and promiscuous," said Rama.

"Some Hindus favor the myths in the 'Purnanas' while others prefer the 'Vedas and Upanishads'. We cherish our epics, 'The Ramayana' and 'The Mahabharata'," said Rama.

The conversation about the sacred texts continued for several hours until it was interrupted by the hostess.

"Ladies and Gentleman, please fasten your seatbelts, we will be arriving in Kathmandu in twenty minutes. Kindly remain seated until the plane comes to a complete halt at the Tribuwan National Airport."

"Dad, I fell asleep watching the movie," said Kathy. "I just woke up because we'll be landing shortly."

"There's the Himalayan Range," said Samitra, looking out the window. "Right now we're near the Everest Region. I thought we'd be delayed because of the monsoon rain. The sky is clear," said Rama.

"The glaciers in the Himalayas are melting rapidly, which caused the torrential flooding and the collapse of mountains in India, leaving thousands of Hindus and tourists stranded only a few weeks ago," said Carl.

"Oh, look! There's Pashupatinath, the Lord of the Animals," said Samitra. "It's dedicated to Shiva. And there's Bodhnath, the second largest Tibetan Buddhist Shrine in the valley. We'll be landing in a few minutes."

Chapter 18
"The Kathmandu Valley"

"Ladies and Gentlemen, welcome to the Tribuwan International Airport in the Kathmandu Valley. Please remain seated with seatbelts fastened until the plane comes to a halt.

"We'll be landing at 8:35 a.m. After leaving the plane, passengers with visas for Nepal may go through customs after retrieving their luggage. Those without visas go to the Visitors Desk to purchase them before entering the country.

"Thank you for choosing Qatar Airlines. We hope that your flight has been memorable," said the hostess.

"What a relief to finally be in Kathmandu," said Kathy, standing up in the crowded aisle where passengers were removing their luggage from the upper compartments.

"Kathy, we'd like you to stay with my brother, Dipak, and his family for a few days before you do your rotation at Shanta Bhawan Hospital," said Samitra.

"Thanks for the offer, but a driver from the hospital will be waiting to take me to my living quarters there. I'll begin working in the Emergency Room tomorrow," said Kathy.

"Please call me on my cell phone once you get to the hospital," said Carl. "Be sure to send your mother an email, informing her that we arrived safely."

"I'll call you and send mom the message," said Kathy, following her father and his friends down the stairs and toward the terminal.

"Once inside the building, Samitra and Rama led the way

to the luggage retrieval station. Carl and Kathy followed them, noticing a long line of tourists and Arab businessmen from their flight, waiting in line to purchase their visas.

After gathering their luggage, they went through customs without any trouble by showing the guards their passports.

Carl and Kathy were amazed that their luggage wasn't even inspected. Within a few minutes they left the terminal with Samitra and Rama, where taxis, cars, and buses were parked in the bright sunshine.

Within a few minutes several of Samitra's relatives rushed towards them, speaking rapidly in Nepali.

Samitra introduced her brother, Dipak, and his wife, Uma, to Carl and Kathy. While they were talking, Rama and their relatives were busy carrying their luggage to their parked cars.

Kathy, noticed a taxi coming to halt. A uniformed chauffer stepped out carrying a sign, "Attention Doctor Kathleen Brecht." She waved to the chauffer and then gave her father a hug and kiss on the cheek. After saying goodbye to everyone, she entered the taxi while the driver placed her luggage in the trunk.

As they departed, Kathy rolled down the window and shouted, "Have a wonderful trip to Mount Kailash. Please come and see me at the hospital when you get back!"

"Your daughter is very beautiful," said Uma.

"I'm worried about her being at the hospital by herself for a whole month," said Carl.

"Don't worry about Kathy. Shanta Bhawan's the best hospital in the Kathmandu Valley. She'll be welcomed there with open arms," said Dipak.

"Carl, you'll be staying at our house in Dhasipati for four nights before our departure for Tibet. It's about a half hour drive north of the airport, depending upon traffic." said

Dipak. "You can ride in the front seat with me. The backseat will be used for your luggage.

"My sister, Samitra, is riding with my wife, Uma, and her twin sisters. Rama will be travelling with their husbands and the rest of the luggage."

As they departed from the airport Carl stared out the window, bewildered by the heavy traffic "Everything has changed since I was here last!"

"When was the last time you were in Kathmandu?" asked Dipak, honking his horn at pedestrians, and rickshaws stalling the traffic by crossing from side streets.

"My daughter and I came to Nepal to attend a Shaman Convention in 2001. We didn't expect to be here during the assassination of the Royal Family," said Carl.

"That's twelve years ago," said Dipak. "So much has happened since then. Please excuse the condition of our roads. The traffic is heavy at this time of day with so many people going to work and students to school."

"I'm confused by the heavy congestion of vehicles here. I've never seen so many motorcycles, taxis, buses, and foreign cars. The streets are as crowded as Bombay and Calcutta," said Carl.

"There are lots of school children waiting for their buses to arrive," said Dipak. "Those long yellow buses are responsible for most of the congestion.

"The students are all wearing uniforms," said Carl, glancing out the window at the girls in jumpers and the boys with white shirts and ties.

"We have a large number of private schools that require students to wear uniforms. The tuition is high because most classes are held in English, "said Dipak.

"I've saw several yellow buses whizzing past us, loaded with children going to Montessori Schools," said Carl, having noticed the bold print beneath the bus's open windows.

"We have several of them here in the Kathmandu Valley," said Dipak. "My youngest son, Chandra, went to a Montessori School, where he learned to speak perfect English. He rarely speaks Nepali at home anymore, which annoys my wife because she doesn't want him to lose our cultural heritage. Our older son, Surya, also attended the school but he speaks to us in Nepali."

"Last week I watched a documentary about Maria Montessori and her son, Mario, establishing a Teacher's College in Italy during the Roaring Twenties with Mussolini's support," said Carl, pausing when Dipak slowed down before coming to a halt at a stop sign.

"If we go east, we'll end up at the Kathmandu Guest House," said Dipak. "We'll continue north toward the suburb, Dhasipati, where we live in my parent's house. Carl, tell me more about Maria Montessori."

"During the Great Depression, Maria was horrified by the rigorous training of the Italian youths in the Fascist Army because it was opposed to her liberal teachings about freedom and harmony in the classroom.

"Maria and Mario left Italy and went to London where they met Mahatma Gandhi. He invited them to come to India to open Montessori Schools, which they did successfully," said Carl.

"I was impressed with the hands on approach of the Montessori School where my sons studied. After finishing high school with the Jesuits at Godavari, they went on to the university and became Civil Engineers.

"Chandra and Surya ride their motorcycles to their office every morning and sit at their desks frustrated because there is no work for them. They'd like to go to Australia, the UK, or America, but they haven't been able to get visas because they don't have a work history.

"In spite of their drawings of bridges and roads, their plans are not materializing due to lack of government funding," said Dipak, shaking his head.

"This is a real problem for most of our educated young men and women. There is no employment for them in spite of their degrees. I told Chandra and Surya to be patient. They both have visas to travel to India to work, but they're reluctant to go there. Some of their friends are working as Civil Engineers in Saudi Arabia and they're investigating going there," said Dipak.

"That's too bad that they can't repair the roads here," said Carl, glancing out the window. "I remember travelling on Ring Road some years ago. I could see the buildings on both sides of the street clearly.

"The road was only one lane. Now it has two rutted lanes, long pipes stretching out in front of the buildings, and deep trenches filled with stagnant water," said Carl.

"That's because of the monsoon rains," said Dipak "The ruts in this road are terrible. The problem is no one is working on the road. It's been dug up like this for three years now," said Dipak.

Chapter 19
"The Day of the Snake Gods"

"What's going on at those shops?" asked Carl, looking out the window of the car. "The shopkeepers are busy putting up posters above their doorways."

"It's because of Naga Panchami, 'The Day of the Snake God'. It takes place every year during our lunar fortnight.

"Every entrance has a rice paper drawing of a snake with red tika powder on its head. Fresh cow dung is used as an adhesive to hold up the picture," said Dipak, slowing down the Honda in front of a shop.

"It looks like the whole family's worshiping the image of the Snake God with offerings of flowers, incense, and oil lamps," said Carl.

"At our house in the suburbs, Uma sets out boiled rice, honey, and curds at the back door for the snakes in the garden," said Dipak.

"Is it true that the Nepalese believe it's a sin to kill a snake?" asked Carl.

"Yes, because centuries ago the entire Kathmandu Valley was a vast lake, called 'Abode of the Snakes'," said Dipak, pausing as they crossed the bridge over the Bhagmati River.

"Why are those farmers milking their cows in the river?" asked Carl, glancing at women and men squatting in the shallow water.

"They're appeasing the snakes by feeding them milk because they still believe that Snake Gods control the monsoon rains," said Dipak.

"When was the lake finally drained?" asked Carl, as they crossed the bridge.

"Several thousand years ago, Manjusri, the Buddhist saint, came to Nepal from China. He removed his sword at Chobar Gorge and struck his blade against a rock, creating a ravine to drain the water from the entire valley."

"It's been many years since I've been to that gorge, where the water cascades between huge rocks," said Carl.

"Most Nepalese believe that snakes inhabit the land for six months of the year. During the other months they dwell underground in Naga-Lok, their Snake Kingdom. Their society is composed of snake families, who live in buildings and palaces, ruled by a snake king," said Dipak.

"Images of Shiva always have a snake coiled around his neck or waist," said Carl. "They are symbols of the eternal cycle from birth to death."

"During this holiday thousands of Hindus will be visiting Shiva's Temple to worship the numerous snake images," said Dipak. "I want to take you there before our departure for Mount Kailash."

The two men continued talking until they reached the suburb, Dhasipati. Dipak swerved the car onto a rutted road and sped through the small town.

"This road is even more rugged than the last one," said Carl, taking a deep breath as Dipak turned left and went up a paved hill away from the town.

He continued on a one lane street with houses soaring to the right and left behind large gates and surrounded by wrought iron fences. He finally came to a halt.

"We're here at last at our home. When I grew up this was a rural community with only a few houses. Now it's a large community.

As Carl stepped out of the car, he glanced across the road through a wrought iron fence where hens were guarded by a red rooster. After walking behind the parked car, he heard the mooing of a Swiss cow munching on hay with her calf at the entrance of a small barn in the neighbor's yard.

"Let me help you with the luggage," said Carl, turning to Dipak, who had unlocked the Iron Gate and was already heading toward his house with a suitcase.

A few minutes later, there was the arrival of Samitra with her twin sisters, and Rama with their husbands.

After Carl was taken to his room on the ground floor, he unpacked and placed his clothes into a drawer, the he heard a knock on the door.

Dipak entered and said, "I wanted to tell you that Uma and her sisters are preparing a lunch for us in the kitchen. Carl, when you're done unpacking please come to the balcony on the third floor for tea before we have lunch in the kitchen."

Within fifteen minutes Carl went up the three flights of stairs to the third floor, where the family dog with one eye was growling from his cage on the roof. Glancing over his shoulder toward the kitchen, there was the aroma of spices drifting down the hallway.

Turing to the right, Carl glanced into a chapel, with pictures of Hindu Gods and Goddesses on the wall, bronze statues on an altar with oil lamps burning and orange cushions on the blue tiled floor to sit on while worshiping.

Going past the shrine, Carl entered the balcony overlooking the suburb with a view of the distant foothills and snow covered Himalayas.

Dipak greeted him along with his sons, Chandra and Surya, who poured him a cup of steaming tea.

"Carl, have you heard of Shiva Puri Baba?" asked

Chandra. "Our grandfather wrote a book about him in Nepali. It was called 'Swadharma, Self-Realization'."

"I remember reading that book given to me by Nina Upadhaya, his devotee. He also showed me, the saint's grave, where his corpse was buried in the nearby woods instead of being cremated."

"We don't cremate the corpses of saints," said Surya. "Shiva Puri Baba was born in Kerala, India. His parents died when he was nine years old, and he was raised by his grandfather, an astrologer in the court of a sultan.

"After the death of his grandfather, he stayed in the forest meditating for 25 years. Upon achieving enlightenment, he travelled on foot throughout India.

"While touring the country, he became acquainted with the poor, the middle class, and the wealthy. He shared his spiritual knowledge with all.

"His goal in life was to be at peace with himself and friendly toward everyone. He kept his body healthy through exercise, and his mind cleansed through prayer, meditation, and helping others," said Dipak.

"Carl, are you a Christian?" asked Chandra. "We now have 3,000,000 Nepalese Christians living in Nepal."

"I was raised Catholic, but I try to be opened minded and tolerant of people from all religions," said Carl.

"Have you been to Kerala in South India?" asked Surya.

"Yes, while touring India, I learned that Saint Thomas travelled to Kerala, where he converted thousands of Hindus to Christianity," said Carl. "It also has the Jewish Synagogue and a large Communist population."

"Please come to the kitchen, where my sisters, Tara and Saraswoti have rice, dal, lamb and cauliflower curries," interrupted Uma. Also please tell Rama, Kumar and Hanuman, that lunch is ready.

Chapter 20
"Traveling to Dakshan Kali Temple"

On the morning of August 7th, Carl awoke with the rooster crowing from the yard across the street. He glanced at his watch. It was 5:30 a.m. A few minutes later, he heard the cow mooing from the shed in the neighbor's barn, where she was waiting to be milked. He glanced out the window into the garden, where he heard two dogs barking across the fence in the alley.

Carl got out of bed and stretched. He left the bedroom in his underwear with a towel, crossed the hallway, and entered the bathroom to take a shower.

Upon returning to his room he got dressed, and began his morning meditation. A few minutes later the household servant, Jyote, knocked on his door and entered his room carrying a steaming cup of tea, which he set down on a table in front of Carl.

"Yo bihana maile dherai sarpaharu hamro bagainchama hereko, I saw several snakes this morning in our garden," said the ten year old boy.

"Kun kisimko saapaharu hereko tyo? What kind of snakes did you see?" asked Carl.

Jyote informed him that Dipak's wife, Uma, had put food into the back yard because of the Snake Festival.

"Malai thulo dhar lagne nag hereko. Angreji ma, cobra, bhancha, I saw a large snake. In English it's called a cobra."

Carl warned him to be careful when he's in the garden; so he wouldn't be bitten by the cobra. He paused upon hearing a knock at the door, followed by Dipak entering.

"Jyoti, go back to the kitchen and help my wife with breakfast," said Dipak.

The boy bowed to them and backed out of the room, leaving the door open. He hurried down the hallway with his bare feet thumping up the three flights of stairs.

"I hope that Jyoti wasn't annoying you this morning. He's always poking his nose into the guest room when we have company staying here over night."

"I enjoyed talking to him. He told me that he saw several snakes in the garden this morning, including a cobra."

"I've never seen a cobra in my yard," said Dipak. "That boy has a vivid imagination. Are you planning to go with Samitra and Rama to the Dakshan Kali Temple after breakfast?"

"Yes, we were hoping to go there before leaving on the pilgrimage," said Carl.

"I have a good friend who's a taxi driver. He'll take you there for 500 rupees. There are about 100 rupees to a dollar. For 1000 rupees he'll do a round trip. I'll call him on my cell phone to come in an hour.

"Please come with me to the kitchen. Breakfast will be ready by the time we get there," said Dipak, leading the way.

Upon reaching the third floor, the dog growled inside his screened cage, located on the ledge of the roof.

"Let's stop at the chapel for a few minutes before we go for breakfast," said Dipak, removing his shoes at the entrance.

Carl followed him into the chapel, where they folded their hands and bowed to the images of the deities. After lighting oil lamps and burning incense, they sat down on the cushions to pray and meditate for ten minutes before heading down the hall to the kitchen.

While eating a breakfast of rice and lentils with chapattis and cups of steaming tea, Carl was startled as he looked out of the kitchen window at a flock of raucous crows, cawing on the extended roof.

"Don't mind the crows," said Dipak, shouting at the servant boy to feed the crows leftover food from yesterday.

The ten year old opened a window and threw handfuls of white rice to the flock of crows. They flapped their wings and cawed as they were being fed.

Noticing that the crows had finished eating, Dipak rose from his chair and stood at the open window, clapping his hands at them until they flew away.

"That was a huge flock of crows," said Carl.

"We feed the crows because they transport the souls of the dead to the next world," said Dipak, pausing upon hearing footsteps in the hallway.

"Forgive us for being late for breakfast," said Samitra, sitting down next to Rama at the table.

"Jyoti, dal bhat, ra chapatti liera au, Jyoti bring them rice, lentils and chapattis," said Uma, rising from the table.

"We slept late this morning after that long flight from Chicago and then Qatar," said Samitra. "Did Carl tell you about the oil tanker exploding at the airport in Qatar?"

"We heard about the explosion while we were coming home from the airport yesterday," said Uma. "Let's focus on something positive."

"Carl and I have been talking about going to Mt. Kailash for twelve years," said Rama, changing the subject. "That's where Shiva meditated in a cave for many centuries before meeting Parvati, his servant girl. She meditated with him for several thousand years before he asked her to marry him."

"We're anxious to visit the Dakshan Kali Temple this morning. There's also a temple there dedicated to Shiva and

Parvati at the top of the hill," said Samitra.

"Our taxi driver should be here in fifteen minutes," said Rama, glancing at his watch while eating a chapatti.

"Dipak and I went to both temples there last week. We won't be joining you today because I have a doctor's appointment at ten o'clock."

"It's just a routine checkup before we leave for Mount Kailash with you. We hope you'll enjoy your trip to the temples," said Uma.

"Taxi aiyo, Taxi, aiyo," shouted Jyoti, looking out the window at the taxi parked in front of the locked gate

"Uma, thank you for the wonderful breakfast," said Carl.

"We'll see you later for supper." said Uma.

Dipak led the way through the hallway past the growling dog and down the stairs, followed by Carl, Rama and Samitra. They left the house and walked toward the locked gate, waiting for Dipak to open it with his key.

When the taxi driver pulled into the driveway, Carl sat next to Moti Lall in the front seat while his friends sat in the backseat. A few minutes later they headed down the hill toward town.

Carl glanced at goats and sheep grazing in the pasture behind a butcher shop, where carcasses of chickens and goats were hanging from hooks. Several customers were waiting, while the butchers sliced and wrapped the meat at the outdoor counter.

"Motiji, Dakshan Kali Mandir yaha deki kati tara cha? Moti, how far is the Dakshan Kali Temple from here?" asked Carl, as the taxi headed north away from the suburb.

"Yaha deki adda ghanta lagcha? From here it's about a half hour drive," said Moti, turning left onto a rutted road with trees on both sides toward the distant mountains.

"The temple is about 24 kilometers from here or 14 miles.

It might take longer because it's rush hour," said Rama, startled by the driver slamming on the breaks as a school bus swerved in front of them from a side road.

"I heard that animal sacrifices still take place at that temple, especially during harvest time," said Carl, as the taxi followed the school bus.

"When Emperor Ashoka converted to Buddhism, animal sacrifices came to a halt throughout India, except in Bengal and Nepal," said Rama.

"It was because Buddha taught reverence for life. His devotees replaced animal sacrifices by offering incense, fruit, and flowers at their shrines," said Samitra.

"Many centuries ago human sacrifice was common throughout India and Nepal. In some isolated villages it still happens," said Rama.

"Human sacrifice is central to the plot in the film, 'Indian Jones and the Temple of Doom', where people are sacrificed to Ajima Shakti Dev, the blood thirsty Mother Goddess," said Carl. "That movie gave Hinduism a bad reputation."

"Human sacrifice ended in the Near East when Abraham took his son, Isaac, into the mountains to sacrifice him as an offering to Yahweh. God spoke to Abraham, forbidding him to do it. This was a great leap for the future of the Israelites and all of humanity," said Rama.

"The Jews celebrated the Passover by sacrificing goats in the precinct of the temple in Jerusalem, remembering that the Angel of Death spared them because they placed the blood of the lamb over their doorways prior to the Exodus," said Carl.

"The Bible contains historical facts, mythology, theology and spirituality. It's up to the reader to sort out reality from fiction," said Samitra.

Moti Lall honked the horn because the school bus ahead

of his taxi was almost struck by a car, zooming past them in the opposite lane.

"That was a close call," gasped Samitra, clinging to her husband's arm in the back seat. "All of us were almost human sacrifices to the Goddess Kali!"

The driver turned onto the narrow paved road leading up the side of a mountain with a forest to the right and terraced rice fields on the left. In the distance was the grandeur of the Himalayan Range.

"Euripides wrote the Greek tragedy, 'Iphigenia', which involved a human sacrifice. After Paris eloped with Hellen of Troy, her husband, Menelaus, wanted his wife back. He was unable to sail to Troy with his troops because there wasn't a favorable wind.

"His brother, Agamemnon, decided to offer his daughter, Iphigenia, as a human sacrifice to Apollo the Sun God, in an exchange for a favorable wind," said Carl.

Once again Moti Lall slammed on the brakes to avoid a collision. After reaching the top of the mountain, they continued down the forested road while a semi-truck was coming toward them full speed. Everyone felt relieved when it whizzed past them.

"I hope the trip to Mount Kailash won't be as dangerous as this road," said Samitra, gasping as the school bus in front of them loaded with children came to a screeching halt blocking the road again.

The taxi driver slammed on the breaks to avoid hitting the school bus. He took deep breaths, waiting for the children to board the bus before going up the mountainous road.

After several more stops and starts due to the heavy traffic, the taxi arrived at the parking lot, located on the side of the mountain. Below them in the forested area was the Dakshan Kali Temple near the Bhagmati River.

Chapter 21
"Arrival at the Temple"

"We're fortunate it's not raining," said Carl, noticing the puddles in the parking lot as he left the taxi with his friends.

Moti Lall led the way down the paved hill, which was filled with open air shops, where merchants were selling fruit, incense, flowers, and red tika powder.

There were also postcards, pictures, and statues of the Mother Goddess in her various incarnations along with images of Shiva, Parvati, Ganesh, and Kumar for sale to the devotees and tourists.

"Let's buy a bouquet to offer Dakshan Kali," said Samitra. "As you know Dakshan means the southern direction and Kali means black. Many Hindus are fearful when they hear the name of the Mother Goddess in her form as Kali."

"They're frightened because of the way artists depict her. Her black images scare most people because they bring out the goddess' wildest instincts," said Rama.

"What foreigners find confusing is that Kali holds weapons in both of her hands to frighten away evil spirits and inflict punishments on her enemies," said Carl.

"What scares me the most is when she's naked, wearing, a rosary of decapitated human heads hanging from her neck," said Samitra. "In other pictures she covers her nakedness with severed heads and arms."

"I don't like the pictures of Kali with her tongue hanging from her mouth, thirsting for blood," said Samitra.

"The most horrifying image is when Kali is stepping with

one foot on the prostrated image of her husband, Shiva. Strangely enough he is totally at ease and smiling while lying on the ground with his eyes closed, giving the goddess permission to dominate him," said Rama, as they approached the temple.

"Shiva was worried about her addiction to blood so he interfered by lying down at her feet so that she would stop the frenzied violence," explained Samitra.

"Kali is sometimes portrayed with ten arms and ten heads. When I see her with so many arms and heads, she reminds me of Ravana, the Demon King, who kidnapped Sita and took her to Sri Lanka, which led to a fierce war between the forces of good and evil," said Carl.

"Rama, with the help of Hanuman and his army of monkeys, killed the ten headed Demon King and liberated his wife, Sita, bringing her back to his palace in Northern India," said Samitra.

"Here we are at Kali's temple. There are a lot of people making offerings to the goddess in her shrine over there. She's just as frightening as some of her pictures," said Samitra, waiting in line to offer flowers to the goddess.

Carl paused staring at the huge stone sculpture of Kali with six large arms. Her huge feet were stepping on the sleeping image of her husband, Shiva.

"In spite of her fierceness her devotees are offering her fruit, flowers or incense," said Samitra. "I'm grateful that her sculpture's not splashed with blood like it was when we came here some years ago."

"I noticed that a few goats were taken to be sacrificed behind the temple," said Rama.

"The lady standing in front of us just sprinkled tika powder on her statue," said Samitra, placing her bouquet of flowers near the goddess' feet. "Red tika powder is used in most shines these days rather than blood."

"The best time to visit Dakshan Kali Temple is either on Tuesday or Saturday," suggested Moti Lall, offering two oranges to the goddess. "During Dasain, the longest Hindu holiday of the year, thousands of animal sacrifices takes place here drenching Kali's image with blood."

"That's when animals are sacrificed for ten days at the Hindu temples throughout Nepal," said Carl, offering incense to the goddess.

"Dasain or Durga Puja begins during the bright lunar fortnight and ends on the day of the full moon in late September or early October. The festival is in honor of Durga, the Mother Goddess in her numerous forms, including Kali," commented Rama, bowing to the goddess.

"Animal sacrifices are not performed by everyone. Instead of offering a chicken or goat to the Mother Goddess, many devotees offer her an egg or pumpkin during Dasain," said Samitra.

"Blood sacrifices are still performed by a majority of the people in Nepal in spite of the Animal Rights activists and protestors trying to stop them," said Rama.

"Throughout India, Hindus offer fruit, flowers, incense, or red tika powder to the Mother Goddess. There are almost no animal sacrifices during the Dasain Holidays, except in Bengal, where Calcutta is located," said Carl.

"Calcutta is the largest city in Bengal. It's now called Kalkot," said Samitra.

"Now that we have made our offerings, let's go to a restaurant and have a cup of tea before visiting the Temple of Shiva and Parvati at the top of the hill," said Rama.

"I'm going back to the taxi to take a nap," said Moti Lall. "I didn't get much sleep last night because we were entertaining family members from Pokhara. They came to

Kathmandu to celebrate Gunla, the Buddhist Holidays."

"We'll meet you in the parking lot in about two hours," said Rama, heading toward a restaurant with his friends.

Twenty minutes later they were climbing the cement steps to the top of the hill to make an offering at the temple.

"You probably know all about Shiva meditating in the cave at Mount Kailash. When Parvati arrived at his cave, she immediately fell in love with him. Because Shiva was a yogi, committed to prayer and meditation, he paid no attention to her," said Samitra.

"Parvati decided to be his servant. She was influenced by Shiva's austerity and eventually became a yogini, who practiced prayer and meditation. Because she was so devoted and spiritual, Shiva started to notice her sincerity and devotion," said Rama.

"The gods sent Kama, the Cupid of India, to the cave to encourage Shiva to fall in love with Parvati, whose name means mountain because she was the daughter of the God of the Himalayan Range," said Samitra.

"Shiva became angry with Kama, who interrupted his mediation. His third eye, located in the middle of his forehead, emitted a flame of fire, which burned him to ashes," said Rama.

"After many centuries of asceticism in the cave together, Shiva finally fell in love with Parvati and decided to marry her," said Samitra, pausing. "Here we are at the shrine. Let's go inside and make an offering of incense."

Once inside the shrine, Samitra was the first to notice a smoldering log in front of the images of the Shiva and Parvati.

As she placed incense into the fire pit, Samitra said, "Kali Dass is the poet, who wrote memorable stanzas about Shiva and Parvati's wedding in his classic, 'The Birth of Kumar'. I memorized a few of the Sanskrit stanzas which I'll recite to you in English

"By going around the blazing fire at night, the couple radiated light. Like day and night, joined together, they circled Mountain Meru's slopes."

"The bride and groom circled the fire three times and then closed their eyes while touching their fingertips. The priest then asked Parvati to throw rice into the fire, which blazed upward.

"When the royal priest recited the ritual that joined them in wedlock, they bowed to the Creator, Brahma, seated on a lotus blossom."

"Later, when the lovers were alone in bed, Kali Dass wrote these stanzas about the consummation of their marriage," said Rama, lighting his incense from the smoldering log and placing it into the fire pit.

"When her lover pretended to be asleep and curiosity made Parvati look at Shiva, he opened his eyes and smiled. She quickly closed her eyes as if struck by lightning.

"Alone and naked in bed with Shiva, Parvati covered his eyes with her palms, but her effort was in vain because the third eye on his forehead was looking at her," added Rama.

"In spite of her fear, Shiva embraced his wife and made passionate love to her. He then took Parvati on a tour of the Himalayas, where they enjoyed the grandeur of the forests and beauty of the mountains during their honeymoon," said Samitra.

"Most scholars say that Kali Dass, lived around the fifth century," said Carl, lighting his incense and placing it on the smoldering log.

"The classic culminated with Shiva and Parvati's honeymoon. Their son, Kumar, wasn't born in the book in spite of having his name on the title. In the final chapter the eroticism of the lovers seemed to have a religious and metaphysical dimension," said Rama.

"It looks like rain," said Samitra.

"We should head back to your brother's house so that we won't get caught in rush hour traffic again," said Carl, leaving the temple.

"That's a good idea," said Rama, noticing the dark clouds while heading with them down the flight of cement steps.

Upon arriving at the parking lot, Moti Lall was still asleep inside the taxi. Carl knocked on the window until he woke up and unlocked the car.

After they were seated, Moti drove out of the lot a few minutes before the thunder, flashes of lightning, and heavy rain. The driver turned on the windshield wipers, which flapped like wings of a prehistoric bird.

There was a peculiar silence as he swerved the taxi onto the winding road and headed slowly back to the suburb.

Chapter 22
"Early the Next Day"

Carl woke up the next morning while the rooster was still crowing, the cow mooing, and dogs barking in alley. He yawned glancing at his watch on the night table. It was 5:30 a.m., August 8, 2013. His first thought was of his wife, Barbara. He had promised to send her an email upon arriving in Kathmandu, but he still hadn't done it.

He got out of bed and did fifteen minutes of stretch exercises before leaving for the bathroom. After shaving and showering, Carl returned to his room, got dressed, and began his meditation.

Sitting on the floor in the lotus position, Carl opened the book, "Upadesha Saram, The Essence of the Teaching," turning to the chapter dealing with Astanga Yoga, The Eight Limbs of Yoga and focused upon the first five steps.

1. Yama: Avoid: anger, resentment, fear.
2. Niyam: Pursue: forgiveness, tolerance, patience.
3. Asana: Posture: sit in lotus position or upright.
4. Pranayama: Breathing: inhaling and exhaling.
5. Pratyahara: Control of senses: hearing, looking, tasting, smelling, touching.

Carl's meditation was interrupted by the bedroom door swinging open. Jyoti entered his room, carrying a cup of steaming tea.

"Namaste, Hajur. Tapailai sanchai hunuhuncha?" Greetings Sir, I hope you are well." said the servant boy, handing him a cup of tea.

"Danyabad, thanks," said Carl, reaching for the cup and setting it down on the floor next to his book. "Aihle ma dhyana gardai chu. I am now doing my morning meditation."

"Hajur, maph garnos na. Aja, bihana ko khana sat baje tira cha, Sir, please forgive me. This morning's breakfast is at 7:00 o'clock," said Jyoti, bowing his head and departing from the room, leaving the door open.

After closing the door, Carl sat down and concentrated upon the last three steps of the meditation.

   6. Dharana: Focusing upon one object: peace, harmony, nature, mountains.

   7. Dhyana: Returning to the object: each time the mind wandered

   8. Samadi: Complete absorption: awareness, total silence, no thoughts, absence of duality.

After finishing his meditation, Carl went into the living room across from the stairway where Dipak was reading "The China Daily."

"May I use your computer to send an email to my wife?"

"Of course, it's over there on the desk," said Dipak, setting down the newspaper and turning on the computer.

After a brief conversation with Dipak about the weather report for the day, Carl sat at the desk typing an e-mail.

   Dearest Barbara,

     The flight from O'Hare to Doha, Qatar was 12 hours. The service was wonderful on the jumbo jet. Every seat had a TV screen with multiple films to watch during the trip. The stewardesses were kind and pleasant. They served us our meals without any problem.

     After several hours of flying, Kathy was summoned over the loud speaker because she was the only doctor on the flight. She went to the back of the plane where she delivered a baby.

We arrived safely at the airport and boarded three buses to take us to the terminal

While continuing toward the terminal, we noticed numerous oil tankers zooming past us on the rugged road. All of a sudden our bus came to a halt due to an explosion of one of the tankers, which burst into flames. Our driver managed to turn away from the explosion although several people on our bus were injured after falling onto the floor.

Upon reaching the terminal, ambulances were waiting to take the injured to the hospital. Several guards were stationed at the entrance because of rumors that terrorists might have blown up the oil truck.

All the passengers went into the terminal except for Kathy who left the plane with Shanti, her baby and two children. Her husband was also there waiting. They all went to the hospital in Doha for further care of the mother and newborn child.

After nearly six hours of waiting at the airport, Kathy returned and we all boarded the flight to Kathmandu. I wanted to let you know that your first dream didn't come true. Rather than the plane exploding and crashing at the airport, the oil tanker exploded and the driver was killed.

In spite of the turbulence, we arrived safely in the Kathmandu Valley two days ago. You wouldn't recognize the place because of the traffic and congestion, reminding me of Calcutta or Bombay.

I hope you're doing well at the museum. Please say hello to Father Lorenzo when you see him after mass. Don't forget to say hello to Renee, Sammy, and Emily for me. Have you heard from Mark? Any news about his divorce? I presume your father, Sam, is helping him with the paper work. I'll write to you again soon.

    With all my love, Carl

After sending the email Carl sat staring at the screen of the computer, thinking about Barbara.

"You're worried about your wife, aren't you?" asked Dipak, folding, "The Times of India."

"I promised to send her an email as soon as I arrived," said Carl. "I finally sent it two days later."

"It looks like we might be getting more rain. It's been very hot here for two of days," said Dipak. "Carl, take a look at the screen on your computer. Someone just sent you a message."

    Carl glanced at the screen, noticing an email from his wife, which he quickly opened.

Dear Carl,

    I've been a nervous wreck after watching the fire at the Qatar Airport on BBC News. I was horrified when I saw so many Qatari soldiers lined up at the terminal. The cause of the explosion of the oil tanker wasn't disclosed by the reporter. I suspect it was done by terrorists. There was no report of your plane exploding. Thank God!

    Your email arrived after I told Emily and Sammy to go outside and play on the swing in the back yard. As soon as they left, I went right to the computer, where I saw your message.

Kathy emailed me after you arrived in Kathmandu on August 6th. She told me all about the baby being born on the airplane. She didn't mention the oil tanker being blown up at the airport in Qatar. However she told me that she went to the hospital with the mother and the baby in the ambulance and didn't come back until a half hour before departure for Kathmandu, wearing a burqa.

I've been going to mass every day at St. Eymard's, where I light candles and pray that you and Kathy will be safe in Nepal and Tibet.

I had another horrible dream about an earthquake hitting Nepal, resulting in the death of thousands of people with others injured and homeless. The earthquake destroyed buildings, temples and shrines throughout the Kathmandu Valley. It was just horrible to wake up sweating and trembling because of that dream.

Please be extra careful travelling to Tibet, I read in the "New York Times" that Chinese guards in plain clothes were harassing a cameraman on the Nepalese border. I also read it was almost impossible for Tibetan refugees to cross over into Nepal due to the tight security.

Carl, I hate to say this, but I had another dream that you had been arrested at the Tibetan border by Chinese guards and thrown into jail.

When I told Father Lorenzo about my dreams after mass this morning, he told me to light a vigil light and pray for the safety of you and Kathy.

He said he'd offer masses this week for both of you, including the Nepalese pilgrims travelling on the bus to Tibet on August 10th.

Sammy and Emily have just come back to the kitchen because it's so hot outside. They wanted me to say hello to you for them. My mother, Renee, is pouring lemonade for them. She also wishes you a pleasant trip to Tibet.

Be extra careful at the Tibetan border. Please say hello to Rama and Samitra and her family. Don't forget to send me another email before you leave for Tibet. I miss you terribly, especially at night.

With all my love, Barbara

"How's your family doing, Carl?" asked Dipak, setting

down the newspaper.

"They're all fine although I'm worried about Barbara. She's been having more dreams. This time she dreamt that an earthquake struck the Kathmandu Valley and caused a lot of damage to the temples and shrines throughout the valley."

"We haven't had an earthquake since 1936, during the Great Depression. I wasn't even born yet. My parents were living in this house at the time. Fortunately they weren't injured because the house was well built.

"When that 8.2 earthquake hit Nepal, it killed 10,000 people and left thousands injured and homeless in the valley. About 7000 people were also killed in India from that same earthquake.

"I don't think we have to be concerned about your wife's dreams. India's still recovering from the terrible floods, which left thousands of pilgrims stranded in the Himalayan Mountains," said Dipak.

"I believe there's a connection between glaciers melting in Himalayas and earthquakes. The connection is due to Climate Change. When the glaciers melt, the heavy ice pressing against the earth is no longer there to hold down the tectonic plates.

"Once the ice is gone there's a release of pressure due to the shifting of the plates. The size of the earthquake and the number of tremors, depends upon the amount and duration of the shifting," said Carl.

"The seismologists at the university agreed to alert us a week ahead of time if we're in danger of having another earthquake here in Nepal," said Dipak.

"Bihana ko khana tayar garyo. Banchama aunos na. Breakfast is now ready. Come to the kitchen," announced Purosotam, entering the living room and picking up an empty tea cup before departing for the kitchen.

Dipak and Carl hurried up the three flights of stairs, where they got a glimpse of the growling dog prior to entering the Prayer Room. They folded their hands and bowed to the images of the gods and goddesses, recited a few prayers, and hurried down the hallway to the kitchen.

After breakfast Dipak informed their guests that he and Uma would like to the celebrate Janai Purni or Raksha Bandhan, "The Sacred Thread Festival".

"We need to buy the sacred thread in the market place" said Uma, gathering up the plates from the table and taking them to Jyoti, who was washing the dishes in the sink.

"Today, I'd like to take you to the market place and the Sacred Pond, Kumbeshwar, in Patan, where a lot of people will be celebrating the holidays."

Chapter 23
"The Trip to Patan"

As they travelled along the rutted road in Dipak's Honda, Carl noticed heavy equipment imported from America. He said, "There are a lot of cranes, bulldozers, and trucks parked alongside the road and in the alleys, but I don't see anyone working today even though the sun's shining and there isn't a cloud in the sky."

"We often have two days of sunshine, which makes the roads dusty, followed by a couple of days of rain making them muddy. The Department of Transport Management increased our heavy equipment here in the valley by150 % this past year. We have over 3000 heavy duty trucks and machines alongside the roads throughout the valley," said Dipak.

"The problem is the trenches that were dug out by the cranes are filled with water from the monsoon rain, but there are no pumps to drain the water," said Uma. "Just look out the window. You can see the pipes, waiting to be installed."

"Those pipes have been there for months, even before the monsoon season started," said Dipak. "We have equipment, drivers, and laborers, but we don't have the money to finish the rutted roads here in the valley."

"Our citizens have submitted petitions to complete the construction of a 13-km road, which was supposed to be finished in 18 months. It took the workers three years to complete eight kilometers," said Uma. "Some of our friends contacted the District Development Committee and discovered that the contractors spent 60 million rupees for a road that's not finished."

"Three private companies were involved with the blacktopping before they ran out of money," said Dipak, irritated when his Honda struck a rut in the road.

"That was quite a bump," said Samitra, clinging to Rama's arm in the back seat. "I hope it didn't do damage to your car."

"The Honda's is well constructed," said Dipak, shaking his head. "We'll soon be turning onto New Road, which was built and paved by the Chinese, prior to the death of Mao in the summer of 1976."

"The local people in Shanku are threatening to take actions against the contractors by bringing the petition to the Prime Minister," said Uma. "I doubt whether anything will get done."

"The worst road is the one going to Buddha Nil Kantha the Old Blue Throat, shrine," said Dipak.

"Years ago Samitra and I walked the six miles from Kathmandu to that shrine," said Rama. "It was in the fall when the villagers were harvesting their rice. You can't even see the rice fields now because of the five and six story buildings on both sides of the road."

"The contractors displaced the two-story buildings where the farmers used to live and raise their children, filling the area with poorly constructed suburban houses," said Dipak.

"A lot of those buildings are vacant or still unfinished," said Uma. "The problem with the housing industry is that the government doesn't place sanctions upon them."

"The urban population in the Kathmandu Valley was about a million ten years ago. We now have about 2.5 million people in the valley," said Dipak.

"There's been a huge migration of ethnic groups from

distant villages, looking for work here. All of them were hoping to have electricity, clean drinking water, and satellite television," said Dipak. "Most of them are disappointed."

"Several years ago New Zealand's consulting engineers won a United Nations award to develop a building code here in Nepal. Our structural engineers worked with New Zealanders to study the faults in the Himalayas, the historic earthquakes, and the ground conditions," said Dipak, "They also drafted a building code, which came to halt because the Maoist Revolution.

"Several businessmen, who financed the construction of buildings were experts at bribery, encouraging inspectors to take their money and look the other way. Those poorly constructed buildings will collapse if we have another earthquake," said Dipak.

"I get nervous when you talk about earthquakes," said Uma. "The New Zealanders predicted that we'll have another earthquake during the summer of 2015."

"Uma, you worry so much about the future. It's important to take things a day at time," said Dipak.

"We're finally here in the city of Patan. I hope we can find a parking space in the crowded city," said Carl.

"There's a taxi over there leaving that space," said Dipak, entering the crowded lot and parking the Honda.

Chapter 24
"The Sacred Thread Festival"

"The city of Patan has a long history," said Dipak, walking out of the parking lot with his friends. "The Emperor Ashoka from India was responsible for the construction of Buddhist stupas here in 250 B.C. They are located in the four corners of this city."

"Of course the Newars were responsible for the construction of the temples and shrines because they were among the indigenous inhabitants of the valley," said Uma.

"In the 15th century Malla Kings speaking Newari, ruled the three cities of the valley. They were conquered by Pritivi Narayan Shah who introduced the Nepali language to the entire country," said Rama, leading the way into the crowded bazaar, where customers were shopping.

"What are those shopkeepers doing over there?" asked Carl, noticing several customers buying threaded bracelets.

"They're celebrating Janai Purni," said Uma.

"Tell me more about the festival. Janai means the holy thread and Purni is a shortened form of Purnima, which means the full moon," said Carl.

"That's right. The upper castes in Hinduism are the Brahman priests and the Chetris, warriors, who rule the country. Only men from these two castes are allowed to wear the sacred body thread over their shoulders.

"The other castes are Vaisyas, the merchants, shopkeepers, and Sudras, farmers, selling fruits, vegetables, and flowers in the open air market places. They must wear the thread on their wrists," explained Dipak.

"There are a lot of people shopping today," said Samitra, walking past a bearded man holding a bunch of bananas and a woman standing in front of bushels of tangerines and apples.

"I was given my sacred body thread by a priest when I was a teenager during the ritual, which initiated me into the Brahman caste of Hinduism," said Dipak, pausing to unbutton his shirt to show them the triple cord around his neck and looped under his arm.

"I must wear this thread every day of my life. As you can see the yellow threads are frayed and dirty. It's my duty to change them once a year during this festival," said Dipak.

"The word caste is often misunderstood by foreigners because it implies inequality and injustice. No doubt the corruption among some members of the wealthy upper castes were responsible for our Maoist Revolution, which dragged on several years here in Nepal," said Samitra.

"The amazing thing is that in spite of the revolution, the Maoists allowed the Nepalese people freedom to practice their religion and celebrate our sacred holidays. They didn't destroy the Hindu and Buddhist temples and shrines in Nepal like the Maoists did in Tibet." said Rama.

"Maoist terrorists often gave Nepalese Christians, Moslems, and Jews a hard time, but they didn't stop them from attending their churches, mosques, and synagogues," said Uma.

"Some violent Maoist terrorists bombed the local Catholic Church, which killed a few people here in Patan during the revolution. Since then the church was repaired and the Nepalese Catholics are back to attending their services," said Dipak.

"The only serious problem is that some Maoists are still trying to prevent the Tibetan Buddhists living in Nepal from celebrating the Dalai Lama's birthday. However many Buddhists do it secretly without drawing attention.

"After Mao's death, there was loosening of government regulations, which led to the reconstruction of the Jokang Temple and restoration of damaged monasteries in Lhasa.

"In comparison to the Maoist revolution in Tibet, our revolution in Nepal was tame," said Dipak, pausing to look at the shopkeepers, selling the sacred threads.

"Dipak ,what is the meaning of the triple thread that you showed us?" asked Carl.

"The threads symbolizes that upper caste males must control their thoughts, words, and emotions after their initiation into Hinduism," said Dipak.

"Our Gurus taught us to treat teachers and elders with respect, including members of different castes and religions. Since God is the Creator, Preserver, and Destroyer of all life, we believe that the Supreme Soul is present within all human beings, plants, and animals.

"At a very early age we're taught prayers and meditation so that our individual soul may be united with the Supreme Soul by practicing Yoga," said Rama.

"Later this afternoon, Dipak's guru will come too our house with a new triple thread. We'll gather around the priest in the garden while he blesses the threads in the name of Vishnu and places it around his neck," said Uma, pausing to examine the colored wrist threads.

"I'd like to buy them here," said Uma. "Men, women, and children from all castes are allowed to purchase wrist threads during this festival."

"The thread is called Raksha Bandhan, which means the 'Bond of Protection'. We only wear it for three months," said Samirta. "It must be removed when we celebrate the Festival of the Lights, Tihar, in honor of Goddess Lakshmi during the month of November."

    Uma paused to speak to the shopkeeper, who was selling the yellow thread. She handed him ten rupees, and he nodded to the Brahman priest, who was sitting on a blue cushion in front of the counter. Uma folded her hand and bowed to him. She smiled as the priest tied the sacred thread to her wrist. Next in line was, Samitra, and then Carl.

    While the priest was tying the thread on his wrist Carl asked, "Samitra, you never told us why you must remove the thread during the autumn festival?"

    "We replace the frayed and dirty thread with a new one to honor Lakshmi, the Goddess of Wealth, who takes the form of the sacred cow. We believe that owning a cow is a symbol of wealth because she produces milk, butter, yogurt, and cheese. In the villages and towns cow dung is used as fuel for cooking, and her leather for sandals and shoes.

    "After worshiping the cow, a Brahman priest ties the faded wrist thread to the tail of a sacred cow. We believe that the spirit of a cremated corpse clings to the thread on her tail while she carries the soul across a sacred river and releases it to travel to the Gate of Judgment," said Samitra.

    "It's unfortunate that villagers often go into debt to buy a cow so that a family member's soul can be transported to the next world," said Rama.

    "It also bothers us because some Brahman priests refuse to perform the death rituals unless a sacred cow is present. Others insist that the deceased must give the priest the cow to take home with him after the ritual," said Uma.

    "It's unfortunate that there's corruption among priests as well as politicians," said Dipak, walking toward the temple.

    "The Kumbeswar Temple has five stories and a pool in the courtyard," said Samitra. "The ceremony began late last night, but is still packed with worshippers."

"Inside the temple are two large Shiva Lingams, which are phallic symbols. The first lingam is a pillar with five carved faces of Shiva, facing north, south, east, west, and upward. The second lingam contains the body of Shiva, covered by golden snakes," said Uma.

"Here we are at the temple. It used to be two stories high, but it was reconstructed during the reign of a Malla King. It's now the highest temple in Patan.

"Kumbeswar, Lord of the Water Pot, is dedicated to Lord Shiva. His shamans have come from remote villages in the mountains to celebrate the Sacred Thread Festival. They are over there wearing colorful headdresses with feathers and bowing to the images of Shiva," continued Uma.

"Where's all that noise coming from?" asked Carl.

"It was worse last night when hundreds of Hindus were waiting for the image of the goddess, Bagala Muki Ajima, to arrive from her temple. Her name means, 'Grandmother's Powerful Face'," said Samitra. "Eventually several men arrived with her statue to present to Shiva.

"The officiating priest wore a scarlet robe and was carrying a Shiva Lingam with garlands of flowers on it to the pool. With each step that he took, a Brahmin priest in front of him read a passage from a sacred scripture, while the musicians were blowing trumpets and beating drums," added Samitra.

"What kind of power does Ajima have?" asked Carl.

"By reciting prayers to her, she gives her devotees power to control their thoughts and emotions. By chanting the mantra 'Hireem', she drives away evil forces, coming from gossip, slander and violent actions," said Uma.

"Notice that the goddess' complexion is golden. She's wearing a brilliant yellow dress and sits on a throne among lotus blossoms," said Samitra.

"There are also terrible images of her destroying enemies by ripping their tongues out of their mouths," said Dipak.

Upon arrival at the pool, they saw a decorated Shiva Lingam on a platform in the water, surrounded by men and teenage boys wearing loin cloths. They were standing in a circle bowing to the sacred image.

"What's that floating in the water?" asked Carl.

"Those are offerings of rice, flowers, and fruit thrown into the pool by the devotees," said Dipak.

"Look over there, where the women are scooping water with their hands and sprinkling it on their heads to purify themselves. After this ritual, they stand in line and wait to receive their sacred thread from the Brahman priests in the courtyard under that banyan tree," said Uma.

"When we received our sacred threads, the priest gave us each a blessing, linked to King Bali," said Carl, noticing teenagers and young boys leaping into the pond and splashing water at each other.

"The priest said these words," said Dipak. "Thus, I tie the Raksha Bhandan around your wrist, the same which bound the arm of mighty Bali, the king of the Danavas. May its protection be eternal?

"Many centuries ago King Bali was known for his devotion and piety. He took a vow to grant his people any wish that they requested, which made him very popular.

"As a result of the king's popularity, the Hindu gods and goddesses were jealous of him. They approached Lord Vishnu and asked him to get their devotees back," said Uma.

"After Vishnu took the shape of a dwarf, he asked Bali to fulfill his wish, which was to give him as much land as he could have in three strides.

"Once Bali consented to give him the land, Vishnu changed his shape into a giant. In two strides he stepped across the Earth into Heaven. Then Vishnu produced a third leg from his navel and stepped unto Bali's head, pushing him into the Underworld, where he continues to rule, wearing his sacred thread on his wrist," said Samitra.

"Whenever the equilibrium of the earth was threatened Vishnu became an Avatar. In his form as a dwarf, he was called Vamana," said Samitra.

"I wish that Lord Vishnu would return to earth and do something about the glaciers melting in the Himalayas. I'm afraid that if it doesn't stop, Nepal will be either destroyed by floods or earthquakes," said Uma.

"Stop being so pessimistic, Uma. Here it is a holiday and you're worried about disasters," said Dipak.

"After the holidays Shiva will leave the Kumbeswara Temple with Parvati to visit Gosainkund, the sacred lake in the mountains about 25 miles north beyond the Sherpa settlement at Helembu," said Dipak.

"Several years ago I went on a trek with friends to Gosaindkund during the month of August. Because of the monsoon it rained every day during our eleven day trek.

"At that time thousands of pilgrims from Nepal and India were trekking to the sacred lake to celebrate Janai Purni and to worship Shiva and Parvati.

"That long narrow trail was slippery and muddy due to the rain. Our small group hiked for six days before reaching the Sacred Lake.

"By the time we arrived, most of the pilgrims had already departed although a few were still bathing in the lake and worshipping Shiva. I noticed a chill in the air since the entire lake was covered by a strange white mist," said Carl.

"Because Gosainkund is located at 14,200 feet, pilgrims often become weak and dizzy while bathing in the lake at the high altitude," said Dipak.

"Some of them believe they are being exposed to the polluted water that Lord Shiva drank from the ocean in order to save the human race," added Samitra.

"Others faint due to oxygen deprivation and have to be carried back to Kathmandu on the backs of Sherpa guides from Helembu," said Rama.

"Several years ago my friends and I witnessed an exorcism at the Sherpa settlement. We arrived there late in the afternoon on our way to the sacred lake and stayed overnight," said Carl.

"I was amazed how the whole Sherpa community turned out to watch the shaman perform the exorcism that evening. Since the monsoon rain was pouring down, everyone took shelter in a community hall.

"The Sherpas were silent when the shaman entered the room wearing a loin cloth, a feathered head dress, and a string of bells around his bare chest. He circled the sick man several times with bells ringing from his ankles and his bare feet thudding on the wooden floor," said Carl.

"After several hours of clashing cymbals, chanting prayers, and pounding on the drum, the shaman drove the evil spirit from the sick man.

"The healed Sherpa rose from the blanket, where he had been lying on the floor and was greeted by family members."

"The two ponds here at Kumbeswar are symbolically linked to Gosainkund Lake. Shiva reclined in the water to rest after drinking the poison from the polluted ocean," said Rama. "He drank the poison to save the fish, whales, sea creatures, including humans who need water to survive."

"I wish Shiva had come to the Himalayas to drink the monsoon rain which caused the collapsing of the mountains, leaving pilgrims stranded in India," said Uma.

Chapter 25
"An Accident on the Highway"

Early the next morning Carl was awakened by the crowing of the rooster. He glanced out the window amazed that the sun was so bright, pausing to hear the cow mooing and the dogs barking.

After shaving, showering and doing his stretch exercises, he meditated for a half hour before being interrupted by Purosotam with a cup of tea.

Carl continued with his meditation until the servant knocked on the door and told him that breakfast was being served. He rushed out of his room and hurried up the three flights of stairs to the kitchen.

"Namaste," said Carl, bowing to his friends. "Namaste, please excuse me for being late."

"Jyoti, khana hamro satilai lyaunos na! Jyoti, bring our friend his breakfast," said Uma.

Rama and Samitra were seated at the table across from Dipak and Uma. They were talking about going to the Pashupatinath Temple for a special ceremony for pilgrims travelling to Mount Kailash.

"There's a legend about the origin of Shiva's famous temple," said Dipak. "He became tired of numerous gods being worshipped by his devotees. So he left Benares in India and came to the Kathmandu Valley. Upon arrival he decided to change himself into a gazelle and live in the forest with other wild animals.

"Many gods also left their palace on Mount Kailash and went to Kathmandu to find Shiva who had been missing for a long time. They heard that he was masquerading in the forest as a gazelle," said Uma.

"Mount Kailash is to the Hindu gods and goddesses like Mount Olympus is to the Greek deities," commented Carl.

"Upon reaching the forest the gods seized Shiva by the horns hoping to capture him and bring him back to their palace at Mount Kailash. While struggling with the gazelle, they broke off his horns," said Rama.

"After Shiva leapt across the Bhagmati River, where his temple is now located, he changed into his human form. He shouted across the river to the gods, who were holding his horns. 'Since I have lived in the woods as an animal, in the future my name shall be Pashupati, Lord of the Animals,' " said Dipak.

"Lord Vishnu took Shiva's broken horn and propped it up, making it into a lingam, which he placed into a shrine. Immediately all the gods began worshipping the sacred image," added Rama. "A temple was then built over the shrine which lasted for generations but eventually collapsed from an earthquake.

"The Shiva lingam was buried in the rubble. After the debris was cleared, a sacred cow was grazing in the area and sprinkled her milk over the spot where it had been buried. A herdsman dug up the sacred horn and later enshrined it in the new temple," said Samitra.

"We better get going so that we're not late for the ceremony at the temple," said Uma, rising from her chair and gathering the plates. She took them to the sink where Purosotam was waiting to wash them.

While leaving the house, Dipak said, "Carl, you can sit with me in the front seat. I hope the rest of you won't be too cramped in the backseat."

After opening the lock on the cast iron gate, Dipak

shouted to Jyoti to come down from the kitchen on the third floor to lock the gate after they departed.

"I hate going into Kathmandu during rush hour," said Uma, sitting in the back seat with Samitra and Rama.

A few moments later Dipak drove past the neighbor's house where the rooster strutted among the hens. He continued driving past the barn on the right where the Guernsey cow nibbled on grass with her calf.

As they headed down the hill, Carl noticed goats behind the meat shop, where customers were buying meat. He saw a sign that stated no chickens or eggs for sale. "Why are there no chickens or eggs available for sale?" asked Carl.

"The city of Bhaktapur is shut down due to the Avian Flu," said Dipak, driving through the small town where the shopkeepers waited on customers from the suburbs.

"I read in the newspaper that the farmers were angry when our soldiers arrived to kill their chickens and burn their remains in the nearby fields," said Uma.

"Throughout the valley the meat shops aren't selling chickens to the public. Even the restaurants have stopped serving chickens because of the Avian Flu," said Dipak.

As they rode along, Carl noticed a plastic statue of Shiva attached on the dashboard. He glanced over his shoulders and asked, "Because you are devotees of Shiva, could you tell me the meaning of Siva's Cosmic Dance? I like this image on the dashboard."

"We call that statue, Nataraja, which means 'King of the Dance'," said Samitra. "Shiva's dancing is symbolic of his transcendent identity as Creator, Preserver, and Destroyer of all beings."

"We're all dancing with Shiva every moment of our lives from conception until death. Even after death, we continue to dance until we're reincarnated and eventually united forever with the transcendent, Mahadeva, the Supreme God.

"If you look closely at the image of Shiva on the dashboard, you'll see that his head is balanced. His right earring contains a snake, which represents the male, but his left ear with an earring, suggests the female," said Uma.

"The symbolism here is that Shiva is ultimately the Creator of both sexes; however, he transcends them. His fiery third eye in the middle of his forehead indicates spiritual knowledge and wisdom," said Uma.

"Some years ago I visited the Island of Elephanta off the coast of Bombay" said Carl. "There were numerous statues of Shiva on display in the Great Cave Temple, which was built in the sixth century.

"The temple is an architectural wonder. The exterior has soaring pillars at the entrances. The interior is a huge cave made into a vast hall with side chapels. It also has pillars supporting the ceiling and the weight of the hill above the temple," said Carl.

"You're right! That temple is a showcase with sanctuaries depicting Shiva's multiple identities," said Rama, pausing as Dipak slammed on the brakes.

"What's happening?" screamed Uma, alarmed by the stalled traffic on New Road.

"Why are so many cars stalled with their drivers honking their horns. I'm getting out to see what's happened," said Dipak, leaving the Honda.

"I'll come with you," said Carl, opening the door on the passenger's side and joining him.

"You women wait here for us to return. Be sure and lock the car," said Rama, departing while the women looked out the windows trying to see what was causing the delay.

"There's a crowd of people blocking traffic straight ahead," announced Dipak, leading the way past a long row of honking vehicles.

As they hurried toward the crowd, Rama stopped to ask a cab driver, standing next to his vehicle and smoking a cigarette, about what had happened.

"We've been waiting here over two hours for the police to disperse the crowd," said the taxi driver, throwing his cigarette butt into the street and stamping it with his foot.

"Brother, what happened?" asked Dipak, annoyed by the constant honking of the horns.

"A truck driver was speeding along the highway, when a calf darted into the traffic from a side street. The alarmed cow went charging into the street after her calf. Her baby was killed instantly, and the mother was severely injured. The cow is lying in the street gasping for breath with her legs broken," said the taxi driver.

"The shopkeepers and their customers are furious with the driver of the truck for killing the calf and injuring the sacred cow," said the taxi driver.

"They have been throwing stones at that huge truck and pounding on the driver's windows. If he leaves his vehicle, the crowd will stone him to death," said the taxi driver. "The problem is that he's a Sikh driver, who came from Pokhara with a truck load of cement for repairing the roads.

"The neighborhood police have been trying to protect the driver from being killed by threatening to arrest the crowd."

"Here comes the National Guard now," said Dipak. "They're bringing a veterinarian with them."

Within a few minutes the leader of the National Guard, using a megaphone, announced to the crowd to back away from the wounded cow and her dead calf.

While he spoke, numerous guards surrounded the truck with their rifles aimed at the crowd as the veterinarian gave the bleeding cow a lethal injection. Within a few minutes the cow died near her mutilated calf.

By the time Carl, Rama, and Dipak arrived, the guards had dragged the cow and her calf out of the street and placed their corpses on a wooden cart, which took them to be cremated along the river.

The Sikh driver, suffering from shock, finally came out of his truck, surrounded by guards. He stood there trembling, while the crowd shouted that he should be arrested and put in jail for careless driving.

Carl was amazed to see a Nepalese guard signal the Sikh driver to enter the truck on the passenger side and sit down. The guard boarded the vehicle and started the engine before driving away, leaving behind the angry protestors.

A guard signaled for the row of cars to move along.

As the cars and trucks started moving slowly forward, the three men rushed back to their parked Honda, where the women were waiting for them to continue their journey.

When Dipak informed Uma and Samitra about what had happened, everyone was silent for a few minutes.

"Where did we leave off with our conversation?" asked Rama. "Fortunately, we weren't delayed long in the traffic."

"We were talking about the temple on the Island of Elephanta," said Samitra. "I feel badly about that calf dying and then having to put the injured cow to sleep."

"The cow is an incarnation of Lakshmi, the Goddess of Wealth," said Uma, trying to console Samitra.

"Our custom about allowing cows and bulls to roam the streets in the Kathmandu Valley is still a problem here," said Dipak. "There's a law forbidding cows to wander the streets, but it's not enforced by the police."

"Nepal hasn't recovered from the Maoist Revolution," said Dipak, taking a deep breathe.

"Let's forget the revolution for now," sighed Uma. "I

remember visiting the main hall of the Cave Temple at Elephanta years ago. There was a large shrine in the shape of a cubicle with entrances on four sides, called the Garbagraha or Womb House."

"In the center of the shrine were the Shiva lingam and yoni, symbolizing the eternal union of the Male with the Female," said Samitra.

"The union of opposites reminded me of the Yin and Yang symbol in Taoism," said Carl. "I was in awe when I saw the huge sculptures of Nataraja, the King of the Dance in three different chapels. I was also puzzled by a statue called 'Ardanarisvara', which means, Lord Shiva is Half Female."

"Carl Gustav Jung , the psychiatrist from Switzerland, believed in the importance of the individual's quest for wholeness by the integration of the opposites," said Rama. "Jung came up with the theory that every human being possesses male and female archetypes."

"He probably got the idea from the ancient Romans, who believed we had two souls, the Animus, the intellect and the will, located in the brain, and the Anima, the emotions and feelings, connected to the heart," said Samitra "In Latin animus is the masculine gender and anima, feminine."

"Jung claimed that while a man is sleeping the female archetype is expressed in his dreams. The opposite is true of the female who manifests a masculine inner personality while dreaming," continued Rama.

"I believe that when Shiva is depicted as being half male and half female it means the Lord is present in both sexes. Since humans and mammals are both conceived from a sperm and an ovum, each individual has genetic traits from both the mother and father," said Samitra.

"Recently, we've had a protest in Kathmandu by The

LGBT protestors, who were largely high school, college or university students," said Dipak. "I don't believe most them know anything about Jung's philosophy, which is similar to the Chinese, Yin and Yang symbol."

"We're all children of God. I feel sorry for those, who are rejected by society because of their sexual orientation," said Rama. "By the way when Samitra and I visited the temple at Elephanta we saw two statues of the Goddess Uma."

"I liked her statues more than the others because my wife was named after her," said Dipak.

"Uma is the Goddess of Light and Beauty. She's an avatar of Parvati, the wife of Shiva," said Samitra.

"I was horrified when I saw a stone image of Shiva with vampire like teeth at the temple," said Uma, glancing out the window. "Look over there! It's the bronze bull Nandi, Shiva's vehicle, in front of the Pashupatinath Temple."

Chapter 26
"Arrival at Pashupatinath Temple"

"We are now a short distance from the Pashupatinath Temple. The traffic is heavy here," said Dipak, "We still have twenty minutes before we meet the pilgrims who'll be travelling with us to Mount Kailash. Most of them are followers of Shiva."

"When you look at Shiva's statue on the dashboard, you'll notice his wild hair," said Carl. "He looks like a yogi, who doesn't care about his appearance."

"Shiva's flowing hair is a symbol of the Ganges River coming down from the Himalayas in honor of the Goddess Ganga. It represents descending grace. The Crescent Moon symbolizes Shiva's fertility and creative power while the skull reveals his destructiveness," said Samitra.

"Where did you learn about those symbols?" asked Carl.

"It's in the book, 'Dancing with Shiva: Hinduism's Contemporary Catechism'. It's here in my purse."

"It's still early in the morning and there are plenty of parking spaces here," said Dipak, entering the parking lot. After leaving the Honda, they joined the crowd heading toward the temple.

"I'm impressed by the pagoda style architecture of the main temple," said Carl.

"The two levels of the roofs are made from copper with layers of gold that sparkle in the sunlight," said Dipak. "Don't' overlook the designs carved in the wooden rafters."

"Excuse me for interrupting you. Did you see that woman coming out of the taxi over there? She's wearing red high heels and a scarlet dress. She's certainly getting a lot of attention from the young men, staring at her. I can't believe she'd wear such a seductive outfit," said Uma.

"That woman's Margaret Porter!" said Carl. "She's coming with us on the pilgrimage to Mount Kailash."

"That's her all right," said Samitra. "I tutored her on Skype for a couple of months because she wanted to practice her Nepali. She told me that she hadn't spoken it since her husband died."

"She looks like Marilynn Monroe with that dyed blonde hair," said Rama. "She's very attractive for her age."

"The last time I saw her was in 2001 here in Kathmandu. After the assassination of the Royal Family, Margaret had a nervous breakdown because her son, Nigel, was accused of murdering the abbot of at the Bodhanath monastery.

"She eventually married her Nepalese psychiatrist, who helped her recover from shock. Unfortunately, her husband, Krishna, died from an automobile accident several months ago in London," said Carl.

"So that's Margaret Porter," said Uma. "Samitra told me she was planning to come with us to Mt. Kailash. She also plans to visit Nigel, who's a Buddhist monk, studying the Tibetan language in Lhasa."

"That taxi driver escorted Margaret to the building where we'll be having our orientation for the pilgrimage," said Dipak, pausing to look at the sacred cows grazing in a lot near the temple and pigeons being fed kernels of corn by a caretaker.

"Hurry up or we'll be late," said Rama, rushing past curio shops selling statues and postcards.

"We only have ten minutes before the ceremony begins" insisted Dipak, leading the way to the entrance gate, where they were stopped by armed guards.

Carl noticed Margaret Porter with her taxi driver hurrying past a large water fountain toward a brick building. He watched her remove her red high heels putting them into her handbag, before walking barefoot up the steps to the entrance.

Dipak explained to the uniformed guards that they were going to an orientation for a pilgrimage to Tibet in the building on the other side of a fountain. They continued past the guards and the fountain.

"Dipak, how many entrances are there to the temple, Pashupatinath?" asked Carl, noticing a gate on his left where an armed guard stood next to an enclosed booth with a ticket collector. The entrance fee for foreigners was 1000 rupees or ten dollars.

"There are four entrances to the Pashupatinath Temple. This is the main one. If you buy a ticket you may go to the shrines on the exterior of the temple, but you won't be allowed to go inside the Sacred Temple. Being Nepalese there is no fee for us to roam around the grounds. We're able to peek at the statues inside, but we're not allowed to enter."

"Thanks for the information," said Carl, removing his shoes and placing them on a wooden rack before going up the stairs of the brick building to the entrance. He was followed by Dipak and Uma.

"That building across from us is Pashupatinath. It contains the Maukhalinga. It's a phallic symbol a meter high with four faces. The male lingam is supported by a silver, female yoni with a serpent around it. The large stone image is covered with golden vestments," said Samitra. "I had the privilege of going into the building the last time we were here." said Uma.

"If we have time after the orientation, we can also take a closer look at the bronze bull, Nandi, Shiva's vehicle. It's almost 8:00 o'clock," said Dipak.

Upon entering the interior of the hall, Carl noticed that most of the Nepalese pilgrims were seated on cushions in the lotus position. There were also young Brahman priests, wearing white shirts and trousers, sitting to the left of a painted mural with images of Shiva and Parvati, Nandi, and Vishnu with Lakshmi.

Carl glanced around the room while his friends sat down on their cushions. He noticed that Margaret was sitting alone in a chair on the opposite side of the room. Within a few moments when their eyes met, Margaret rose from her chair and hurried across the room.

"Carl, it's so good to see you," she said, giving him a hug by pressing her body against his chest.

"It's been a long time since we met," said Carl "My friends are anxious to meet you. I understand you've been studying Nepali on Skype with Samitra."

"I'm sorry for being so emotional," said Margaret, sobbing while clinging to him. She backed away, reaching into her purse for handkerchief. "It's been eight months since my husband, Krishna, died from that auto accident."

"I'm terribly sorry about that," said Carl, glancing at his watch, noticing that it was 8:15. He also was aware that the pilgrims and priests were staring at Margaret's low cut dress and whispering to each other about her appearance.

Everyone was waiting for the tourist guide, Hari, to arrive so that the young priests could begin chanting for the protection of the pilgrims while travelling in Tibet.

Carl felt uneasy, because Margaret was getting so much attention. He said, "Margaret, would you like to go outside for a few minutes so we can talk more privately?"

"Maybe later," she said. "Samitra told me that you were staying with her brother and his wife in the suburb."

"That's right. I've been with them ever since we arrived three days ago," said Carl.

"I didn't get here until yesterday. I stayed overnight at the Kathmandu Guest House. I'm sorry that I've made such a spectacle of myself in front of everyone. I feel awkward because they're all looking at us," said Margaret, removing a lace shawl from her purse and wrapping it around her shoulders and covering her cleavage.

"Here comes Samitra. She was so patient with me while I studied Nepali on skype. She invited me to go with her and Rama on this pilgrimage."

"Margaret, I expected you to call me as soon as you got to Kathmandu," said Samitra, giving her a hug.

"My flight was cancelled due to fog in London," said Margaret. "I waited for hours at the airport. It didn't leave until yesterday morning. Please forgive me for not calling you. I've been a nervous wreck due to the delay."

Samitra glanced at her watch. It's nearly 8:30 and our tour guide still hasn't arrived."

"Would you mind if I sit down?" asked Margaret. "I'm quite exhausted from the flight. I came here by taxi."

"There are vacant chairs behind the pilgrims," said Samitra, taking them to area.

"I'd be glad to keep you company during the orientation," said Carl, sitting down beside Margaret.

"Here comes our tour guide, Hari. He's a half hour late. I better get back to my cushion. I'm sure the chanting will begin shortly," said Samitra, returning to her cushion.

"Margaret, how is Nigel doing?" asked Carl. "Is he still in Lhasa studying Tibetan?"

"He stayed in London with us for several months back in 2001. After our wedding, Krishna and I travelled with him to Tibetan Buddhist monasteries in the Alps. We were hoping he would join a community nearby so that we could visit him more often. Instead he returned to his monastery at Tyangboche in Nepal.

"After studying Tibetan for several months, the Chinese government encouraged Nigel to become a tour guide for English speaking tourists. Since he is a Buddhist monk, he donates his salary and tips to the monastery where he is staying," said Margaret, pausing to listen to the tour guide.

"Hari's speaking so fast in Nepali that I can't understand a word that he saying. What's he saying, Carl?"

"He's explaining the ceremony, involving the chanting by the priests," said Carl." I'm sure he'll switch to English to let us know what is happening."

After speaking in Nepali for about five minutes, Hari translated everything into English. He said, "The priests will be chanting passages from the Vedas, our ancient scriptures, while the Head Priest performs the ceremony.

"As you know Rudra, the Fierce One, is another name for Shiva," said Hari. "When I give the signal the priests will begin chanting, while their Guru performs the Rudrabhishek Ceremony.

"The word Abhishek means the pouring of water. The guru is now pouring water from the Ganges River over the bronze Shiva Lingam in front of the room. This cleansing frees us from enemies, ghosts, and evil spirits.

"The continuous stream of water flowing onto the lingam throughout the ceremony removes our worries, anxieties, and fears as we travel on the long road to Mount Kailash.

"There are fruits surrounding Shiva, and their juices will be mixed with water and poured over the lingam while the priests chant for us to have a safe pilgrimage.

"The mixture of sugarcane and water will be offered to the Goddess Lakshmi to provide us with food, clothing, and shelter during our journey.

"Honey mixed with water supplies us with money to fund the trip. Clarified butter, ghee, will also be offered to improve our health as we travel.

"Milk mingled with water will bring you a son or a grandson to assist you during old age and at your funeral rituals," said Hari.

"The young priests dressed in white will now begin chanting the Vedas, while the guru pours the water and juices over the Shiva Lingam for the next three hours.

"After the chanting there will be a Fire Ceremony honoring Agni, the God of Fire, a friend of Shiva.

"Don't forget early tomorrow morning, we'll all meet at the bus stop with our luggage so that we may begin our journey from Kathmandu to Tibet," said Hari, sitting down on a cushion in front of the guru and the Shiva Lingam, giving the signal for the ceremony to begin.

Chapter 27
"A Surprise Meeting at a Restaurant"

Carl sat patiently next to Margaret while the young Brahman priests chanted without stopping for the next three hours. The guru performed the Rudrabhishek Ceremony by pouring water mixed with the other liquids over the lingam.

The event was culminated by the Fire Ceremony for a final purification of sins of the past.

Several Hindus pilgrims waited in line so that they could pour water over the lingam before leaving. Others were eager to talk to Hari or congratulate the young priests for their fine chanting. A few lingered to visit with relatives.

While leaving the building, Dipak introduce Carl and Margaret to the Canadian couple, who planned to join them on the pilgrimage.

"It's a pleasure to meet you," said Allen, shaking hands with them "This is my wife, Casandra."

"We're originally from Bulgaria. Allen and I met at the university while we were studying Herbal Medicine. After our wedding, we moved to Quebec," said Casandra.

"We look forward to seeing you tomorrow at the bus stop," said Dipak, noticing that Margaret was reaching into her hand bag for her high heels.

"We'll be there by 8:00 o'clock sharp," said Allen, sitting on the steps to put on his shoes while the others were busy removing them from the wooden rack.

"Oh there's my taxi," said Margaret, noticing that the driver was smoking a cigarette in front of the fountain. "I asked Akrodha to meet me here. I must go now. I'll see you all tomorrow at the bus stop."

All eyes of the pilgrims, coming out of the auditorium, were focused on Margaret as she hurried toward the taxi driver in her scarlet dress with matching high heels.

Upon reaching the fountain, she waved to Carl, throwing him a kiss with her right hand, not expecting her lace shawl to fall onto the ground, which exposed her cleavage. While covering it with both hands, she watched the taxi driver pick up the shawl and give it to her.

With nearly everyone still watching, Margaret wrapped the shawl around her shoulders. Taking the Akrodha by the arm, she hurried with him through the gate toward the taxi.

While walking to the parking lot, Uma said, "We need to get something to eat before going home."

"Let's go to Patan. My daughter, Kathy, sent me and an email informing me that she's been going to a restaurant close to Shanta Bhawan Hospital for lunch. I wanted to say goodbye to her before we leave for Tibet." said Carl.

"There's a good restaurant called the Himalayan Café in Patan near the hospital. Usually doctors and nurses go there for lunch," said Dipak, entering his Honda.

After every one was settled, Dipak left the parking lot and headed toward Patan. Within twenty minutes they arrived at the Himalayan Café.

Upon entering the restaurant, the waiter took them to a table for five in the middle of the room and handed them each a menu with Mount Everest on the cover.

"They have the best mushroom and potato curry here, said Uma. "That's what I'm going to order."

"I'd like to try it," said Samitra.

"I'm going to order the scalloped potatoes with cheese and herbs", said Rama.

"I hope you vegetarians don't mind if I have the fish curry," said Dipak.

As Carl glanced at the menu, he heard a familiar laughter coming from a corner booth. He was startled when he saw Kathy sitting there with a young man.

While the waiter was taking their orders, Carl skimmed the menu, deciding to order Kukhura Ko Tarkari (rice and chicken curry).

"It looks like Kathy is here having lunch with someone from the hospital. I'll be back in a few minutes," said Carl, heading toward their booth.

"Why Dad, what are you doing here?" asked Kathy, startled by his unexpected appearance.

"Kathy, I was going to stop by the hospital to say goodbye to you because we're leaving tomorrow for Mount Kailash."

"Dad, I don't think you recognize Om. He's a doctor working in the Emergency Room at Shanta Bhawan."

"Of course, I remember Om. His father is the Limbu Shaman, who attended the Shaman Convention at Bir Hospital back in 2001," said Carl. "Om, it's good to see you again after twelve years. How's your family?

"They're all fine. It's a pleasure to see you, Doctor Brecht," he said. "I've been working with Kathy in the Emergency Room. She's very skilled dealing with patients, suffering from serious injuries."

"Om graduated as a Medical Doctor from Tribuwan University four years ago. This is the first day we were able to leave the hospital early for lunch because of the long line of injured patients."

"We've been here nearly an hour," said Om, glancing at his watch. "We'll be going back to the hospital shortly."

"Please say hello to Rama and Samitra before you leave,"

said Carl. "I'd also want you to meet Dipak and Uma."

"Of course," said Om, paying the waiter and leaving a tip for the waitress.

A few minutes later, Carl introduced Kathy and Om to his friends, seated at the table, waiting for their meals.

After greeting everyone and shaking hands. Kathy said, "We need to get back to the hospital."

"Om, very few people have such a sacred name. What's your middle and last name?" asked Samitra.

"My name is Om Prasad Limbu. My father and my mother live near Tribuwan University in Pokhara with my wife and two sons."

"Om's wife, Maya, is expecting another baby during 'Tihar, the Festival of Lights,' in November," said Kathy.

"My family will be coming to Kathmandu to celebrate the Dasain Festival in October. They'll be staying with my grandparents who live near Bodhanath, the Buddhist Shrine," said Om.

"Om's father and grandfather are both Limbu shamans," said Kathy. "I met them when I was here twelve years ago."

"We must leave now or we'll be late," said Om. "It was a pleasure meeting all of you."

"Are you taking a taxi?" asked Uma, glancing out the window where taxi drivers were smoking cigarettes.

"Om's giving me a ride to the hospital on the back of his motorcycle," said Kathy, giving her father a hug. "Don't forget to email mom tonight before you leave for Tibet."

"Have a great trip to Mount Kailash. I hope to see you again when you get back," said Om, leaving with Kathy.

All eyes turned toward Om mounting the motorcycle with Kathy sitting behind him. They departed with a roar, leaving a stream of exhaust behind them.

"Our dinner has finally arrived," said Dipak, observing

the waiter setting down his rice and fish curry.

"I'm the one who gets the scalloped potatoes with cheese and herbs," said Rama'

"Carl, your daughter is very beautiful. Has she known Om for a long time?" asked Uma, glancing at her plate of mushrooms and curry.

"I brought Kathy to Nepal after she graduated from high school. We came to Kathmandu to attend the Shaman Convention at Bir Hospital in 2001," said Carl, tasting his rice and chicken curry.

"Later we met Om in Pokhara where he was a student at Tribuwan University. I have to admit that Kathy was attached to him for a few weeks.

"When we returned to the states, Kathy kept in touch with him by email while studying microbiology at college. She lost contact with Om when she was accepted at the University of Chicago, where she graduated as a doctor. Kathy is now doing residency at Rush University Hospital.

"I'm sure she's enjoying the motorcycle ride back to the hospital because Kathy likes adventure," said Carl.

"Om seems well educated," said Dipak.

"He's also a doctor, who works with Kathy in the Emergency Room," said Carl.

"Why didn't Kathy's boyfriend come to Nepal with her?" said Samitra.

"He's doing a rotation in Quito, Ecuador for the next month," said Carl, finishing his lunch.

"We must get going. I still have to pack a few things for the trip. I'm going to invite Margaret to sit next to me on the bus tomorrow," said Samitra. "Rama wants to talk to you about the history of Tibet while I'm giving Margaret a Nepali lesson.

Chapter 28
"Email from Barbara"

Early the next morning Purosotam entered Carl's room with a cup of steaming tea, informing him that it was 5:00 a.m. and that breakfast was being served at 6:00. He left quickly leaving the door wide open.

He got up and did his stretch exercise and then took a quick shower and got dressed. He sat in the lotus position doing his morning meditation. At 6:30 he left his room and hurried up the stairs to the kitchen.

"I hate to rush you but two taxis will arrive promptly at 7:00 this morning to transport us with our luggage to a bus stop in Kathmandu," said Dipak.

"We are scheduled to depart for Zhangmu, the border town of Tibet, by 8:00 a.m. We'll be there in four hours if the bus leaves on time."

"Purosotam maki ra dahi hamro paunalai dinos na! Purosotam, bring our guest his cornmeal porridge and yogurt," said Uma.

"Thank you so much," said Carl, noticing that Rama and Samitra were already finished with their breakfast.

"That was delicious porridge," said Rama, rising from his chair. Please excuse us. We'll meet you outside as soon as the taxis arrive."

"We still have some packing to do," said Samitra, following her husband down the hallway.

"Would you mind if I use your computer?" asked Carl. "I must send an email to my wife before departing for Tibet."

"Go right ahead," said Dipak.

After finishing his breakfast Carl went down stairs to the living room and sat down in front of the computer, reading his email.

Dear Carl, I've been concerned because you only sent me one email. I'm, also, really worried about Kathy. She emailed me yesterday mentioning that she met you and your friends at a restaurant in Patan.

She was surprised to see you while having lunch with Dr. Om Prasad Limbu. She informed me that she was working in the Emergency Room with him ever since she arrived. I've gotten emails from her every day. Each time she comments about how she likes working with Om.

I remember meeting him when Mark and I came to Kathmandu after you escaped from the Medicine Cave, where you and Kathy were being held hostage by terrorists.

I was frantic when Kathy informed me that she was still in love with Om, even if he's married with two children. She said his wife was a expecting a third child and was living with his parents in Pokhara.

I asked Kathy if she was going to breakup with her boyfriend, Greg, who's recently left for Quito, Ecuador to do his rotation. He's been emailing her every day asking how she's doing in Nepal.

Kathy told me that she still loves Greg, but that he was totally different from Om, who's so much more mature because he's married and has children.

Om told her that his father, Muktuba, arranged the marriage ceremony for him while he was senior at Tribuwan University.

When Om came home to his village in the mountains north of Pokhara during a winter break from the university, his father surprised him by having a wedding ceremony. Om was in shock because the whole Limbu community was invited to attend his wedding.

   Om didn't want to offend his parents by saying no to the marriage. His mother reminded him that the arrangement with the bride's family had been made when he was ten years old.

   Om had only met his former bride once before he was initiated into the Limbu community at age fourteen. At that time his parents expected him to get married. He told them if they tried to force him to get married, he would run away and never come back.

   After Kathy came home with us back in 2001, Om wrote to her once a month for two years. All of sudden he stopped sending emails to her because he was married. Kathy never expected to see him again. Eventually, she started dating Greg because they were both students at the University of Chicago.

   Upon arriving in Kathmandu, Kathy went straight to Shanta Bhawan Hospital, where she met Om again. He invited her to have tea with him after work at a nearby café.

   By the way Kathy sent me an email informing me that some of the Limbus in his community had more than one wife. I don't know what to think about it. I'm still tense over my dreams about you falling off the mountains.

   Please email me before you leave for Mt.Kailash. I can't believe that pilgrims from India are still stranded in the Himalayas even though a couple of months have gone by since the flooding.

   I'm thinking about purchasing a plane ticket and coming to Kathmandu to bring Kathy home before she decides to marry Om and become his second wife. I also want to take a helicopter to Tibet and bring you home before you fall off Mount Kailash.

   I've already sent an email to Hari, your tourist guide.

He said that all the pilgrims were Nepalese except for you and a female doctor from Naperville. There's also a Canadian couple from Quebec, and Margaret Porter from London. That makes five foreigners.

I understand that Margaret stood out like a sore thumb yesterday at the orientation. Hari said she was wearing a bright red dress, which is only worn by Hindu brides at their weddings.

Carl, if I don't hear from you soon, I'm contacting the American Embassy and the CIA to track you down. I already talked to my mother, Renee, about me coming to Nepal to bring Kathy home before she gets more involved with Om.

She told me to calm down and stop worrying. Renee has been taking Sammy and Emily to the park every day since you left. The kids are behaving quite well for her. I haven't heard a word from Mark about his divorce.

Out of desperation I called my father, Sam. Of course, he's willing to hire a private jet and come with me to Kathmandu to bring both you and Kathy home before something happens.

I'm on the verge of having a nervous breakdown worrying about Mark's divorce, Kathy's love affair with Om and you falling off the mountain. I'm leaving now to go to mass, followed by a talk with Father Lorenzo.

With love and tears,
    Your stressed out wife, Barbara.

Carl paused and took a deep breathe, glancing at his watch. It was already 6:50 a.m. He quickly wrote a brief response to his wife's email.

    Dear Barbara,   August 9, 2013
    I'll soon be leaving Dahasipati with Rama and Samitra. We'll be boarding the bus at 8:00 a.m. and

departing for Zhangmu the border town in Tibet. It's about a four hour ride from Kathmandu.

    I'm also concerned about Kathy and Om. However, they're both adults and not children. I don't think it's a good idea to come to Kathmandu with Sam. I'm pleased that you've decided to go to mass and talk things over with Father Lorenzo. He's given you good advice in the past.

    It may be ten days before you hear from me again. It won't be necessary for you to contact the American Embassy. If there's an emergency, they will contact you.

    Samitra agreed to ride with Margaret Porter on the bus to Tibet. She needs a female companion on the trip to console her over the loss of her husband, Krishna.

    After going through customs in Zhangmu, we'll be travelling to Nylam where we'll stay for two nights.

    Tomorrow after breakfast, we will all be climbing the nearby mountain to get a view of the Himalayas and acclimated to hiking on narrow trails in Tibet.

    I must go now. The taxis drivers are honking their horns outside. Dipak has just entered the living room to inform me that it's time to leave for the bus station in Kathmandu.

        I love you Barbara!
        Your husband, Carl

Chapter 29
"Departure with Memories"

"I'll be right with you," said Carl, shutting down the computer. He hurried into his room where he picked up his back pack and suitcase and departed from the house. He saw Dipak and Uma going through the open gate to enter the taxi. Within a few moments they were gone.

Carl put his suitcase in the trunk of the second taxi and entered the front seat on the passenger's side. He glanced over his shoulder at Samitra and Rama holding hands in the back seat.

"We are now beginning our journey to Mount Kailash," said Carl, as the taxi driver backed into the alley. He glanced at Purosotam, waving to them as he closed the huge iron gate and locked it.

"I haven't slept too well since we arrived," said Rama. "It takes me a couple of weeks to get used to the time change."

"I really haven't had any time to relax. I'm exhausted from going on tours during the day and then visiting with my relatives every night,' said Samitra.

"You'll have plenty of time to spend with them during the trip," said Rama. "We'll be seeing your twin sisters and their husbands at the bus stop."

"Hari mentioned that during our two nights at Nylam, Rama and I will have our own room. After that we'll have four people to a room for the rest of the trip.   Carl, you'll be sharing a room with the female doctor from Naperville and the Canadians," said Samitra.

"I'm not going to worry about that right now," said Carl, glancing out the window. "It looks like we might get some rain today."

"Carl while we were at the restaurant yesterday, you started to tell us about travelling with Kathy and Om to the Tyangboche Monastery in 2001. You never finished the story," said Samitra.

"I didn't travel with them. Kathy, Om and his father, Muktuba, flew in a small plane to Lukla. From there they trekked to Namche Bazaar and stayed overnight in the Sherpa settlement near the base of Mount Everest.

"The next morning they hired a Sherpa who took them up the nearby mountain to take pictures of Mount Everest. Afterwards they trekked for four hours before reaching the Tyangboche Monastery," said Carl.

"Upon arriving at the monastery, they were startled by helicopters flying over the monastery, leaving behind armed guards. The soldiers began searching the monastery for Nigel Porter and his Buddhist friends, who had escaped from jail in Kathmandu."

"Why were they in jail?" asked Rama.

"Nigel was a friend of Crown Prince Dipendra, who invited him to come to the royal palace to teach him how to meditate. The prince wanted to be free from his addictions to alcohol and marijuana.

"Since Nigel was present at the royal palace during the assassination, he was arrested along with two Buddhist monks and a yogi. After breaking out of jail, Nigel and his friends fled to the Bodhanath Monastery," said Carl.

"I remember seeing Nigel's picture on the front page of the 'New York Times' after escaping from prison. He was accused of murdering the Abbot at that monastery and then fleeing into the foothills with his friends and then to

Tyangboche Monastery," said Rama.

"The real culprits involved with the assassination were two former soldiers, expelled from military in India," said Carl. "They also arrived at the Tyangboche Monastery with Nepalese soldiers hoping to find Nigel. Instead they handcuffed Kathy and her boyfriend, Om, and took them to a Medicine Cave in the mountains north of the monastery."

"How terrible," gasped Samitra, glancing out the window, as the taxi came to an abrupt stop. "There's Hari standing on the corner, surrounded by Hindu pilgrims with their luggage waiting for the bus."

Carl paid the taxi driver and followed his friends to retrieve his luggage in the trunk.

Samitra said, "Carl, you still haven't finished your story about what happened in the cave?"

"Well I received a message from my daughter via an email that she was very sick and had been taken to the Medicine Cave along with Om to recover from hepatitis. She begged me to come to Tyangboche."

"Carl, where were you when you received the e-mail?"

"I had trekked with Moksha to Terhatum and then to his farm where I met his wife, Shraddha.

"After receiving the message that Kathy was sick, Shraddha contacted a pilot via a short wave radio. He was flying a helicopter and searching the mountains for Nigel and monk friends.

"The pilot agreed to fly Moksha and me to the Tyangboche Monastery and transport Kathy and Om back to Kathmandu for medical treatment at the hospital in Patan.

"When we arrived at the monastery the Abbot showed us the mutilated corpses of the three Buddhist monks who had escaped from jail with Nigel. He mentioned that a yak herder had seen Nigel murder the monks and hide their corpses behind the rocks on the trail to the medicine cave," said Carl.

"I remember reading in the 'Chicago Tribune' that Nigel was roaming in the Everest region and had massacred the outlaw monks. A shepherd claimed that he had seen Nigel killing a sheep and eating its raw flesh," said Rama.

"Well it looks like the bus has finally arrived," said Carl.

"We still haven't found out what happened to Kathy and Om at the Medicine Cave," said Rama.

"I'll tell you more once we get seated," said Carl, watching the pilgrims give their luggage to the driver's assistant for storage in the compartment under the bus.

"Where's Margaret Porter?" asked Rama. "If she's late today, she'll miss the bus."

"Here she comes with that taxi driver carrying her luggage," said Samitra. "I feel sorry for her because she's still grieving the loss of her husband. She's worried about Nigel, because she hasn't heard from him for a month."

"Margaret! We're over here!" waved Samitra. "Come and join us. You can sit next to me on the bus. Rama's sitting next to Carl in front of us. I'll give you a free Nepali lesson as we travel."

"Samitra, you're such a darling," said Margaret, handing the taxi driver a crisp $20 dollar bill. She glanced at the pilgrims staring out the windows of the bus at her low cut pink blouse and her tight black slacks. Margaret quickly covered her cleavage with a lace shawl.

"Carl, it's so good to see you. Have you heard from Barbara? I was surprised when I opened my email at the Guest House last night. I certainly didn't expect to get a message from her.

"Barbara wrote to me that she's planning to come to Nepal with her father, Sam, the president of Havlett

Industries," said Margaret.

"I sent my wife an email this morning," said Carl. "She's worried about me travelling to Tibet because thousands of Indian pilgrims are still stranded in the Himalayas due to flooding earlier in the summer."

"I don't blame her for being worried," said Samitra, boarding the bus.

"Margaret, you should go next," said Rama.

"Oh thank you so much. Samitra told me that you've never said an unkind word to her, during your twenty-five years of marriage," said Margaret with her hips swaying as she climbed the steps onto the bus and headed down the aisle. All eyes were upon her as she sat down in the vacant seat next to Samitra in the back of the bus.

"Why is everyone whispering in Nepali?" asked Margaret. "I can't understand a word they're saying."

"They're talking about your stylish clothing, the death of your husband, and newspaper articles about your son, Nigel's involvement with the assassination of the Royal Family," said Samitra. "Don't pay any attention to them."

"I shouldn't have worn this pink blouse," said Margaret, waving to Carl as he boarded the bus, and sat next to Rama. Across the aisle from them, Dipak and Uma had already taken their seats.

Once everyone was seated, Hari greeted the 36 pilgrims in Nepali. He used the microphone to wish them a pleasant trip to Zhangmu. He then handed the microphone to Radha, who began chanting prayers as the bus departed on the road toward Bhaktapur.

Chapter 30
"On the Bus to Tibet"

"Margaret, why is Rada screaming into the microphone in front of the bus?" asked Samitra.

"It's because she's never used one before. I learned how to use a microphone many years ago when I was studying voice and piano in London.

"I found it difficult to teach music and play for the symphony orchestra after Krishna's death." said Margaret.

"Radha's bellowing that prayer to Ganesh so loudly in Sanskrit that it's giving me a headache," said Samitra.

"My husband taught me that prayer," said Margaret, reciting it in English. "Behold the deity with a trunk and body, which is brilliant as the sun. May Lord Ganesh remove the obstacles from my life and grant me prosperity."

"Hindus always pray to Ganesh first and then the other gods," said Samitra, as Radha bellowed a prayer to Shiva.

Carl listened to the chanting for a half hour before putting in his earplugs. He removed "The Bhagavad Gita" from his carry-on, noticing that Rama ignored the chanting and was reading the "China Daily."

"We just drove past Bhaktapur. The city's shut down because of the Avian Flu," said Rama.

Carl responded, "The Avian flu has been a serious problem in other areas of Nepal as well."

After listening for nearly two hours to Radha, the pilgrims were irritated and murmured among themselves, trying to drown out the noise of the chanting.

In spite of the restless passengers, Radha didn't stop screeching. She finally announced that she would take a break before singing the "Gayatri Mantra".

"That is the most sacred of all hymns," said Samitra.

"My husband taught it to me. I used to sing it in Sanskrit while he played the melody on his guitar. I even sang it at his funeral in London," said Margaret.

"Margaret, please sing it for us ?" requested Samitra. "We're all tired of Radha screeching."

"I'd love to sing it to the pilgrims," said Margaret, taking a deep breath to overcome her stage fright.

Samitra left her seat and spoke to Radha about Margaret singing to the passengers. Exhausted from singing, Radha agreed to her request.

All eyes were on Margaret walking up the aisle covering her cleavage with a lace shawl as Samitra introduced her.

"My dear friends, today we are privileged to have Margaret Porter, a pilgrim from London, with us. She is a concert pianist who plays for the Symphony Orchestra, a singer and a music teacher. She will now sing the Gayatri Mantra," said Samitra, handing the microphone to her.

Margaret bowed her head and sang the sacred words in Sanskrit, "Om bhu bhuvah suvaha, tat savitur varenyam, bhargo devasya dhimahi, dhyo yo naha prachodayat." When she stopped singing everyone applauded.

"My dear friends, thank you for allowing me to sing this ancient Vedic hymn that's been chanted by Hindus for thousands of years. I will now sing it in English.

"May Lord Savita, the Sun, the source of our life, send his brilliant light to dispel the darkness within us, and lead our intellects to a higher plane of consciousness," sang Margaret, bowing again. "Thank you for the privilege of allowing me to sing this sacred song again."

After handing the microphone back to Radha, Margaret noticed that her face was crestfallen. She advised Radha not to scream into the microphone, but to back away from it to reduce the amplification.

Radha took her advice and sang for the first time in a soothing manner. The change of amplification attracted the attention of the pilgrims, who began singing the popular verses and hymns with her.

As the bus continued north, Rama said, "Carl did you happen to see that 96 foot statue of Shiva on the hill after we went through Bhaktapur some time ago. It's the highest statue of him in the world.

"Samitra and I visited that park and saw his soaring statue at the top of a long flight of stairs with a beautiful garden below. On his right side were four life size statues of him and his family. There was Shiva, Parvati and their sons, Ganesh and Kumar. On the left side was a statue of Nandi, the scared bull.

"Between them at top of the stairs was a shrine, attended by a priest, offering prayers for visiting devotees and flowers to the Shiva Lingam," said Rama.

Uma who was sitting across the aisle overheard Rama's conversation, said, "I'd like to see those statues when we come back from Mount Kailash."

"I'd like to see them with you," said Dipak, pausing. "Someone's crying in the back of the bus."

"What's wrong Margaret? Everyone liked your singing a few minutes ago?" said Samitra.

"I miss Krishna terribly. He was a good husband and a wonderful psychiatrist. He got my bipolar illness into remission without me taking medications."

"How did he do that?" asked Samitra.

"Krishna taught me how to meditate, which helped me

control my unrealistic expectations of myself and others.

"It was because of his faith in me that I returned to teaching piano and voice. Eventually, I went back to performing with the symphony orchestra and singing at concerts.

"Krishna introduced me to his doctor friends at the hospital where they worked with patients, who were drug addicts and alcoholics. Several were mentally ill, suffering from bipolar depression or schizophrenia.

"My husband taught me to set boundaries and not to overextend myself. He, encouraged me to exercise daily and not isolate from society

"I decided to come to Nepal to visit Nigel, and go on the pilgrimage instead of staying home and feeling sorry for myself over Krishna's death," said Margaret.

"I'm amazed by your courage," said Samitra. "You're truly a remarkable woman."

"My first marriage was a disaster because I foolishly married for security and wealth. I made a serious mistake by fleeing to Katmandu from London with my two sons, Christopher and Nigel, back in 1976. However, my second marriage to Krishna was a great success."

Margaret suddenly paused, glancing at Carl sitting next to Rama. He had stopped reading the "Bhagavad Gita".

She stood up and waved to him to come down the aisle. A few minutes later, she said, "Carl, do you remember when I had a nervous breakdown and you came to visit me at Shanta Bhawan Hospital in Patan? It happened after Yorg murdered Christopher and kidnapped Nigel."

"Of course, I remember visiting with you at the hospital," said Carl. "That's where you met your future husband, Krishna Manandhar, the psychiatrist."

"I'll never forget you promised me that you would find

Nigel even if you had to go to the end of the world," said Margaret.

"After searching for him for months in India, I finally found Nigel at a cottage near Pokhara, where I was, also, taken hostage by the London Coven.

"A yogi helped Nigel to escape during a terrific storm, which caused the building to collapse, killing Yorg and several members of the coven," said Carl. "I managed to escape before the roof caved in. I hurried toward the pier, where I saw the yogi with Nigel in a boat going down the river," said Carl.

"I didn't hear from Nigel for several years. He finally wrote to me, informing me that he had stayed with the yogi in a cave for three years before going to the Tyangboche Monastery, where he was studying to be a Buddhist monk. After he became a monk, I made an effort to come to Nepal once a year to visit him," said Margaret.

"He'd meet me at the Bodhanath Monastery in Kathmandu during the month of August, where I helped him and the monks prepare food for poverty stricken beggars and homeless refugees from Tibet for three weeks.

"During Nigel's free time, he'd take me on tours of Buddhist and Hindu temples in the valley. Toward the end of the month Krishna and I went on a seven day retreat before, returning to London," said Margaret, listening to Hari speaking over the loudspeaker.

"We have now arrived at the Log Cabin Restaurant along the river. I hope you'll enjoy the Nepalese buffet with a view of the waterfall from the dining room windows. The modern restaurant has electricity, restrooms and overhead fans."

"I can't wait to meet your son, Nigel," said Samitra, as they departed from the bus. "Maybe he can teach me something about Tibetan mysticism."

"I'm also eager to see him. Nigel sent me several emails from Lhasa, where he's studying Tibetan scriptures. I want to go there after the pilgrimage to meet him."

"The restaurant looks like an Alpine chateau that you'd find in Switzerland," said Rama, following Carl, Dipak, and Uma into the restaurant.

Hari stood at the entrance, giving the passengers directions to the restrooms, since they had been traveling for four hours without stopping.

Within a few minutes the pilgrims were in the lunch line. They heaped their plates with fried or white rice, a variety of curries and numerous vegetarian dishes.

All the pilgrims were encouraged to return to the buffet a second time for bottled water, coffee, tea, and desserts. They sat in booths or at table eating their lunch and enjoying the grandeur of the nearby water fall.

Chapter 31
"Arrival at Zhangmu"

"What a marvelous lunch," said Dipak, leading the way back to the bus. "Hari, how far is it to Zhangmu?"

"We'll arrive at the border in about twenty minutes and might have to wait in line at customs in the new terminal," said Hari, boarding the bus.

"It took a number of years to build that terminal," said Dipak, sitting across the aisle from Carl.

"The last time I travelled to Tibet, there wasn't a terminal at the border. When we got off the bus, the pilgrims had to walk across the bridge. At the end of bridge a customs officer was sitting at a table, checking our passports and stamping our visas.

"We travelled for an hour on the back of a truck on a dirt road before reaching Zhangmu, which was a city built into the side of the mountain," said Carl, noticing that Margaret wasn't on the bus yet.

"We stayed in a hotel over night with six people in a room on the third floor with a bathroom at end of the hall.

"After leaving Zhangmu, we travelled all day through the mountains before we reached a second guesthouse. The outdoor toilets were quiet a distance from the rooms. The next morning when we were ready to leave, the bus wouldn't start because the battery was dead," said Carl.

"Four hours later, the driver installed a new battery so we could continue our journey. After travelling through the mountains for several hours on a rugged road, our bus got stuck in the mud. We were delayed for hours. A truck driver stopped and pulled the bus out of the mud with a cable attached to his rear axle.

"The following day the engine of our bus died in a remote area, where we waited for hours for another bus to arrive to take us to Lhasa.

"In spite of the delays, we finally arrived in Lhasa where we toured for two days before flying back to Kathmandu," said Carl.

"This time we'll be going in the opposite direction to Mount Kailash in land cruisers. By the way Zhangmu has expanded considerably. The city has expanded to the base of the mountain and begins once we cross the terminal," said Dipak, watching the last group of pilgrims board the bus and move down the aisle to their seats.

After everyone was seated, Hari announced over the speaker that Margaret Porter was missing. He paused as the driver started the engine and honked the horn.

"I saw her fifteen minutes ago in the restroom," said Uma, glancing out the window.

"Here she comes!" announced Carl, while the driver opened the door for her.

Margaret was running toward the bus carrying a bouquet of purple lilies. After boarding, she was gasping for breath as if being chased by a wild boar.

"Where have you been?" asked Hari. "We were about to leave without you."

"I just had to take pictures of the waterfall and pick a few lilies down by the river," she said, sliding into the seat next to Samitra.

The driver revved the engine and then turned onto the road where several huge trucks whizzed past them coming from Chinese occupied Tibet. The traffic was heavy as they approached the border town of Zhangmu.

"What are the Chinese transporting into Nepal in those semi-trucks?" asked Carl.

"The trucks are loaded with cell phones, computers, televisions, clothing, and artifacts, manufactured in Chinese factories," said Rama.

When the bus stopped near the terminal at the border, Hari called off the names of the pilgrims and the order they were to stand in line at customs with their passports. Carl was surprised that his name was the last one on the list and Margaret's was just before his. In front of them was the couple from Quebec, Canada.

The thirty-two Hindu pilgrims from Nepal went into the air conditioned terminal and through customs, showing their passports without having to open their handbags or back packs. Rama and Samitra who were American citizens, had no trouble with their passports. The Canadians from Quebec went through the line without difficulty because they had once been citizens of Bulgaria, a Communist satellite. Even the Hindu doctor from Naperville, Illinois had no difficulty crossing into Tibet.

When Margaret handed her passport to the Chinese border guard, he refused to let her to go through the turnstyle to cross into Tibet. She was taken into a nearby room by a guard to be interrogated.

Carl glanced at the luggage going through the terminal on a conveyor belt. He was startled when he saw an officer pull Margaret Porter's suitcase and his own from the conveyor belt for inspection by guards.

Feeling anxious, Carl was puzzled by the delay. He saw Rama and Samitra standing at the exit of the terminal about two hundred feet away in Zhangmu. They were waiting for him to join them in Chinese occupied Tibet, where Hari was assigning the pilgrims to their land cruisers.

In an aisle to his right, Carl noticed Sherpa porters carrying bundles of cotton from India on their backs to be transported to clothing factories in China.

After waiting nearly an hour, he was pleased to see Margaret coming out of the office. Her blonde hair was disheveled, and she was sobbing while wiping her eyes with a handkerchief. After receiving her passport, she hurried across the terminal with a guard carrying her luggage.

"Please follow me Doctor Brecht," said the Chinese guard. "Your passport is in order, and we found nothing unusual in your suitcase. Come with me into this room."

Carl followed the guard into the office where he was introduced to Wang Lee, who was sitting behind his desk, leafing through a stack of papers.

"Doctor Carl Brecht, please sit down. I've been checking your credentials. You're an anthropologist from the University of Chicago," said Wang.

"I taught anthropology there for 30 years, before retiring a couple of years ago," said Carl.

"Doctor Brecht, my records show that you're still teaching part-time at the university, and that you're an expert on Nepalese Shamanism."

"I studied history in Beijing before getting my master's degree in Political Science at the University of London. My government assigned me to work at the Nepalese boarder because we had 4,000 Tibetans crossing illegally into Nepal and India without passports for many years," said Wang.

"I heard that the number of Tibetan refugees has dropped over the past few years," said Carl.

"We only had four hundred illegal Tibetan refugees escape last year. They bribed the local police at border towns that are now guarded by Chinese soldiers," said

Wang.

"Doctor Brecht, why are you travelling with Hindus to Mount Kailash? My colleagues believe you're working for the CIA."

"The Dalai Lama's brother worked for the CIA. He was involved with the training of Tibetan terrorists in Hale, Colorado and Mustang, near the Tibetan boarder," said Carl.

"I'm aware of those hit and run terrorist attacks made by Tibetans against the Chinese. When Nixon was president their training came to a halt because of his negotiations with China to stop the Vietnam War," said Wang.

"Numerous Tibetan terrorists were stranded in Mustang because of Nixon's decision. Instead of attacking the Chinese soldiers at the border, the terrorists fought among themselves, resulting in a bloody massacre," said Carl.

"You certainly know your history Doctor Brecht," said Wang. "Please tell me about your relationship with Margaret Porter."

"Just call me Carl. I met Margaret and her two sons when they boarded the plane in London for Kathmandu in the fall of 1976. Her children caused plenty of trouble on that flight."

"At that time you stayed at the Kathmandu Guest House after arriving in Nepal," said Wang, glancing at his notes. "It says here that Margaret Porter checked into the Royal Hotel, but was asked to leave because her sons were out of control. She then moved into the Kathmandu Guest House where you were staying.

"In an article from the 'Nepal Daily' from 1976 it says that Margaret Porter collapsed in the garden of the guest house from shock when she saw her son, Christopher, hanging from a rope in the pomelo tree," said Wang. "It also states that Yorg Schmidt, the leader of a London Coven, kidnapped her son, Nigel. He took him with his coven to a town in India near the Nepalese boarder.

"At that time Indira Gandhi was the Prime Minister, attempting to control the population of India by encouraging birth control.

"After leaving India, Yorg took Nigel to a cabin along the river near Pokhara. According to the newspaper you were also taken hostage there," said Wang.

"That's right," said Carl. "I had promised Margaret Porter that I'd try to find her son, but I didn't expect to be kidnapped by the coven."

"There was a brutal slaying of a pregnant woman. Her fetus was offered to Nigel, who had been drugged by the coven members.

"Yorg was about to sacrifice me to the demon, Ravana, but he was stopped by a sudden storm with a harsh wind that shook the whole cabin," said Carl.

"Fortunately, a yogi entered the cottage and helped Nigel escape. Even though my hands were tied, I was able to get out in time before the roof collapsed, killing Yorg and several members of his coven.

"I hurried to the dock where I saw the yogi leaving in a boat with Nigel. The yogi waved to me, shouting that he was taking the boy to his cave and then a Buddhist monastery," said Carl. "When I finally got back to Pokhara, I reported the incident to the police. I was then interviewed by several newspaper reporters.

"In spite of trips to Nepal to study shamanism, it wasn't until I came back in 2001 to attend a Shaman Convention that I met Margaret Porter again. I heard from friends over the years that Nigel had become a Buddhist monk, living at the Tyangboche Monastery in Eastern Nepal," said Carl.

"According to the newspaper, the 'Nepal Daily', Nigel

was 33 years old when Crown Prince Dipendra, invited him to come to the palace to teach him how to meditate. In reality the prince was hoping to become liberated from his addiction to alcohol and drugs," said Wang.

"Nigel was present on the palace grounds during the assassination of the Royal Family on June 3, 2001 by Crown Prince Dipendra, who was suicidal and died from a bullet wound to his head after the death of his parents," said Wang.

"Nigel was arrested in the garden on the palace grounds by Yama Raj and put in jail along with three Buddhist monks and a yogi. The prisoners escaped to the Bodhnath Monastery, where Nigel was accused of murdering the Abbot and then fleeing with his friends," said Carl.

"In fact Nigel was photographed killing the Abbot. and some weeks later murdering three monks and two Maoist terrorists on the trail leading to the Medicine Cave, north of the Tyangboche Monastery," continued Carl.

"That's where you and your daughter, Kathy, were held hostage," said Wang, glancing at the article on his desk. "It's amazing that Nigel was never brought to trial for all of those brutal murders," said Wang.

"Nigel was falsely accused by Yama Raj, who wore a rubber mask made in China of Crown Prince Dipendra when he assassinated the royal family. Later he wore a mask of Nigel, while murdering the two Maoists and the three Buddhist monks on the road to the Medicine Cave.

"Yama Raj then sent photographs of Nigel, hovering over the corpses with his gun, which got international attention," said Carl.

"You've defended Nigel as if you were a lawyer, Carl. Did you know that Nigel came to Lhasa to study Tibetan Buddhist scriptures? Instead of studying, he was asked by the Chinese government to become a tourist guide.

Unfortunately he once again has gotten himself into serious trouble," said Wang, shuffling through the newspapers.

"Margaret Porter never told me that Nigel was a tourist guide in Lhasa," said Carl.

"I'm surprised that she's travelling with you and the Hindu pilgrims. Our records show that Margaret has returned to Nepal every year to visit her son, Nigel, during the monsoon season. It's strange that she's going to Mount Kailash rather than Lhasa."

"Margaret's planning to travel to Lhasa after returning from Mount Kailash," said Carl.

"I've been studying 'The China Daily' for several days. Here's the article written on August 7, 2013 about Nigel."

Carl glanced at the headline on the front page, which read, "Murder of Security Guard at the Jokang Temple." Under the title was a photograph of Nigel wearing his maroon monk's robe beneath a statue of "Avalokitesvara, The Lord Looking Down With Compassion".

"Please read the article to me," requested Wang.

"Of course," said Carl. "Nigel Porter, a Buddhist monk from Nepal, came to Tibet to study Buddhist scriptures over a year ago. After a few months of studying in Lhasa, the Chinese governor asked him to become a tourist guide for English speaking travelers.

"Nigel agreed to take the job and donate his salary to the Buddhist monastery where he was living. His job was to take tourists to the Jokhang Temple and Potala, the former living quarters of the Dalai Lama and presently the location of the Buddhist government.

"Nigel was with a group of English speaking Chinese students and professors from Beijing, when suddenly a woman named Ping Lee accused him of stealing her wallet while in the Jokhang Temple.

"She immediately called a guard, who found her wallet in Nigel's satchel. The guard also found fliers entitled, 'Free Tibet from the Chinese Occupation'.

"Nigel denied that he stole the wallet. He insisted that when his back was turned, someone put Ping's wallet and the fliers into his satchel.

"While he was arguing with the Chinese guard, the lights in the Jokang Temple went out. There was murmuring and a temporary panic occurred within the temple. About five minutes later the lights came back on.

"The tourists were shocked when they saw the armed guard, lying on the floor in a pool of blood with a knife in his back with the fliers scattered around the corpse, clinging to the empty wallet of Ping Lee," read Carl.

"I believe that Nigel Porter not only murdered the Chinese guard but fled with the money from Ping's wallet after scattering leaflets on the corpse," said Wang.

"The following day the Chinese police went back to the monastery. The Abbott informed them he had come down with typhoid and was quarantined in the infirmary. The guards told the Abbott that Nigel was under arrest for the murder of the guard at the Jokang Temple.

"When the guards returned a few days later, the Abbott told them that Nigel had died from typhoid and had been cremated near the river.

"However, Chinese guards searched the monastery and claimed they found fliers about liberating Tibet under Nigel's bed. They believed that he had escaped from Lhasa and was hiding somewhere in Tibet.

"The Chinese governor of Lhasa offered a reward of 50,000 yuan to anyone with information leading to the arrest of Nigel Porter," said Carl, handing the newspaper to Wang.

"Carl, it's obvious that you're an honest man, but I'm

concerned that Margaret Porter has a history of being bipolar. She foolishly brought her sons to Kathmandu and exposed them to danger. Within a few weeks Christopher was murdered, and Nigel was kidnapped. I understand that Margaret was hospitalized from the shock and her history of mental illness.

"I'm concerned that Nigel may have inherited some of his problems from his mother since there's been a great deal of genetic research about mental illness," said Wang.

"That's possible," said Carl. "After she leaves, he returns to his schedule at the monastery, which includes daily meditation and helping trekkers and Sherpas at the clinic with respiratory illnesses due to the high altitude."

"Once again you have defended Nigel," said Wang. "I told his mother, that her son has been accused of murdering the Chinese guard and has fled from Lhasa. If Nigel is found, he will spend the rest of his life in prison. That's when she burst into tears," said Wang.

"Margaret's suffering from the loss of her husband, who was killed nine months ago in an automobile accident in London. Now she must cope with Nigel being accused of murder and his disappearance.

"Frankly I'm also worried that she might end up in the hospital from the stress during our pilgrimage," said Carl. "Wang, is it true that 100 Buddhist monks burned themselves to death in Tibet during the past year?"

"Yes, it's a serious problem for us when the monks commit suicide," said Wang. "Our government believes that the Dalai Lama should come to Lhasa from Dharmasala to speak to the Tibetans about this problem, since he's a nonviolent world leader and Nobel Peace Prize winner. We've had no responses from him in spite of numerous emails, letters, and phone calls."

Chapter 32
"Travelling to Nylam in Tibet"

"You may now leave the terminal and cross over into Zhangmu, Carl. I hope you'll have a pleasant pilgrimage to Mount Kailash with your Hindu friends," said Wang, standing up at his desk.

"I forgot to mention that I received an email from a Chinese friend, who is studying psychology at the University of Wisconsin in Madison. His professors have done scientific testing on Tibetan Buddhist monks. They've concluded that daily mediation reduces stress," said Wang.

"I've read about Professor Richard Davidson. He used an MRI to monitor the brain waves of a monk, who suffered from depression because of pain." said Carl. "After numerous tests, the professor concluded that the monk's pain was greatly reduced because of his daily meditation routine."

"Paul Ekman, a psychologist from the University of California, also discovered that Buddhist monks, who meditate daily, identify their emotions, but don't react to them. Their training gives them the ability to deal with fear, guilt, shame, remorse, and anger to an extent unheard of by Westerners," said Wang, opening the door for Carl.

"I apologize for the delay. Most of your Hindu friends have departed for Nylam already. A guard is waiting for you with your backpack, luggage, and passport. Have a great trip to Mount Kailash."

After shaking hands with Wang, Carl departed with the guard through the empty terminal into Zhangmu.

"We've been waiting for you for almost an hour and a half," said Hari, unlocking the trunk of the land cruiser for the guard to put Carl's luggage into the vehicle.

"I'm sorry about the delay. I didn't expect to be interrogated that long," said Carl.

"Margaret was an emotional wreck after being questioned by Wang Lee about Nigel fleeing from Tibet after murdering the guard at the Jokang Monastery.

"She didn't settle down until I put her in the land cruiser with your friends, Rama and Samitra. They left some time ago for Nylam," said Hari.

"Here's your passport," interrupted the Chinese guard, handing it to Carl, who gave him a five yuan tip.

"Margaret's still grieving the loss of her husband," said Carl. "Now she has to face the disappearance of Nigel and the possibility of him being arrested for murder."

"I read in the 'China Daily' this morning that the police shut down a monastery in Lhasa and arrested the Buddhist monks for harboring Nigel and helping him to escape," said Hari, noticing that the women in the back seat of the land cruiser were frowning because of the delay.

"I'll be sitting with the baggage. You and the women can communicate with me through the open space between the back seat and the trunk," said Hari, watching Carl entering the front seat across from the driver.

Carl introduced himself to the driver and the two gray haired women in the backseat. He said, "Didiharu, ma dherai dillo bhayo. Kripaya malai maph garnos na. Sisters, I was very late. Please forgive me."

The angry women did not respond to his apology. They scowled, crossing their arms, refusing to speak to him.

Hari spoke to Carl through the opening from the trunk, informing him that the driver's name was Rajan and the women in the backseat were Sushma, and Sita.

Rajan startled them when leaving the terminal and slamming on the brakes as he entered the heavy traffic. He honked his horn at pedestrians dashing into the congested main street between the parked cars.

During the afternoon rush hour, Carl glanced out the window at the Chinese shops, restaurants, and hotels on both sides of the street. They were crowded with Chinese customers, rickshaws and taxis, but there were no Tibetans in sight.

"Didiharu, ke pardnu huncha, Sisters, what are you reading?" asked Carl, noticing they were trying to recite passages from a book.

"Ke bhanu bho? What did you say?" asked Sushma, restless as the vehicle crawled along in the traffic.

Sita, who was more alert, informed Carl in Nepali that they had been reading verses from the "Bhagavad Gita."

The women were both surprised when Carl recited the verse back to them from memory. He also joined them as they chanted in unison, "Aham Atama gudakesa sarva bhutashya sthitah. Aham adisdca, madhyam ca, bhutanam anta eva cha."

"Give us the translation in English," insisted Shusma.

"I Am the Soul, O' Conqueror of Sleep, of all living beings. I AM the beginning, the middle, and the end of all of life," said Carl.

Sita praised Carl for being able to chant the verse in Sanskrit, asking him where he had studied the language.

Carl informed her that he took lessons every Sunday for three years at the Hindu Temple of Greater Chicago in Lemont.

"You must be an avatar like Krishna sent to us from heaven by Vishnu," said Sita. "I'm so pleased that we have a chance to be with you, Carl."

Sita informed him that she was a widow and that her travelling companion, Sushma, was a retired elementary teacher, whose husband died five years ago from cancer.

"Why do you have to tell the whole world about my husband's death?" shouted Shushma in Nepali. "I dream about him all the time! He tells me that he's not happy in Narga, the Underworld, and wants to be born again so that he can be with me! I don't know why you believe that Carl's an avatar like Krishna or Rama?"

"I'm sorry for offending you, but I'm tired of you talking about your husband, Artha," said Sita, quarrelling like a competitive hen in the presence of a rooster.

After a few minutes Sushma stopped yelling. She folded her arms across her breasts and angrily stared out the window as the driver suddenly came to an abrupt halt.

Carl removed granola bars from his coat pocket and offered them to the women. Sita smiled, thanking him as she removed the wrapper, while Sushma murmured she would eat hers later.

Sita said, "I still believe that you're an Avatar sent to us from heaven."

Sushma blurted out, "Carl's an old man with gray hair and definitely not sent from God. He's probably a devotee of Ravana."

He informed them in Nepali that he wasn't an avatar nor a devotee of the Demon King, but only an average man. He paused when Hari spoke to them in Nepali through the opening in the trunk.

"My dear lady friends, this is Doctor Carl Brecht, an anthropologist from the University of Chicago in America and an expert on shamanism."

Sushma apologized to Carl and began munching on her

granola bar. When she was finished, she asked Carl if he knew of a shaman in Kathmandu who could perform an exorcism so that her husband could leave the Underworld and be reincarnated.

"Once I get back to Kathmandu, I will contact my Newar friend. I'm sure he knows a shaman, who can help you out."

"I'm so sorry that I shouted at you," said Sushma. " I didn't sleep last night because my husband, Artha, was begging me to help him get out of the Underworld."

"I have to admit that I've also been jealous because Sita's giving all her attention to you and forgetting that I exist."

"Let's read another passage from the 'Bhagavad Gita'," said Sita, as the driver crawled through the city stopping due to the heavy traffic.

After finally leaving Zhangmu in the late afternoon, the two women fell asleep in the backseat while Hari dozed in the trunk. Carl turned his attention to Rajan, who refused to talk to him while driving.

After another forty minute delay, they finally left the border town and were speeding on a newly paved road constructed by Chinese engineers and laborers.

Carl was stunned by the beauty of the barren mountain ranges in the distance and the snow covered Himalayas. He was amazed by the extensive green pastures where Tibetan herders were grazing flocks of sheep and goats.

He noticed that all road signs were written in Chinese, not Tibetan. He was surprised at the sight of the electric poles, soaring alongside the two lane road for miles and the electric power plants in small towns along the river.

After travelling for several hours, they arrived in Nylam, which was a large town filled with numerous Chinese gift shops, restaurants, and hotels.

Chapter 33
"Arrival at the Hotel"

When they finally reached the newly constructed hotel, where the pilgrims were staying, Hari helped them check in at the information desk. He told them that they would all meet in the dining room at 8:00 p.m. on the ground floor of the hotel near the kitchen.

Several Chinese bell boys arrived to carry their luggage up a grand, carpeted staircase, which reminded Carl of a scene from "Gone with the Wind" when Rhett told Scarlet, "Frankly my dear I don't give a damn!"

Carl waved to Sita and Sushma as they followed the bellboys down a hallway to his right while he went straight ahead on the second floor.

Upon reaching his room, the bell boy opened the door with a key, handed it to Carl, and turned on a light to show Carl the tiled bathroom. As he left, Carl handed him a five yuan tip.

After taking a shower, Carl dressed and departed for the dining room. He went back down to the grand staircase to the desk and asked the clerk about the location of the kitchen and the dining room.

He walked down a long corridor on the first floor and arrived at the dining room. Opening the double doors, he noticed that there were no tables in the room. The pilgrims were seated on wooden chairs, placed against the four walls. Carl sat down next to Rama and Samitra, who had saved a chair for Margaret Porter.

Hari glanced at his watch and then spoke to the crowd in

Nepali. "Good evening ladies and gentlemen. I hope you had enjoyed the scenery while travelling here.

"We'll be staying at this hotel for two nights. Please enjoy the hot showers. Once we leave Nylam we won't have private bathrooms and bedrooms. There'll be four people to each room at the guest houses. The accommodations have only outdoor toilets without running water."

While Hari was talking, Margaret Porter walked through the double doors of the room, wearing a pair of tight black slacks, a low cut red blouse, and red high heels. She sat down next to Carl in the only vacant chair in the room.

"I'm sorry that I'm late," whispered Margaret.

"We will now proceed to the kitchen where dinner will be served to us by waiters. Each person will be handed a tray. Once we get the main course, we'll return to this room where we'll be seated while eating.

"After finishing the main course, we'll go back a second time to the kitchen for soda, water and dessert. Will the guests sitting in front of the wall to my right, please leave for the kitchen," said Hari.

Carl watched as the Hindu pilgrims passed through the double doors into the kitchen. A few minutes later, he and his friends were standing in line waiting to be served.

"I was very disturbed by Wang Lee questioning me at the border," said Margaret, standing in front of Carl, while the waiter filled her plate with rice, chicken curry, mo mo dumplings, and grapefruit salad.

"The meal certainly looks delicious," said Carl, trying to change the subject.

"I don't believe that Nigel murdered that guard," she insisted, her voice quivering. "I'm certain that he's still alive in a monastery somewhere in Tibet."

"We'll talk about it further while eating," said Carl,

heading back to the dining room.

"You've been very understanding," said Margaret, sitting down next to him with her tray.

"I cried for nearly an hour in the land cruiser on the way to Nylam. I was afraid that I would end up in the hospital again with a nervous breakdown. Samitra reminded me that my husband taught me to meditate upon the wonder of God's creation when I was stressed.

"As soon as we got back to the hotel, I took a hot shower and fell asleep in my room. Samitra telephoned my room to tell me that dinner was being served in dining room. I'm so glad that she woke me up when she did and that you saved me a seat. I felt embarrassed coming late and interrupting Hari's speech."

After everyone finished their main course, Hari stood up and spoke to the group once again.

"My dear friends, desserts are now being served with drinks in the kitchen. You'll have a choice of coffee, tea, or bottled water. For dessert there's mango ice cream cones, donuts made from coconuts and raisins, and delicious purple balls in syrup."

While their friends left to get their dessert, Carl and Margaret continued talking.

"I actually thought Mount Kailash was near Lhasa in eastern Tibet, because I never checked the map.

"Wang Lee told me that Nigel walked from the monastery early in the morning and then returned in the evening. He had been a successful tour guide for a whole year before the brutal slaying of the Chinese guard.

"When Wang showed me the map where Mount Kailash was located, I was horrified. I didn't know that there was such a distance between Lhasa in western Tibet and Mount Kailash in the east.

"Nigel wrote to me that he was overworked as a tour guide in Lhasa and needed to spend more time studying the ancient Buddhist scriptures, especially the teachings of Milarepa, a Tibetan Buddhist saint and poet, who spent most of his life meditating in a cave."

"Let's talk about it after getting some dessert and something to drink," said Carl, heading toward the kitchen.

Upon returning with their bottled water and mango ice cream cones, Carl and Margaret resumed their conversation, which was interrupted by Rama.

"I overheard you speak about Milarepa," said Rama.

"Tell me more about him," said Margaret.

"Did you ever hear about 'Yoga of Inner Fire'?" asked Rama. "It involves the four upper chakras."

"My husband, Krishna, took me to yoga classes regularly," said Margaret. "He taught me the names of the seven Hindu chakras."

"Milarepa compared the cleansing of the chakras to the untying of knots on a white handkerchief."

"The chakras are the seats of our thoughts, and emotions," said Samitra.

"The cleansing of the chakras is like driving the crows out of the garden," said Margaret. "When my husband and I were driving from London to Stonehenge we took a wrong turn because the highway was being repaired.

"Krishna stopped in a village to ask for directions from an elderly man working in his garden. While he was giving us directions, a crow flew into his garden. Within a few moments a whole flock of crows landed there.

"Krishna told me that Hindus believed that crows were symbols of death. They are the birds that transport the soul to the next world. I panicked and was trembling from fear hearing the crows cawing."

"Don't worry about those crows," said the villager. "I'll take care of them."

"I was terrified that he would go into his cottage and come out with a shotgun to shoot them," said Margaret. "Instead he clapped his hands loudly.

"Upon hearing the clapping, the leader of the crows flew away but was only followed by two others. When the villager clapped his hands loudly three or four times about twenty-five crows soared into the sky."

"That's a good analogy," said Rama. "Did you ever get to Stonehenge?"

"Yes, but we couldn't go near the ancient stones because the Druids were protesting. The police finally arrived and arrested them for driving away the tourists," said Margaret, pausing to listen to Hari speaking into the microphone.

He informed the group that it was time to leave the dining room and that breakfast would be served the next day from 7:00 - 8:00 a.m. Afterward everyone would meet in the courtyard before climbing the nearby mountain.

"Samira and I are going to the computer room to email the British Embassy to find out if they have any information about Nigel," said Margaret.

"I'm going to go for a walk around town. When I get back I'll send an email to Barbara."

Carl glanced at Margaret leaving the dining room. Feeling restless, he departed from the back door of the hotel after going through the kitchen instead the lobby.

He wandered down the deserted street, stopping at a Buddhist monastery where monks were chanting. He stayed with them for an hour. After returning to the hotel, the desk clerk informed him the computers were shut down for the night because it was after 10:00 p.m.

Chapter 34
"Ascent of the Mountain at Nylam"

Carl had a restless night tossing and turning. He was wondering if he should get up, put on his clothes, and knock on Margaret's door to console her. He knew that she'd be upset after writing a letter about Nigel disappearance to the British Embassy. Instead he decided to take a cold shower before going back to bed.

The next morning he got up early and went to the computer room to send an email to Barbara. He told her that they had crossed into Tibet and travelled on to Nylam, where they would be climbing the nearby mountain after breakfast to get acclimated to the altitude.

Carl didn't mention that he was questioned by the guard at the border, nor did he say anything about Margaret Porter's son, Nigel. He asked her to write back, and he'd check his email for her response later in the evening.

After going to the dining room, Carl was greeted by Rama and Samitra. He sat down next to them, anticipating the arrival of Margaret.

When Hari announced that breakfast was being served, Carl followed his friends into the kitchen. He returned with a tray containing grapefruit salad, cornmeal porridge, and Nepali donuts.

Samitra came back with her tray, glancing at the vacant seat beside her. She said "I hope Margaret's all right. She was disturbed after we sent the letter to the British Embassy last night and worried she'd never see Nigel again. I stayed with her for a long time before she took a sleeping pill and dozed off," said Samitra.

"Don't worry about Margaret," said Rama. "She'll be here in a few minutes, wearing a stunning outfit to get everyone's attention."

After finishing breakfast, the pilgrims were leaving the dining room when Margaret arrived. She was wearing a kaki army uniform and black boots that echoed on the floor.

"I'm terribly late," she said glancing at her watch. "I wonder if they're still serving breakfast."

"Margaret, you must go to kitchen before it shuts down. Rama and I are going back to our room to put on our hiking boots. We'll see you in the courtyard shortly," said Samitra, departing with her husband.

"We were worried about you," said Carl, noticing that Margaret's dyed blonde hair was disheveled and her forehead wrinkled.

"I overslept," said Margaret putting her purse on a chair, reaching for her compact and lipstick. "Carl, please stay with me while I put on my makeup."

"I'd rather bring you a tray from the kitchen with fruit salad, toast, and scrambled eggs," he said, leaving the dining room.

When Carl returned with her tray, he was surprised that Margaret had combed her hair and her wrinkles were gone.

"You certainly look beautiful," said Carl.

"Thank you so much," she said, tasting the grapefruit salad. "I'm starving. I didn't eat much last night. I also had a restless night with awful dreams."

"I didn't sleep so well either. I have to go back to my room now," said Carl, looking at the pilgrims entering the room with hiking clothes and boots. They smiled, greeting them as they passed through the kitchen into the courtyard behind the hotel.

Carl departed for his room on the third floor, where he brushed his teeth and put on his hiking boots, returning to the vacant dining hall. He hurried into the kitchen, where Nepalese chefs, hired to cook for the pilgrims were washing dishes. They smiled, nodded and pointed to the exit.

When Carl entered the courtyard, he stood at the end of the line watching Hari distribute yellow jackets with a hood and blue sleeves. Each pilgrim tried on small, medium, or large sizes, departing with the one that fit the best along with a walking stick.

Hari encouraged everyone to wear their coats and use walking sticks, while ascending and descending the mountain, which would take three to four hours.

The pilgrims were led by Hari's assistants from the courtyard to the nearby highway, free from morning traffic.

Everyone was amazed by the cement wall, soaring on the north side of the paved highway. It was built to prevent sheep, goats, yaks and wild animals from entering the town.

Hurrying along Carl tried to catch up with Dipak and Uma, who were way ahead of him with Samitra, Rama, and Margaret. He paused when Sita called out his name and ran toward him, leaving her companion behind.

Glancing over his shoulder, he overheard Sushma trying to catch up with them, shouting in Nepali, "Carl, you're an old man with gray hair, looking for a young wife."

"Don't pay attention to her. She's been up most of the night with diarrhea from eating too many desserts at dinner," said Sita, scowling.

"Where did you learn to speak English?" asked Carl.

"I went to St. Mary's boarding school and my brothers went to St. Xavier's," said Sita. "When I was home for summer vacation, my father taught me how to meditate."

"I have a stomach ache," sighed Sushma. "I didn't eat anything for breakfast this morning."

"You need to clear your chakras by meditating," said Sita, giving her friend a pill from her back pack.

"Tell me what you know about the chakras," said Carl, crossing the highway and entering a horizontal path above the northern wall with the two women.

"The word, chakra, means wheel. There are seven chakras located along the spinal column from the tail bone to the top of the head," said Sita. "They need to be cleansed during daily mediation to prevent them from becoming clogged, which leads to illness,"

Carl glanced toward the pilgrims leaving the narrow trail behind the wall and beginning the trek up the mountain on the vertical path.

"I'll tell you the Sanskrit name and the medical symptom for each clogged chakra," said Sita, walking beside Carl.

"The first is Muladhara, which causes overweight, sciatica, and arthritis.

"The second is Svadhisthana, involving sexual and urinary problems.

"The third is Manipura, which causes digestive pain, fatigue, and hypertension.

"The fourth, Anahata brings on allergies, heart, and lung disease.

"The fifth is Vishuddha, dealing with throat, neck and thyroid.

"The sixth is Ajna which causes vision and headaches.

"The seventh is Sahasrara, leading to depression, withdrawal, and confusion."

"I'm surprised by the number of medical issues that take place when the chakras are clogged," said Carl.

"The Tibetan Buddhists only have six chakras, which

they cleanse while chanting the mantra, 'Om Mane Padme', which means, 'Behold the Jewel in the Lotus Blossom'." said Sita, leaving the trail behind the wall to start trekking up the mountain.

"Wait for me," shouted Sushma, hurrying after them.

"I am sorry, older brother. You are not an old man."

Carl said, "I'm seventy one years old, and I'm not offended by being called an old man. I'm also not looking for a wife."

"Where is your wife?" asked Sushma.

Carl told her that he was married for 35 years, and his wife, Barbara was working at a museum in Chicago.

Sushma smiled, telling him she was amused by his wife's strange name. Carl left the two women sitting on large rocks to rest while he continued up the mountain.

Upon reaching the top, he admired the snow covered Himalayas, soaring beneath a blue sky. Carl surveyed the hills and valleys with no nomads in sight.

He walked toward a chaitya, a Tibetan Buddhist shrine, built from stones in memory of the departed ancestors of nomads. He looked around, hoping to find his friends, but they were nowhere in sight. He sat down on a rock to rest, enjoying the solitude and peacefulness of the area.

After resting for a while, he trekked east until he heard voices coming from a cluster of trees. As he approached them, he recognized the familiar faces of pilgrims. Carl talked with them for a few minutes, before excusing himself to explore the area.

Glancing into the valley, he saw a Tibetan nomad family standing in front of their tent watching their sheep and goats grazing near the river.

He glanced at his watch, deciding to trek down the mountain on a steeper trail using his walking stick.

Chapter 35
"Descent of the Mountain at Nylam"

While climbing down the mountain, Carl noticed that an elderly gentleman was sitting on a large rock, resting. He had removed his coat and was wiping his forehead with a handkerchief.

"Daju, namaste. Tapai sanchai hunuhuncha," Greetings, older brother. Are you all right?" asked Carl.

The gray haired man answered him in English. "I'm tired because I'm eighty years old, and I didn't sleep well last night at the hotel. This trail is steeper than I expected even though it's shorter than the other one.

"My name's Subir Bahadur Shrestha," he said, removing a water bottle from his back pack and taking a sip.

After introducing himself, Carl fetched a water bottle from his own back pack and sat down next to him.

"I used to teach Shakespeare's 'Macbeth,' to the high school students at the Jesuit boarding school in Godavari. They wouldn't let me teach 'Romeo and Juliet,' because it was a love story," said Subir.

"Most of the students came from wealthy families. After graduating nearly all of them went to universities in India, China, or London. A few of them went to America.

"You must have known Father Marshal Moran, and Father Thomas Downing? They were Jesuits from the Chicago Province."

"I knew both of them," said Carl. "They've been dead for some years now. Father Moran travelled with Nehru trying to stop the violence between the Hindus and Moslems after India achieved Independence from the British.

"The violence was terrible after Gandhi's assassination in 1948," said Carl. "Over a million people lost their lives during the Partition when East and West Pakistan separated from India and became independent Muslim countries."

"East Pakistan is now called Bangladesh," said Subir. "We had a lot of violence in Nepal during the Maoist Revolution. At that time my son, Rajan, was teaching Science at the high school in a town, a day's walk from Kathmandu.

"He never expected Maoist soldiers to invade the school and take the students and teachers up the nearby mountain for indoctrination into Communism.

"When the headmaster, Mahesh Rana, refused to go with them, a Maoist soldier shot him in the head in front of the students and faculty. They were all terrified by the brutal murder.

"After the indoctrination, several Nepalese students joined the Maoists because they promised them food, clothing, shelter, and military training," said Subir.

"Did the students willingly join the Maoists or were they forced to do it?" asked Carl.

"The Maoists threatened to kill their parents and burn down their shops and houses if they refused to join them," said Sabir. "Most of the students conscripted into the army were Newars from the merchant caste or Tamang farmers.

"Because I'm from the merchant caste, I was terribly worried that the Maoists would force my son, Rajan, to leave teaching and join the Maoist army to fight in the revolution against the monarchy."

"Why didn't the Maoists conscript Brahmans from the priestly caste, and Chettris of the warrior caste?" asked Carl.

"Students from the upper castes were spared from being conscripted into the army if their parents donated money, clothing, and bedding to support the Maoist Revolution. In spite of their donations, some students from the upper castes were forced to join the army at gunpoint.

"After training the students from the towns and villages, the new recruits were put in charge of guarding the Maoist Army Camps while the experienced Maoist soldiers fought the Royalist Army in the foothills and mountains throughout the country."

"Prachandra was the leader of the Maoists and a renegade Brahman. He spent time with the Maoists in India before taking over the Kathmandu Valley and deposing the monarchy," said Carl.

"It's time for us to continue down the hill," said Subir, putting on his back pack.

"How did your son deal with the Maoists?

"After the departure of the Maoists, Rajan left Nepal and went to Bihar, India where he got a job teaching at a Jesuit high school in Patna."

"What do you think about Pope Francis, who was a Jesuit priest from Argentina?" said Carl. "His name is Mario Jorge Bergoglio and his ancestors are from northern Italy."

"It's the first time the Catholic Church has a Jesuit Pope, who refuses to live in luxury at the Vatican." said Subir.

"Pope Francis rents a room at a nearby hotel and pays for it out of his own pocket," said Carl. "Some of the Cardinals and Archbishops don't like him because he is focuses upon the poor and the underprivileged people of the world."

"He was concerned about the slum dwellers when he was living in Argentina," said Subir. "He wrote an encyclical, 'Laudato Si, Praise Be'. It deals with Climate Change brought about by industrial pollution, deforestation, soil erosion, and the lack of conservation."

"Pope Francis blames Capitalism and Communism for the climate change," said Carl. "The three countries with the most pollution are China, India, and the United States."

"In Nepal everyone used to blame the monarchy for all of our problems. Now they blame the Maoists since the revolution is over and nothing has changed. The rich are getting richer and the poor, poorer," said Subir, starting down the trail using his walking stick for balance.

"I read an article in 'Time Magazine' about Sir Edmond Hillary commenting about the pollution along the trail to Mount Everest due to the carelessness of trekkers leaving oxygen tanks, plastic containers, and garbage behind them," said Carl. "The Sherpa guides are marching and protesting because they're overworked and receive low wages."

"I wonder how the Christian Missionaries are doing in Nepal?" asked Subir. "I remember getting a terrible infection in my foot while hiking in the mountains north of Pokhara. I was worried that gangrene had set in and that I'd have to have my foot amputated.

"When I returned to Pokhara, I went directly to Shining Hospital, run by missionaries. They cleansed my wound and gave me antibiotics to treat the infection. Within two weeks, I was healed and released to go back to Kathmandu. I'm grateful to the missionaries for saving my life.

"I was surprised by the number of Nepalese lined up at the clinic each morning, waiting their turn in line to see the doctors. Most of the patients were too poor to even give the missionaries a single rupee."

"They also ran a clinic in Pokhara, and built a shelter for people with leprosy, who were in danger of losing their fingers and toes," said Subir.

"I met Scottish missionaries on a crowded train while

travelling to Patna in India. The train came to a halt on the other side of the Ganges River across from the city.

"While crossing the river on a passenger boat, I spoke to the missionaries, who had spent six years in Nepal, working in a remote village in the mountains," continued Carl.

"Doctor Gavin and his wife, Alyssa, a nurse, had two daughters, who were born in Nepal. They were shy and backed away from me," said Carl.

"When I asked the girls their age, they didn't understand me. Their father told me that Isla was three years old and Cora, five. Neither spoke English so I spoke to them in Nepali.

"The girls told me they wanted to stay with their Nepali friends in the village, but their father decided to take them to Scotland to learn English and learn about their cultural heritage," said Carl.

"When the boat arrived in Patna, I helped them carry their luggage to the street. There were no taxis available to take them across town to the other train station, where they planned to travel to Bombay, and then they would take a steam boat to Scotland. The whole trip would take about a month.

"I was startled when a stagecoach, pulled by two horses, arrived and the driver agreed to take the family to the train station on the other side of town.

"I helped Dr. Gavin with the luggage while his wife and daughters boarded the coach. As they departed the girls peeked out the window and waved goodbye to me.

"I read that film makers in India were imitating Western movies," said Subir. "I also wish we had more Nepalese doctors and nurses willing to go to the remote areas of Nepal. Most of them work in the hospitals in the Kathmandu Valley or the larger towns along the border to India."

Chapter 36
"Returning to the Hotel at Nylam"

While hiking down the steep trail, Subir stumbled and slid several yards on the mountain. He seized a shrub with both hands, which prevented him from falling further.

Carl, who was hiking behind him, came to his rescue by pulling him up and setting him down in the grass alongside of the trail.

Subir was trembling because his face was scratched and his hands were bleeding. Carl administered first aid by applying pressure to his wounds with his handkerchief to stop the bleeding. He washed them with drinking water. He applied an antibiotic ointment to the scratches, followed by bandages from his medical kit.

"Are you able to stand up without falling again?" asked Carl, concerned about the elderly man's health.

"I twisted my ankle and it really hurts," said Subir. "Maybe I can still walk on it."

Carl lifted him from the ground and tried to get him to stand on the slanted trail. Unfortunately, Subir was sweating and trembling because of the pain in his right foot.

"I made a terrible mistake by coming down this trail," he sighed. "I still feel dizzy from the fall."

"You better sit down," said Carl, noticing that Subir's ankle was red and swollen. He was relieved to see Dipak and Uma coming down the trail toward them.

"What happened to Subir?" asked Dipak, hurrying toward them with his wife following a few yards behind.

"I fell down and hurt myself. I'm grateful to Carl for helping me get up and bandaging my wounds. I can't walk because my ankle is either sprained or broken," said Subir, trembling.

Dipak removed his back pack and crouched down next to Subir. He asked, "How much do you weigh."

"I'm about a hundred fifty pounds, mostly skin and bones. I'll never be able to climb Mount Kailash because of my ankle. Maybe I can ride a horse up the mountain with my leg in a cast."

"Don't worry about that right now. I can carry you down the mountain on my back," said Dipak.

"We could make a stretcher using our walking sticks and coats," said Carl.

"That's not necessary. I'll carry him the rest of the way down the mountain!" insisted Dipak.

With Carl's assistance, Dipak succeeded in getting Subir onto his back.

"Dipak, take your time going down the trail," warned Uma, praying to Shiva for protection.

"I use to carry bags of cement that weighed 100 pounds each when I was a young man. Subir's light as a feather in comparison," said Dipak, departing with him down the winding trail.

Carl followed them wearing his own back pack and carrying Subir's while Uma followed chanting to Shiva.

After descending for about twenty minutes, Dipak reached the bottom of the mountain and then crossed the paved road, where he called Hari on his cellphone.

A few minutes later Carl and Uma arrive, noticing that a land cruiser had arrived. They hurried across the road as Dipak place Subir in the back seat of the vehicle.

Carl quickly handed Subir his back pack before the driver

departed for the hospital at Nylam.

"Dipak, you're an amazing man for carrying Subir down that steep trail," said Carl.

"You had bandaged Subir before I even arrived, which made going down the trail with him easy," said Dipak.

"I must send my daughter an email at Shanti Bhawan Hospital once we get back to the hotel. I sent my wife an email this morning. I wonder if she answered it."

"Well, there's only one way to find out," said Dipak, taking his wife's arm. "Let's go back to the hotel."

"Don't forget your backpack," said Uma, handing it to her husband. "I'm so glad we have hot water and a shower in our room. I need to get cleaned up before dinner."

"I'm starving," said Dipak. "Uma, let's get a bite to eat at a restaurant before we go back to the hotel. Dinner won't be served until 7:00 tonight."

"I'll see you later in the dining room," said Carl. "I'm going to check my email."

Carl hurried back to the hotel and went directly to the computer room. Sure enough he had a message from his wife, Barbara.

Dear Carl, I received your email, and I'm pleased you're staying at a hotel in Nylam with plumbing. I hope you'll enjoy the trek up the mountain and get back safely. I received an email from Kathy. She's likes working in the Emergency Room at the hospital in Patan.

Kathy didn't write a word about her boyfriend, Greg, who's doing his International Rotation in Quito, Equator. She told me not worry about Om because he's a married man and that her relationship is platonic. His wife lives in Pokhara with his three children and his parents. He goes home to visit them once a month for a weekend and has invited Kathy to go with him to meet his family.

I'm so glad Renee's staying with me while you're gone. She loves being with Sammy and Emily, but she's exhausted by the time I get back from the work on the late afternoon train.

Frankly, I'm worn out from taking busloads of summer camp children through the galleries every day at the museum. Most of the kids are restless and don't want to listen about the exhibits.

Once I'm home, I fix dinner for the kids. Now that they're older, they're fussy about what they eat. Sammy and Emily used to eat everything I put on the table without any hassle. Now they pick at their food and hide the vegetables under their plates, leaving a mess for me to clean up while they are playing in the back yard until it gets dark.

When I'm at work, Renee takes the kids to McDonald's for lunch and then the park to play for hours before her chauffer arrives and brings them home. Twice a week he drives them to the Elk Grove Theater for an afternoon movie.

Next week is my vacation and we'll be traveling to Springfield to the Lincoln Museum, where we'll spend the afternoon. The next day we'll tour Abraham Lincoln's House and then drive to New Salem to see the log cabins.

I forgot to tell you that my father has been angry lately. He's threatening to come for a visit so that he can bulldoze down our house. Sam's wants to buy us a $500,000 house in Mount Prospect because he still doesn't approve of us living in an old bungalow on Maple Street here in Arlington Heights.

Sam also has been angry with his lawyer for not moving ahead with Mark's divorce. Corrine has been upset over the custody of the children. She doesn't want Sammy and Emily moving to Philadelphia and living in an apartment with

Mark and his new girlfriend.

   Corrine has hired one of the best lawyers in Chicago to get custody of the children. She has filed a complaint against Mark for abandoning her by taking a job in Philadelphia.

   I spoke with her on the phone recently. She told me that Mark only comes home every other weekend to see their children. Having a full time job and raising children without a husband has given her so much stress that she's been ill for the past two days.

   Carl, you won't believe this, but Corrine finally kicked her alcoholic mother out of the house. You already know about Sammy, having black and blue marks from being beaten by her mother. Corrine insisted that I bring the kids to stay overnight at her house now that she has hired a nanny to take care of them on weekends.

   I'm stilled worried about you falling off the mountain. I hope you'll be extra careful. I know once you leave Nylam you might not be able to email me for two or three days.

   Say hello to Margaret Porter for me. Samitra told me that she's has been sitting next to you in the dining room and has been suffering from depression over Nigel. I can't blame her for being upset.

   When I picked up the "New York Times", I was surprised to see Nigel's picture. He was dressed in his monk's robe and pointing to a statue inside the Jokang Temple. The headline was 'Monk Murders a Guard in Lhasa."

   I was horrified when I read that a Chinese guard was stabbed to death by Nigel Porter, who was a tourist guide at the Jokang Temple.

   When the lights went out, the Buddhist monk, Nigel disappeared after the murder. A few days later all the monks in the monastery, where Nigel was living, were arrested for harboring a criminal.

I'm still going to mass every morning at St. Eymard's in Elk Grove Village before taking the train to the museum downtown. Please write to me as soon as you can. Be extra careful climbing Mount Kailash.

With love, Barbara.

Carl took a deep breath before writing to Barbara. He informed her that he enjoyed the trek up and down the mountain in Nylam, but he decided not to tell her about Subir injuring himself since it would cause her more stress. After sending the email to Barbara, he sent a message to Kathy at hospital.

That evening Carl joined his friends in the dining room where everyone was weary from the trek although they were impressed by the grandeur of the mountains and the beauty of the landscape.

After dinner Hari announced that Subir had a broken leg and would be staying at the hospital overnight and would be sent by helicopter back to Kathmandu.

He also informed the pilgrims that they would be leaving for Saga the next day after breakfast, and they should have their luggage in the hallway to be picked up by the bellboys before coming to breakfast.

Chapter 37
"Travelling to Saga"

Early the next morning after taking a shower, Carl put his suitcase in the hallway. He then went to the computer room to check his email. He was pleased to hear from Kathy.
Dear Dad,
I'm really enjoying my stay in Patan. I've been putting in quite a few hours at the Emergency Room at Shanta Bhawan Hospital. I received an email from mom telling me about your trek up the mountain at Nylam yesterday. She said that you didn't say a word about Subir falling down the narrow trail and breaking his ankle. She, also, believes you're being secretive about your relationship with Margaret Porter.

Samitra emailed her all about you giving first aid to Subir and Dipak carrying him down the mountain.

Mom's still worried about her dreams of you falling off Mount Kailash. She's hysterical about me going out to lunch everyday with Om. She treats me as if I'm still in high school, which is so annoying.

Since we both have a weekend off from the hospital the third week of August, Om has invited me to go with him in a taxi to his village to meet his wife and children in Pokhara.

Even though Om was my boyfriend when we were here in 2001, I want to reassure you that I'm not having a love affair with him. He's been teaching me Nepali so that I can carry on a conversation with his family when I meet them.

I received an email from Greg from Quito yesterday. He misses me and can't wait to see me. His rotation is only for two weeks due to flooding in the Andes and problems with electricity at the hospital where he's working.

Because there have been Maoist uprising in the villages and towns in Ecuador, foreigners have been asked to vacate the country due to a possible revolution.

Greg informed me that he wants to fly from Quito to Kathmandu to meet me. Om invited him to stay in a guest room here at the hospital, but he already made a booking at the Kathmandu Guest House.

Om told me to ask Greg to come with us to meet his family when we're off from work. He would like him to help us out in the Emergency Room at Shanta Bhawan.

I think Greg is worried that I'm going to marry Om because mom has been sending him emails. She had a dream about Om and Greg having a fist fight over me at Tribuwan Airport in Kathmandu, where they were arrested and put into jail for disturbing the peace.

I've been reading about Nigel being accused of murdering a Chinese guard in Lhasa. I bet Margaret Porter's freaking about this on the trip.

In today's "Daily Nepal," a Buddhist monk in Lhasa confessed that Nigel didn't have typhoid and never died at the monastery. He confessed that Nigel never returned to the monastery after the murder but escaped on the back of a truck travelling to India, where he'll stay with the Dali Llama in Dharmasala.

Dad, it won't be very long before you'll be climbing Mount Kailash. I'm not worried about you travelling with Margaret Porter, but mom believes that you're in love with her. However, I am more concerned about your safety while trekking up the mountain at your age.

                Your loving daughter, Kathy

After leaving the computer room, Carl hurried to the

dining room for breakfast. An hour later, all the pilgrims were boarding their land cruisers and preparing to depart for Saga. Hari mentioned that they would be travelling at 14,209 feet and ascending to about 15,000 on a long, narrow dirt road. It would take them about seven hours to reach their hotel in Saga, providing there were no landslides.

Hari informed the drivers to have a ten minute interval between the departures of the land cruisers because once they were on the dirt road, there would be clouds of dust obstructing the vision of the drivers if they travelled too closely together.

In spite of the dust, the trip to Saga was an incredible experience. Carl travelled in the land cruiser with Samitra and Rama. He sat in the passenger side next to the driver, looking out the window.

In the distance he saw flocks of grazing sheep and goats with shepherds watching them. Near the pitched tents the children were playing while the women washed clothes in the nearby river.

While travelling on the rugged dirt road up the mountain, clouds of dust drifted toward them, forcing the driver to slow down. He turned on the windshield wipers to clear the dust from the windows.

"Tapai Nepali bhasa bolnu huncha?" Do you speak Nepali?" asked Carl, noticing that the driver was tense due to the smeared windshield.

"Hajur, ma Nepali bhasa boldai chu? Mero nam Kesab ho. Tapaiko name ke ho?" Sir, I speak Nepali. My name is Kesab. What is your name?

After Carl introduced himself, Kesab said, "We were the second to the last land cruisers to leave Nylam because of the delay caused by the women.

"It's my fault," said Samitra from the back seat. "I

encouraged Margaret to go to the computer room after breakfast. We were trying to get more information about Nigel when Hari entered the room after searching the hotel for us, he was angry because of the delay."

"I was worried that something had happened to them," said Rama.

"Margaret's right behind us in the land cruiser with Dipak and Uma," said Samitra.

After reaching the top of the mountain, the dust was no longer a problem. Carl took a deep breath and enjoyed the grandeur of the Tibetan landscape with soaring sand dunes and rocky vistas. The lower savannah was the grazing land for yaks, sheep, and goats with scattered trees and drought resistant shrubs.

As they traveled down the winding road, Kesab, was disturbed by a rumbling noise, which was loose grave from the mountain, falling onto the driver's side of the road. At first only the tires thumped from the gravel, but within a few minutes a heavy shower of gravel and stones were striking the roof. Samitra screamed from fright, clinging to Rama.

Carl glanced over his shoulder when he heard the honking of the horn of the land cruiser behind him them, encouraging them to drive faster.

Kesab sped down the side of the mountain, realizing that they were caught in a land slide. Rocks were now striking the roofs and the windows of the land cruiser.

Carl gasped, "I'm amazed that the windows aren't broken from the stones and rocks hitting them.

"It's because they're shatterproof," said Rama, noticing that his wife was trembling.

As they approached the bottom of the mountain, Kesab lost control of the steering due to the accumulation of debris blocking the road.

Samitra screamed as their vehicle zigzagged hitting the side of the mountain and turning over. She was horrified when she fell onto her husband, moaning from pain.

Carl gasped for breath in the front seat with Kesab, clinging to the steering wheel and leaning toward him.

They were all in shock while trying to get out of the toppled vehicle. They didn't expect Dipak to arrive to help them. After climbing up the debris, he yanked the door open and pulled Kesab and Carl out. He then helped Samitra and Rama out of the back seat.

In the distance Carl saw two shadowy figures materialize from a cloud of dust wearing their orange and blue coats. He was relieved to see Uma and Margaret climbing over the debris, which separated the two land cruisers.

"How are we ever going to get to Mount Kailash?" asked Margaret, wiping her face with a handkerchief.

"Maybe the Tibetan herders in the valley over there can help us," said Kesab.

"Kesabji, ahile hamiharu sabai jana Bhoti bhetnu janu paracha," Kesab, all of us should go to meet the Tibetans," suggested Carl.

"Does anyone here speak Tibetan?" asked Dipak, taking Uma's hand and following their driver, Lall, across the road into a pasture.

"I studied it years ago when I was teaching cultural anthropology at the University of Pennsylvania," said Carl.

"They still teach it at the University of Chicago," said Samitra, clinging to her husband for support. "I feel dizzy from the crash."

"Margaret, are you all right?' asked Carl.

"I'm relieved that our land cruiser didn't turn over like yours did," she said, grabbing Carl by the arm sobbing.

"Margaret, come sit in the shade with me," said Samitra,

taking her by the arm into the pasture, where Uma and Dipak were sitting in the shade of a tree.

Carl went back to the land cruiser. With Kesab's help, they pried open the damaged trunk with a crowbar .They returned with their luggage and a medical kit.

"Look over there! It seems as if nomads are coming towards us on horseback," gasped Margaret.

Everyone got up from the grass as the Tibetans rode toward them, each leading a horse behind them.

"Why are they coming toward us with extra horses," asked Uma, noticing they were carrying ropes on their backs."

"I hope they don't plan to take us back to their camp as prisoners!" said Samitra, her voice quivering.

"The Kampas were notorious for robbing and stealing from the herders. They took advantage of the Tibetan farmers by stealing their barley and other crops. On occasion they'd even attacked the monasteries," said Rama.

"I hope those men aren't Kampas. I wonder if they want to steal our passports and luggage," gasped Margaret..

When the Tibetans pulled up alongside of them and dismounted, Carl spoke to the nomads while Dipak stood beside him.

After introducing themselves, they shook hands with Kalsang, which means Good Fortune and his brother Lhundup, Spontaneously Accomplished.

They informed Carl that they came to help them turn over their car with the help of the horses and ropes.

Kalsang and Lhundup removed two shovels from the back of the horses and cleared the stones and boulders away from the overturned land cruiser. A half hour later they handed the shovels to Dipak and Carl requesting them to take away gravel heaped between the two vehicles.

While they were clearing the road, Carl watched the nomads removing the ropes from their spare horses and wrapping them around the axle and through the open windows of the toppled cruiser. After tying the ropes to the four horses, Kalsang and Lhundup guided them as they pulled up the land cruiser and straightened it out on the road.

Kesab rushed over to start the engine, which worked fine in spite of the damage to the doors and the trunk. He drove the vehicle about 25 feet and then let it run.

The Tibetan herders approached Carl and Dipak with their shovels and helped them remove the remaining rocks and stones between the vehicles.

Once the road was cleared, Lall started his vehicle and parked it behind Kesab's cruiser.

Everyone gathered around Kalsang and Lhundup, who spoke to Carl, in Tibetan. A few minutes later, he informed his friends that the nomads had invited them to spend the night at their camp so they could meet their wife, and children, who took care of their goats and sheep.

Carl asked the nomads how much they wanted for their hard work for helping them. They talked privately together and told him, there was no charge.

The pilgrims were surprised by their kindness. Dipak insisted that each person, including the driver should give them ten yuans, which the nomads finally accepted. They then took a vote about spending the night with the Tibetans.

Dipak, Uma, and Margaret decided to go on to Saga with Lall, even though the sun was setting. Carl, Samitra, and Rama agreed to stay at the camp of the Tibetans.

Carl told them to tell Hari they would leave the camp at dawn, arriving in Saga before they departed for Lake Manasarovar."

Chapter 38
"At the Camp of the Tibetans"

Carl waved to Dipak, Uma, and Margaret as they departed in their land cruiser, leaving a cloud of dust behind them. To avoid inhaling the dust, he put both hands over his face and turned around.

When Samitra began coughing, she backed away from the dust with her eyes closed. After clearing her throat, she said, "I'm worried about Margaret. I didn't expect her to burst into tears because of the landslide. I thought for sure she would be staying overnight with us."

"Dipak was anxious to leave because Uma insisted they go onto Saga. They convinced Margaret to go with them," said Rama.

"I hate to say this Carl, but Margaret's in love with you. She repeatedly told me that you've been ignoring her the whole trip because you're a married man," said Samitra.

"Everyone's been gossiping about you and Margaret being Star Crossed Lovers because of the way she threw herself at you before the orientation. All eyes were on her low cut outfits whenever she entered the dining room and sat down next to you," said Rama.

"You're not the only one who admires her figure. I've heard comments from every man on the trip including the drivers, and guides," said Samitra.

"I almost yielded to Margaret's request about trading places with her, so that you two could be together in the land cruiser. I'm tired of listening to her talk about her husband's death from auto accident. I made a mistake by encouraging her to come on the pilgrimage with us," sighed Samitra.

"I feel sorry for Margaret," said Carl. "I'll never forget how she ended up in the hospital after her son, Christopher, was murdered, followed by Nigel being kidnapped by the members of a London Coven."

"Really!" said Samitra. "She never told me about that!"

"She was hospitalized again from shock when Nigel was present at the palace during the assassination of the Royal Family. He was also accused of murdering the Abbot at the Bodhnath Monastery.

"This time Nigel's being accused of murdering a Chinese guard in Lhasa and involved in a conspiracy to liberate Tibet," said Carl.

"I'm worried about Margaret having another nervous breakdown while we're travelling to Mount Kailash," said Carl.

"Margaret's annoying at times, but her husband taught her how to do deal with stress by meditating. I reminded her several times to take his advice and calm down," said Samitra.

"We better get going," said Carl, putting on his back pack and leading the way toward the Tibetans, waiting for them with their horses.

They paused to watch the nomads put straw saddles onto the extra horses followed by their back packs and sleeping bags. After boosting Samitra and Rama onto the spare horses, Kalsang helped Carl onto his horse, while their driver Kesab, rode with Lhundup.

As they rode along on horseback through the pasture toward the campsite, Rama said, "Carl, since you're an anthropologist, you must know something about the Tibetan nomads."

"I'm amazed by their ability to live without modern conveniences and adjust to the changing seasons. I'm also impressed by their mobility and freedom to roam with their families and herds."

"They remind me of the Sioux Indians, who quickly set up and took down their tepees, to follow the buffaloes," said Rama, riding next to Carl.

"The nomads are exposed to the grandeur of the mountains and the brutality of nature," said Carl. "There are only about two million nomads left in Tibet."

"It's because of the immigration of thousands of Han Chinese to Tibet, who encourage the nomads to raise yak herds (dzomo) for beef and milk like cows on farms and ranches," said Rama.

"On many farms in the United States, hybrid cows and steers never leave the barns to graze in pastures. Even chickens don't leave their wire coops. Numerous farm animals, raised for meat, are given injections of antibiotics and eventually will be cruelly slaughtered," said Carl.

"I hope that the nomads don't abandon their pastures by being influenced by modernization. It would be terrible if the nomads would be deprived of their land that stretches from western to eastern Tibet by forcing their sheep, goats, and yaks to be enclosed in barns, "said Samitra.

"I would hate to see these green pastures being plowed by tractors and turned into wheat fields," said Rama.

"William Davis, a cardiologist from Milwaukee, Wisconsin, wrote 'Wheat Belly', claiming that genetically engineered hybrid wheat has negative effects on the body.

"Wheat in bread and bakery goods causes blood sugar to increase, resulting in cravings similar to those experienced by alcoholics and drug addicts. The heavy amount of sugar triggers cycles of feeling satisfied, followed by appetite stimulation for more. The destructive effects of excessive wheat consumption are obesity, neurological disorders, celiac, diabetes, heart problems arthritis, rashes, and depression," said Carl.

"Here we are at the camp," interrupted Rama, noticing a woman hovering over a fire, heating water in a large kettle.

"Where is that garlic odor coming from?" asked Rama, getting off his horse and sniffing the air. "It's coming from the grass that has garlic seeds sprouting during the summer."

Kalsang leapt from his horse in front of the fire while Carl slid off behind him. A Tibetan boy came running up to the horse, taking the reins and leading it to the stream for drink of water.

"Would someone please help me down from my horse?" asked Samitra, her voice shrill from waiting.

"Sorry about that," said Rama rushing to help her dismount. "Forgive me for ignoring you."

Two more boys quickly arrived to take their horses to the stream with Kesab following them with Lhundhup's horse.

"Our wife, Dorje, is burning dried goat dung because there's no firewood in the valley. She invites all of you to have some Tibetan tea," said Lhundup with Carl translating.

"That garlic smell is very pungent," said Samitra, heading toward the outdoor fire. "It's starting to get cold now that the sun setting."

"These coats that Hari gave us for the pilgrimage will come in handy here in the valley," said Rama.

"Here comes Kesab bringing our sleeping bags with the children carrying our backpacks," said Carl, watching him put them in the grass some distance from the fire.

Kalsang came out from the tent with four square rugs, handing one to each of them. He told everyone to sit down on the rugs while his wife poured tea into bowls.

"These rugs are just beautiful," said Samitra. "Mine has an image of a dragon on it."

"This one has a mountain with a river," said Rama.

"Here's Buddha, sitting on a lotus blossom," said Carl.

"Mine has 'Om Mane Padme Hum'," said Kesab.

Everyone sat down on their rugs near the fire, while Lhundup handed them each a steaming bowl of salted, barley tea, known as tsampa in Tibetan. While drinking their tea, they watched the sun setting behind the mountains.

"It's getting cold out here. Please come inside our tent while Kalsang and I set up yours before it gets dark," said Lhundup.

"The tents and their ropes are made from yak hair. They can be put up and taken down quickly because the nomads are continually moving with their herds," said Carl, who was the first to enter the nomad's tent, illuminated by a lantern and oil lamps.

The others followed him, carrying their bowls and rugs into the dimly lighted tent, where they sat around the cast iron stove with a chimney.

Carl paused to introduce himself and his friends to an elderly couple, the parents of Lhundup and Kalsang.

The grey haired grandfather bowed his head to greet the strangers but continued working the spinning wheel while his eight year old grandson's held a ball of thread, which he fed into the wheel.

The grandmother glanced up from where she was weaving sheep wool into a blanket. She bowed to the strangers while her second grandson was braiding a rope made from yak hair.

Dorje was now crouched in front of the cast iron stove, stirring a large pot with a wooden spoon. Sitting next to her was her oldest son, making a sling shot to use for rounding up the herds of sheep and goats.

She signaled her guests to come forward with their empty bowls to get mo-mo dumplings made from Yak meat, which resembled Italian raviolis.

While the guests were eating, Lhundup informed them that their tent was ready. A few moments later Dorje, asked her husbands, the two brothers, to bring their older sons dinner. They were outside in the cold, attending their herds of sheep, goats, and yaks.

After finishing dinner, the second grandson took their bowls to the stream to be washed while his younger brother held the lantern. Upon returning, the family gathered around the stove and chanted prayers in Tibetan to Buddha.

After a few minutes Kalsang and Lhundup returned to the tent informing his family that a sheep had been killed by a wolf, but their older sons chased away the whole pack with stones from their sling shots.

Since the two brothers hadn't eaten, Carl gave up his space for them to sit down and then left the tent with the others following him. Their hosts bowed to each guest as they departed for their own tent for the night, where a grandson was waiting for them with a lantern.

Once they were settled for the night in their sleeping bags, the grandson left the tent and lit oil lamps near the entrance for those who might need to leave the tent during the night to urinate behind the bushes.

Chapter 39
"The Arrival of Unexpected Guests"

Everyone was sleeping soundly for about an hour, when they were suddenly awakened by a pack of wolves attacking the sheep. Kalsang arrived to tell them not to worry about the incident and that it would soon be under control.

Carl and his friends were startled by the howling of the wolves and the braying of panic stricken sheep as the men and boys drove away the wolves with their sling shots.

The guests were tense and nervous discussing the situation in their sleeping bags. It took some time before the nomads returned to their tent, collapsing from exhaustion.

After everything settled down and everyone was sleeping again, pilgrims and nomads were once again startled by the honking of a horn, coming from a vehicle on the dirt road.

Carl was the first to leave the tent, glancing up the hill toward the rugged road where he saw the head lights of a vehicle flickering. He paused to listen to the echoing of the horn bouncing off the mountains.

"What's going on?" asked Rama, coming out of the tent with Samitra and Kesab following him.

"Those people standing in front of the headlights are wearing orange and blue coats just like ours. They're from our tour group. Maybe they're having car trouble," said Samitra.

"I'm sure they know that we're staying here with the nomads after seeing our damaged land cruiser along the side of the rode," said Carl

"How strange that they've come here so late at night!" said Rama, pausing as Lhundup and Kalsang came out of their tent, carrying a lantern, bridals, and saddles.

They watched the brothers going to the pasture where the horses were grazing. Within a few minutes they saw them riding past them with two spare horses."

"It looks like our Tibetan friends are going to help the stranded pilgrims," said Carl.

"I'm going back to our tent because it's freezing outside. I wouldn't be surprised if we get frost tonight," said Samitra, shivering as she left them.

"I hope no one from that group is having a problem breathing at this altitude. Each vehicle's equipped with an oxygen tank in case of an emergency," said Carl.

"I'm sure they'll be coming here to spend the rest of the night with us. Have you noticed no one's waving their hands anymore or even tooting the horn," said Rama.

"They must be inside the car because it's so cold out here. Here comes Dorje and her children with carpets and straw mattresses to put into our tent for the strangers with Kesab helping them.

"It looks like Kalsang and Lhundup have reached the stranded vehicle. They're getting off their horses in front of the headlights," said Carl.

"Two stranded passengers have mounted the horses and are sitting behind our Tibetan friends. A third one just mounted a spare horse. It looks like they're waiting for their driver to turn off the headlights," said Rama.

He just turned them off," said Carl. "All four of them should be here in about fifteen minutes. It must be close to midnight,"

"It's already 2:00 a.m.," said Carl, glancing at his watch.

They paused listening to the shrill cry of a woman, echoing throughout the valley, surrounded by barren mountains in front of the snow covered Himalayas.

"Help me! Help me! I'm being kidnapped by Kampas," screamed the hysterical woman, louder than before. Her words echoed in the valley bouncing off the sides of the distant mountains.

"That's Margaret Porter screaming!" said Carl. "I wonder if she's been told that Nigel's been arrested."

"I hope not!" said Rama, patiently waiting for the horses to return to the camp.

Each time they heard a shrill cry from Margaret, Carl and Rama were worried because of the harsh echoing which caused the nomads to come out of their tent, wrapped in blankets, including the aging grandparents.

As the riders approached, Rama turned on his flashlight to illuminate the campsite.

Dipak slid down from his horse, followed by their driver, Lall. They were both relieved to see their friends waiting for them. He said, "We've come back to your camp because of another landslide that blocked the road!".

"That's not the only reason we came back," said Uma, who was helped down from her horse by Lhundhup.

Kalsang rode up to their tent with Margaret screaming with her arms wrapped around his waist.

"Help me! Someone help me!" screamed Margaret. "The Kampas are trying to kidnap me!

"Margaret ! These nomads aren't Kampas. They're sheep herders," said Carl. "Give me your hand and I'll help you down."

"Oh Carl! I never thought I'd see you again!" sobbed Margaret, sliding down from the horse and throwing her arms around him.

"When we were stranded, Kampas came out of the field on their horses. We agreed to pay them if they would clear the road for us, but they wouldn't do it. Lall tried to reason with them so they wouldn't take our wallet," said Dipak.

"They went directly to the trunk of the land cruiser and stole our sleeping bags, clothes, drinking water, and the oxygen tank," said Uma.

"The outlaws took my cashmere sweaters and emptied my suitcase on the grass," sobbed Margaret.

"While they were rummaging in the trunk, I hid our wallets and passports under seat of the cruiser," said Dipak.

"The leader of the Khampas shoved Lall to the ground when he told them that he didn't have any money."

"One of the Kampas pulled my arms behind my back while the other one kissed me, stroking me with his calloused hands!" sobbed Margaret, "I screamed when he ripped my dress off and tried to run away from him. When he grabbed me again, I scratched him on the face with my fingernails."

"The six foot Kampa slapped my face and threw me onto the ground. I was afraid he was going kill me when he grabbed me by the hair and held a knife to my throat.

"Dipak rushed toward him like a grizzly bear and knocked him to the ground. His knife went flying from his hand into the grass. The other Kampas knocked Dipak down by hitting him in the stomach. He lay on the ground, gasping for breath," said Margaret, clinging to Carl.

All eyes were on Dorje, coming out of her tent with a lantern, signally the guests to come inside for tea while Lhundup and Kalsang carried blankets into the other tent because their sleeping bags had been stolen.

Upon entering the crowded nomad's tent, Margaret started trembling so badly that she dropped her bowl of barley tea, shattering it on the cast iron stove. Then she collapsed onto floor, having an epileptic seizure.

Lall shouted, "Bhut aiyo! Bhut aiyo! An evil spirit has come here!" His frightening words caused Uma to cling to Dipak's arm.

When Lhundup and Kalsang came into the tent, they saw Margaret flopping on the floor like a fish out of water. They informed Carl that the Mountain Gods and Lords of the Earth were angry because they were awakened in the night by the horn honking and the lights flashing from the car.

"Because Margaret was screaming while riding the horse into camp, our nature gods sent evil spirts to attack and possess her mind, body, and soul," said Lundhup.

"Margaret's having a seizure and could choke to death on her tongue," shouted Carl, asking Dorje for a wooden spoon, which she quickly handed to him.

Kneeling down on the floor beside Margaret, he inserted the spoon into her mouth, which she bit with her teeth while convulsing.

Lundhup left the tent, returning a few minutes later with juniper branches from a nearby tree. He broke the branches and put them into the flaming cast iron stove.

Kalsang said, "Margaret contaminated the stove by shattering her bowl of barley tea on it. The juniper leaves will purify the stove."

While he was talking, Dorje handed him and his brother the prayer wheels to ward off the evil spirits, hovering over Margaret.

Carl noticed that Margaret was perspiring because she was sprawled out on the carpet near the stove, still wearing her coat. He struggled to remove her coat, feeling uneasy since she was lying on the floor convulsing in her pink slip because her dress had been ripped off by a Khampa.

Dorje's elderly father hobbled over to them from the spinning wheel with a maroon monk's robe. He hovered over Margaret, covering her so she wouldn't be cold, while a fierce wind shook the tent, startling everyone.

The two brothers walked around Margaret spinning the prayer wheels reciting the mantra, "Om Mane Padme Hum," while Dorje wiped the sweat from Margaret's forehead with a damp cloth.

A few minutes later, the grandmother set aside her weaving and approached her sons, holding a painted Tanka with images of the Buddha.

She joined the procession, invoking the names of Gautama Buddha and Saint Milarepa, to help drive away the evil spirits from Margaret, who was trembling and gasping for breath.

Everyone paused for a few minutes when they heard the wolves howling again. The grandfather ordered the newly arrived guests to go to the other Yak tent because they were using up the oxygen, which was needed by Margaret.

The Tibetan family asked Carl to stay with them while Dipak departed holding a lantern which allowed the other guests to follow him to their tent.

Carl stayed with Margaret crouched down beside her, holding her hand and wiping the salvia from her mouth with a cloth, while the chanting of the mantras continued for the next hour.

Lhundhup approached Margaret, invoking the Mountain and Earth Gods to help him. He placed his hands upon her forehead and shouted in Tibetan, "Evil Spirits be gone!"

A few moments later his brother, Kalsang recited "Om Mane Padme Hum", repeatedly to cleanse her chakras possessed by demons while his hands moved over her eyes, throat, chest, stomach, hips, and then down her thighs, knees, calves, ankles and feet.

Suddenly the stove started rattling, followed by the spinning wheel being knocked over. The whole tent was shaking from the demons sweeping through the tent.

Lhundhup shouted to Dorje, "Open the flap on the entrance to let them out!"

Dorje tried to open it, but was knocked down by the force of the spirits.

"Evil Spirits Be Gone!" shouted Lhundhup.

All of a sudden the bowls on the nearby shelf were rattling and crashed onto the floor, shattering into pieces.

"The demons are trying destroy everything in our tent!" shouted Dorje, getting up from the floor and holding the flap of the tent open. "You must take that woman outside so that the Mountain and Earth Gods will know that she's been punished by the evil spirits!"

Kalsang hurried out of the tent, carrying a lantern and a rolled carpet that he stretched out on the grass.

"Carl, help me drag Margaret outside!" shouted Lhundhup.

After lifting Margaret from the floor, the two men carried her quivering body outside. After putting her on the carpet, she rolled over into the grass.

Carl crouched down, noticing that Margaret was breathing heavily but no longer convulsing. He removed the wooden spoon from her mouth, pulled her unto the carpet, and covered her with the monk's robe.

"Dorje! Hold the flap open so that the evil spirits will leave the tent," shouted Kalsang.

"I can't," she shouted, falling to the ground and releasing the flap on entrance of the tent. Everyone could hear the grandparents shouting inside while more objects from the shelves were crashing onto the floor.

Lhundhup reached for his knife, slashing the flap from the entrance. Immediately white clouds of cold, misty vapors left the tent, soaring into the darkness.

The grandparents came outside the tent with duct tape to mend the slashed entrance flap to the tent.

Carl over heard the grandfather say, "All the evil spirits are gone now. You can bring that woman back inside."

"Wait until I purify the interior," said Kalsang, entering the tent and invoking the name of the Bodhisattva, Avalokiteswara, to cleanse the tent from evil spirits.

Carl recalled that a Bodhisattva is Buddhist saint, who after many reincarnations, decides to return to earth to help others. The name "Avalokiteswara," means "The Lord Looking Down with Compassion," referring to the current Dalai Lama, Tenzing Gyatso, the spiritual leader of the Tibetan people, living in India.

A few minutes later Lhundhup and Carl carried Margaret inside, where the aging grandfather was holding a bottle of herbal medicine.

"Carl lifted up her head and put a straw pillow behind it, while Margaret sighed, opening her eyes.

"Here's some medicine for you," said the grandfather, giving her a spoonful of green syrup.

"Where am I?" asked Margaret, glancing at the family, sweeping up the broken bowls and debris with hand brooms.

Kalsang said, "Carl, we set up a bed for you and your wife with clean blankets in the other tent.

"Margaret's not my wife! She's a friend," said Carl.

"Please tell me what happened! I remember that our land cruiser was stalled because of a land slide," said Margaret.

"I'll tell you about it tomorrow," said Carl, glancing at his watch. "We need to get some sleep so we can continue travelling on the long road to Mount Kailash."

Chapter 40
"Leaving the Nomad's Camp"

Early the next morning, Carl was the first to get up. He looked at his watch. It was 5:30 a.m. and the sunlight was already illuminating the inside of the Yak hair tent, where the others were still sleeping.

He got out of his sleeping bag, put on his clothes and went outside to urinate. Carl shivered in the cold, noticing that smoke was coming out of the chimney from the nomad's tent.

While walking back to the tent, Carl saw Dipak and Rama coming towards him wearing their coats.

"We didn't sleep well last night due to the chanting," said Rama, following Dipak away from the tents to urinate.

"Even though the sun's coming over the mountains, it's still cold! I should have worn my coat," said Carl, entering the tent and returning with it a few minutes later.

"I didn't have a chance to talk to you about the landslide yesterday because of Margaret's screaming and then her seizure," said Dipak.

"It was a difficult evening for all of us," said Carl. "Please tell me about what happened."

"An hour after we left you with the nomads, we were delayed because of another landslide that blocked the road. When we paused to stretch our legs, three Khampas approached us on their horses.

"They were very rough and wanted $200 dollars to

shovel away the debris from the road. When we told them we could give them $100 dollars, they got angry with us and went to the trunk and rummaged through our luggage.

"I quietly told Uma, Margaret, and Lall to give me their wallets and jewelry, which I hid under the front seat of the car. When Margaret saw the outlaws throwing her clothes and makeup into the field, she became hysterical and screamed at them. The oldest Khampa got angry and pushed her down.

"She got up screaming while the leader stuffed her cashmere sweaters into his saddlebag. He was about to mount his horse when Margaret ran toward him and scratched his face with her fingernails.

"That's when he ripped off her dress, slapped her on the face, and knocked her out." said Dipak.

"We were afraid that Margaret was dead. We backed away from them as they mounted their horses and took off into the field.

"As soon as they left, I found a bottle of water among the scattered objects from the trunk. I lifted up Margaret's head and poured the water onto her face, noticing a bruise on the side of her head. When I gave her a drink of water, she began coughing at first and then became conscious.

"She began screaming when she realized that she wasn't wearing her dress, but only a transparent slip exposing her bra and underpants," said Dipak.

"Margaret insisted that she had been raped by the leader of the Khampas, who stole some of her clothes and makeup.

"Uma tried to comfort her by picking up her clothes, scattered in the pasture and putting them into her suitcase. She told Margaret that she still had blouses, skirts, and a satchel with makeup and medications.

"Margaret told us that she had stopped taking Zanax

because it was addictive but she still took Tylenol when she had headaches.

"After the Khampas left, we all pitched in trying to clear the rocks blocking the road, but we weren't successful with the huge boulders. Because we couldn't continue to Saga, we decided to come back to the nomad camp to spend the night," said Dipak.

"Because Margaret was terribly upset, Uma gave her a Zanax to calm her down. She was fine until we got back to your land cruiser. When Lhundhup and Kalsang arrived with the extra horses to take us back to their camp, she began screaming. She thought we were being kidnapped by the Khampas!" said Dipak.

"So that's what happened!" said Carl. "Here comes Kesab and Lall from our tent. Tapaiharu ramro sutnu bhayo?" Did you sleep well?"

"Hoina hami ramro sutneko thiena," We didn't sleep well," they said, heading toward the river.

Upon returning they gathered around Carl, listening to him tell about how the Tibetan nomads chanted and performed the exorcisms on Margaret during the night.

A few minutes later all heads turned toward Samitra, Margaret, and Uma coming out of the tent. The women hurried past them toward the stream, disappearing behind large boulders along the bank to urinate.

When they returned to the camp, Dorje invited them into her tent for a bowl of barley tea. While drinking their tea, they watched the gray haired grandfather working at the spinning wheel and the grandmother weaving another rug.

After finishing their tea, they went outside, where Lhundhup and Kalsang were waiting with several horses to take them back to their land cruisers.

"It's wonderful to see the sun shining above the snow

covered Himalayas. They're so majestic in comparison to these rugged cliffs and barren mountains," said Margaret.

"You were stressed out when you arrived here last night," said Carl.

"I feel as if a heavy burden has been lifted from me," glancing at Lhundhup, signaling her to mount his horse.

Carl helped Margaret mount the horse by crouching down and folding his hand into the shape of a stirrup.

"I vaguely recall that our land cruiser came to a halt because of a landslide in the road. I remember three Khampas coming to help us clear away the debris.

"One of them accidently bumped into me and knocked me down. I felt sorry for him so I gave him two of my cashmere sweaters, one for his wife and the other for his daughter."

"Margaret, do you take medication for epilepsy?" asked Dipak, annoyed by her comments.

"No, why do you ask?" she said.

"We gave you some of your bipolar medication after the Khampas left our camp because you were angry with them for stealing your cashmere sweaters," said Dipak.

"I haven't been taking my medication. I only brought it along in case of an emergency," she replied.

"Yesterday when you were riding the horse you screamed all the way to the camp because you thought you were being kidnapped by Khampas."

"I remember the Khampas were happy because we gave them clothes to take home for the families."

"We didn't give them our clothes and neither did you. They stole our clothes and your sweaters."

"I…I'm not really sure about what happened," she said.

"Do you remember being attacked by the leader of the Khampas? He ripped off your dress and knocked you to the ground after you scratched his face. You were unconscious for quite a while!" said Dipak.

"I remember him accidently hitting me," she said.

"Dipak! Leave her alone! You've said enough!" snapped Uma, mounting Kalsang's horse.

"Margaret's suffering from memory loss after being knocked down by that Khampa! She's so much better this morning because of the exorcisms performed on her by our nomad friends," said Samitra "It's best to forget the past and live in the present moment."

"I don't remember any exorcisms being performed on me last night!" said Margaret. "You've all been so patience and kind. Please forgive me for causing you so much trouble."

"We're grateful that you're feeling better," said Rama.

"Here come our drivers with our sleeping bags and back packs tied to the spare horses.

Lhundhup led the way out of the camp with the other horses following him. Within fifteen minutes they arrived at the land cruisers. While their belongings were being put into the trunks, Carl requested that the men ride together in a land cruiser and the women in the other.

"That's a good idea. Samitra, Margaret, and I will ride together in the other cruiser," said Uma, realizing that her husband was angry with Margaret and wanted to question her further.

"Lhundhup and Kalsang agree to help us clear the other landslide," said Carl. "They left a few minutes ago on their horses with shovels. They will meet us there."

"It's about ten miles from here on the winding dirt road," said Dipak.

Leaving a cloud of dust behind, Kesab drove the cruiser with the women down the road. A few minutes later, the men departed with Lall driving.

After nearly an hour of travelling on the dusty road, the land cruisers came to halt near the landslide, where the nomads were busy shoveling the gravel and pitching it into the nearby pasture.

The women took shelter under a nearby tree, while the men picked up the extra shovels to clear the gravel and roll away the heavy boulders to the side of the road. After two hours of steady work, the road was finally cleared.

Carl took up a collection and gave the Tibetan nomads $100 each for helping clear the road and putting them up for the night.

"Before our friends leave, I want to show them my pictures of Nigel," said Margaret removing them from her purse and handing them to Tibetans.

While glancing at the pictures, Lhundhup seemed puzzled. He said, "I took our wife, Dorje, to the market in Saga to sell her rugs a week ago while Kalsang stayed in camp to watch the herds with our children."

"A truck driver picks us up twice a year and takes us to the market. While we were selling the rugs in Saga, the Abbot arrived from the monastery with three monks. One of them was your son, Nigel.

"He bought all of Dorje's rugs for the monks at the monastery. The Abbot told us that Nigel had been studying Tibetan scriptures in Lhasa and was planning to go to India to visit the Dalai Lama."

"Thank God, Nigel's safe!" said Margaret, after Carl translated the information for her. "Maybe he'll be waiting for me at the hotel in Saga. Thank you so much for the good news! I've been terribly worried about him."

Margaret approached Lhundhup and offered him an extra twenty five dollars, which he refused. However, his brother Kalsang accepted the money before they mounted their horses and headed back to their camp.

Once the brothers departed, the pilgrims boarded their land cruisers and continued toward Saga,

As they rode along, Dipak said, "Margaret doesn't remember how violently she attacked the Khampa leader. She clawed him with her finger nails so hard that his cheek was bleeding.

"The angry outlaw slapped her on the face, ripped off her dress, and pushed her down. That's when she hit the side of her head on a rock," said Dipak.

"Was Margaret really possessed by evil spirits or was she suffering from a brain injury?" asked Rama.

"I was impressed by the way the family handled her convulsions," said Carl. "By chanting the mantra 'Om Mane Padme Hum', a thousand times, the nomads sent healing energy into Margaret's body. Her tremors gradually slowed down and eventually stopped after the mystic, Milarepa was invoked and her chakras were cleared."

"You didn't answer his question. Do you believe that Margaret was attacked by evil spirits, sent to her by the Nature and Mountain Gods?" asked Dipak.

"It's possible that demonic forces attacked her because she was physically and emotionally upset," said Carl. "I, also, believe that a painful injury, intense stress, and severe depression had a negative effect on her mind and body. I'm sure prolonged fear and repressed anger can lead to physical and mental illness."

"You've finally answered my questions," said Dipak, glancing out the window at the Himalayan range.

After several hours of travelling, the two land cruisers came to a halt at the hotel in Saga,

Chapter 41
"Travelling to Lake Manasarovar"

Upon entering the hotel at Saga, Carl and his friends enquired at the desk about whether Hari and the pilgrims were still at the hotel.

"Your friends left early this morning. Hari told me that they were leaving for Lake Manasarovar and were expecting to be at the lake early in the afternoon. Afterwards, they'll be going to a guest house on the other side of the lake for two nights," said the Chinese clerk.

"Did you happen to get a message from my son, Nigel about a week ago?" asked Margaret, showing the clerk a picture of him, wearing a blue shirt and levis.

"Yes, he came here and left a note for Margaret Porter. It's here in my desk drawer," said the clerk, giving it to her.

"Thank you so much," said Margaret, opening the sealed letter and reading the note to Carl. "Mom, I'll meet you behind Milarepa's sanctuary at the top of the hill near the ruins of the guest house with a view of the lake.

With love, Nigel

"I hope, we can find Milarepa's sanctuary. It must be here somewhere in Saga," said Carl.

"He may be at the Buddhist monastery at the top of the hill here in Saga. I believe the guest house was torn down some years ago," said the clerk, opening a map to give them directions.

"I hope Nigel's still there," said Carl, getting the directions from the clerk before departing.

The pilgrims boarded the two land cruisers and headed through town, arriving at the base of the hill, without a lake or ruins in sight.

"The lake's probably in the woods behind all those trees, over there," said Margaret, heading up the hill toward the monastery with Carl while the others followed a path into the woods.

Upon arrival at the monastery, Carl chatted with the Abbott in Tibetan for a few minutes.

"Nigel wore his monk's robe while staying with us here at the monastery and shopping at the market place. He was very kind and bought thirty woven carpets from the nomads. He gave them to our monks here at the monastery.

"The problem was that two days later the police were knocking on the door of our monastery and asking us a lot of questions. They showed us a copy of the 'China Daily', with a picture of Nigel on the front page. He was accused of murdering a guard at the Jokang Temple in Lhasa.

"After the guards left I told Nigel that he must leave before the police returned to search the building for him."

"Where's Nigel now?" asked Carl. "Could he be hiding at Milarepa's cave near the lake in the woods below the monastery?"

"There's no cave, lake, or woods below our monastery," said the Abbot. "There's a monument to Milarepa at the top of the hill near the ruins of a monastery, destroyed by Maoist terrorists. It's located above the Chiu Gompa Guest House on the opposite side of Lake Manasarovara."

"Thank you for helping us," said Carl, writing the information down on a note pad.

"It was a pleasure to meet you," said the Abbott, bowing to Carl and Margaret as they left, hurrying down the hill.

Dipak approached from the woods with the others

trailing behind. "We searched for the lake behind those trees, but we couldn't find anything. There was only a creek, flowing some distance from the trees."

After getting settled in the two land cruisers, they departed from the monastery. As they were heading back to the city, two police cars came toward them on the dirt road.

"I'm sure they're going to search the monastery for Nigel," said Carl. "I hope we won't be stopped."

"You've spoken to soon," said Rama, sitting in the back seat next to Dipak. "They've already pulled over Lall's land cruiser and now they're stopping us."

The Chinese policemen made everyone come out of the land cruisers to search their pockets and then the luggage in the trunks. The senior officer, who spoke English, held up a copy of the 'China Daily' and said, "We are looking for Nigel Porter who murdered a guard in Lhasa.

"He was recently seen in Saga with the Abbott and two monks from the monastery on the top of this hill. I would like to know, why you are visiting this monastery?"

Carl said, "We went to the monastery to look at the Buddhist statues and to take a walk down to the creek to get some exercise. We're planning to join our pilgrim friends at the guest house on the opposite side of Lake Manasarovar because we're on a pilgrimage to Mount Kailash."

The officers wanted to know why they were separated from the other land cruisers. Lall informed them they were delayed due to landslides and had to spend the night with nomads some distance from Saga.

When an officer opened the newspaper and showed them a picture of Nigel in his monk's robe, everyone shrugged their shoulders or shook their heads. Margaret suddenly became pale with fright but was ignored by the police. Within fifteen minutes the police had rummaged through their luggage, sleeping bags and back packs. After a thorough search, the officers departed for the monastery to interrogate the monks.

"Margaret you handled yourself very well," said Carl, opening the back door of the land cruiser, where she entered and sat down next to Uma. Samitra was already in the front seat, sitting across from their driver, Lall.

"What did you do with your photographs of Nigel?"

"I put them in my wallet under the back seat of the land cruiser along with Nigel's note," said Margaret.

"I'm afraid the police are going to arrest the Abbot and the Buddhist monks for harboring a criminal like they did in Lhasa," said Uma.

"I hope not," said Margaret, her voice trembling.

"Maybe you ought to take your medication," said Samitra. "It might help you calm down."

"I'll be all right. I got a nervous when the Chinese policeman was searching my purse," said Margaret.

"Have a great trip to Lake Manasarovar. We'll meet you at the large pavilion. I understand the lake is oval shaped and 55 miles from beginning to end. We'll see you there in about five or six hours," said Carl, closing the door of their land cruiser.

Margaret rolled down a window and thanked Carl once more for giving her courage to continue on the pilgrimage. He paused to wave to her as Lall drove away, leaving a cloud of dust behind.

Carl coughed from the dust as he boarded the passenger side of his land cruiser. Kesab waited for the dust to clear for about five minutes before starting the engine and heading down the dirt road.

While the men were admiring the distant mountains, Dipak asked, "Does anyone know the altitude of Lake

Manasarovar?"

Carl said, "I read in the Karnali Excursion packet. That it's 4590 meters or 15,060 feet. It's higher than Pike's Peak in Colorado Springs."

"We are gradually going higher and higher as we continue toward Mt. Kailash," said Rama.

"Are you familiar with Rakshastal, the smaller lake next to Lake Manasarovar?" asked Dipak. "It means the Lake of the Demon.

"In the Hindu epic, 'The Ramayana,' Rama's wife, Sita, is abducted by the Demon King, Ravana, and taken to Shree Lanka, where he attempts to seduce her.

"Hanuman, the leader of the monkeys gathers his warrior monkeys and helps Rama fight the demons. After years of battle, Rama slays the ten headed, Ravana and brings his wife, Sita, back to Ayodhya in northern India," said Carl.

"Each year during our Harvest Festival, known as Dasera, which goes on for ten days, the Nepalese people celebrate the victory of Rama over Ravana," said Dipak.

"I still get teased by my Hindu students at the university, because my name is Rama. They always ask me if I'm married to Sita. They are surprised when I tell them my wife's name is Samitra," said Rama.

"We're still some distance from Lake Manasarovar. Look, you can see nearly the whole lake with the Himalayas in the back ground," said Rama.

Chapter 42
"Arrival At Lake Manasarovar"

"How far is Lake Manasarovar from Lhasa?" asked Margaret glancing out the window of the land cruiser.

"It's about 580 miles from Lhasa and located in Western Tibet," said Uma.

"The view of the lake from here is breathtaking," said Margaret. "I wish Krishna was here to share it with me."

"You've calmed down quite a bit since we left the camp of the nomads," said Uma.

"I'm so grateful that Krishna taught me yoga. Taking deep breaths while under stress helps me to release my negative thoughts and stay calm," said Margaret.

"I'm amazed at the size of the distant lake with the barren mountains and snow covered Himalayas soaring in the back ground," said Samitra.

"We still have a quite a few miles to go before reaching the pavilion. I hope we can catch up to the pilgrims when we get there," said Uma.

"Why is Lake Manasarovar so important to the pilgrims?" asked Margaret.

"It means 'The Lake of the Mind'," said Uma. "In our religion we have a trinity. Brahma's the Creator, Vishnu's the Savior, and Siva's the Destroyer. We believe Brahma imagined the lake in his mind and then manifested it.

"Most Hindus believe in the 'Paramatma' the Soul of the Universe, which permeates all of creation, including plants and animals." said Uma.

"All of my friends from India are vegetarians," said Margaret.

"In Nepal many Brahmins are vegetarian, although some of us eat goat meat and chicken. We, Hindus, are strict about not eating beef because the cow is sacred," said Uma.

"Members of the Jain religion are strict vegetarians. They only eat vegetables and fruits from plants and trees that don't die when harvested," said Uma.

"I'm afraid we've strayed from the topic, said Samitra.

"We believe that by bathing in Lake Manasarovar, God will forgive us of our sins," said Uma

"Buddhists, also, bathe in the lake because Buddha came here to meditate centuries ago. Even members of the Bon religion come to be cleansed from evil spirits sent by the mountain and nature gods."

"Margaret, did anyone tell you about the exorcisms that the nomads performed on you?" asked Samitra.

"I don't remember anyone performing an exorcism on me," said Margaret. "It's possible that evil spirits attacked me in the nomad camp because I was vulnerable because of my head injury."

"Let's forget about the past and stay in the present moment," said Uma, pausing as Lall drove the land cruiser into the parking lot in front of the pavilion.

"The other land cruiser is arriving now. We should wait for them inside," said Margaret, following the others up the cement sidewalk into the pavilion. They went directly to the restrooms with hot and cold running water, clean stalls and flush toilets.

A few minutes later they were all standing in front of the information desk, where a huge map was painted on the wall, showing the location of Lake Manasarovar next to

Rakshastal, The Demon Lake.

"The Himalayan Range in Tibet is the source of five major rivers which provide water for all of India," said Tara, the clerk. "Their names are the Ganges, Indus, Sutlej, Gadara, and Brahmaputra. The map shows that the source of the Sutleg River is close to Lake Manasarovar. The depth at the center of the lake is 90 meters or 300 feet."

"If those five rivers should suddenly dry up due to global warming, all of India would become a wasteland from drought," said Dipak.

"Come with me to see grandeur of Lake Manasarovar from the veranda. There the other visitors are admiring the view, seated at tables shaded by colorful umbrellas," said Tara.

While everyone gazed at the vastness of the blue lake from the expansive patio, Dipak said, "The lake is close enough for me to go for a swim."

"I don't want to bathe in that lake because I don't know how to swim," said Uma.

"You don't have to worry about the depth," said the clerk. "Our tour buses stop at the sandy beaches as they travel around the lake. The pilgrims are safe because the water is shallow, but there are sharp rocks and stones in the water. Be careful as you enter the water so that you don't stumble and hurt yourself."

"Hari informed me that you can bathe after checking into our guest house on the other side of Lake Manasarovar, where we'll be spending the night," said Rama.

"Buses loaded with Hindu and Buddhist tourists have arrived and departed the whole day. There's a bus leaving right now with tourists," said Tara.

"Your Hindu friends from Nepal boarded a bus and travelled around the lake several hours ago. They bathed in the water and filled their plastic containers before returning to their land cruisers. They departed about two o'clock this afternoon for your guest house," said Tara.

"Let's take the next bus and go around the lake before it gets dark," said Carl.

"It's too late to take another bus," said the clerk, glancing at her watch. "The last bus will return before 6:00 p.m. when the pavilion closes for day. It's already 5:45."

"We were delayed because of landslides blocking the road," said Dipak.

"I'm sorry to hear about your unfortunate delay," said Tara. "If you come back tomorrow morning, I'll reserve a bus for you to take at 9:00 a.m."

"That won't be necessary. We'll drive around the lake in our land cruisers," said Dipak.

"There are eight monasteries that surround the lake. Your guide, Hari, told me that your Nepalese friends will be staying at the Chiu Gompa Guest House," said Tara.

"Let's get going then," said Dipak. "We still have time to bathe in the lake before we reach the guest house, hopefully before it gets dark."

"Your guest house is 25 miles from here. Just follow the circular dirt road north, then west, and south," said Tara.

Everyone paused, getting a final glance of the lake before returning to their land cruisers to get their bathing suits. After changing in the restrooms, they travelled north for a half hour before Lall and Kesab parked the land cruisers along a sandy beach.

"This sand is terribly hot," said Margaret, heading toward the water in her bare feet.

Dipak bolted across the sand and dashed into the shallow water. He stumbled, splashing into the shallow water. Upon surfacing, he shouted to the others. "Be extra careful. There are a lot of rocks here!"

Carl paused scratching his hairy chest for a moment before entering the water. Glancing over his shoulder he saw Margaret following him. She was wearing a pink two piece bathing suit.

He took Margaret by the hand, leading her into the water not expecting her to trip on a rock and fall into the lake.

Carl pulled her out of the water, leading her back to the beach, where she sobbed in his arms.

"I'm...I'm so clumsy," she cried, shivering. "I stubbed my toes on a rock and they're bleeding!"

"Lall! Please get the first aid kit from the trunk of the car!" shouted Carl, feeling uneasy as Margaret clung to him.

Samitra and Uma arrived, wearing modest one piece bathing suits. They decided to take Margaret to the land cruiser and bandaged her toes, if Carl would carry her.

Carl slouched down while Rama lifted her onto his back. She clung to him with her legs around his waist as he hurried to the cruiser, where the women bandaged her bleeding toes.

Feeling relieved Carl returned to the lake, where he dipped into the cold water. After surfacing he bowed toward the Himalayas, reciting prayers to the Universal Soul. Afterwards he helped Rama and Dipak clear away the rocks in the shallow water so that the women wouldn't get hurt.

Fifteen minutes later Samitra and Uma returned to the lake to pray before plunging into the water. Lall and Kesab, also arrived in their bathing suits, chanting prayers before dipping into the water.

When everyone returned to the land cruisers, they glanced at Margaret asleep in the back seat. She was wearing one of Samitra's dresses with the Dali Lama's book, "The Art of Happiness," open on her lap.

Chapter 43
"Arrival Chiu Gompa Guesthouse"

Upon returning to their land cruisers, the pilgrims dried themselves off behind the nearby trees where they changed into their clothes.

As they drove along, the drivers slowed down so the passengers could admire the lake, mountains, and white clouds drifting in the blue sky.

About an hour later they arrived at the Chiu Gompa Guest House, located within walking distance of Lake Manasarovar. Hari came out of the dining hall north of the guest house to greet them.

"We missed you these past two days," he said as they came out of their land cruisers. "Everyone's been worried about you."

"We were delayed because of landslides blocking the road," said Dipak.

"You can tell us all about it in the dining room," said Hari. "Everyone's there, having dinner."

"We'd prefer to get settled in our rooms first," said Samitra. "We're also concerned about Margaret because she hurt her toes while going into the sacred lake."

"I'm sorry about that," said Hari. "Margaret, I'll have a waiter bring a meal to your room."

"I'd rather eat in the dining room," said Margaret, glancing down at her bandaged foot.

"I reserved the last two rooms of the guest house for you late comers. They're closer to the dining room than the others. You'll be staying here two nights with four people to a room," said Hari. "I have your keys. Please follow me to your rooms."

Hari led the way toward the single story brick building with numerous rooms stretching about a city block with windows facing the lake. The two drivers parked the land cruisers in front of their rooms. They removed the luggage and back packs.

Hari opened the door of Room 24 with his keys. He switched on the electric light and showed Rama, Samitra, Carl and Kesab their room.

"I hope you'll be comfortable here," said Hari. "Please come to the dining room once you get settled."

"Where do we put our luggage and back packs?" asked Samitra. "There are no dressers."

"You can slide them under your beds," said Hari.

He approached the other four guests waiting in front of the locked door with their luggage.

After showing them their room, they headed toward the dining room with Margaret limping along clinging to Dipak's arm.

The delayed guests were surprised when the pilgrims stood up and clapped welcoming them as they entered the hall and took their places at the vacant tables.

Within minutes the Nepalese waiters came with trays to serve them - Alu Dum, spicy whole potatoes, and Kerau Ra Tofu Tarkari, peas with bean curry, and Mo-Mo, steamed dumplings.

After dinner Hari informed them about the outdoor restrooms some distant from the building. Each of their rooms also had a pail of water to rinse their hands and a towel near the entrance.

The sun was setting when the pilgrims departed from the

dining room. The late comers were weary from travelling and talking about their overnight stay in nomad tents because of the landslides.

It was already dark when they reached their rooms, discovering the electricity had gone out. They walked sideways between the beds lining the walls, locating their luggage. After removing their flashlights they departed for the restrooms.

Upon returning to their rooms, everyone complained because there were no toilets, only holes in the cement floors with a pungent odor, buzzing with flies and mosquitoes.

Carl tossed and turned wondering how Barbara was doing, trying not to think about Margaret clinging to him with her wet bikini after stumbling in the lake.

He got up twice during the night to use the restroom on the north side of the guest house, but decided not to go inside because of the harsh odor. He urinated behind the brick outhouse in the moonlight.

Upon returning to his room, he noticed that Samitra was sleeping soundly in spite of Rama and Kesab's snoring.

After reciting Sanskrit prayers from "The Bhagavad Gita," Carl fell asleep for about four hours before being awakened by a loud knock on the door.

He leapt from the bed in his underwear and opened the door, where a waiter was holding a tray with four cups of steaming Nepali tea.

Carl held the door open for the waiter to enter the dark room with the tray. He quickly switched on the light, which illuminated the entire room this time.

Samitra sat up in her flannel night gown, startled by Carl standing there in his underwear, barefoot, and scratching his chest. She turned toward the waiter, who handed her a cup of steaming tea and another one to Rama, standing next to her in his pajamas.

Carl quickly put on his shirt and jeans, feeling uneasy about answering the door in his underwear. The waiter handed him a cup of tea while Kesab entered the room complaining about the odor in the men's rest room.

After the waiter departed, Kesab set his cup down on the floor and went over to the window, pushing back the curtain. Everyone was pleased to see the sun rising from the distant mountains, illuminating the lake.

"Hari knocked on the door and entered their room. He said, "Breakfast will be served from 6:30-7:30. Afterwards you can stroll along the lake, sunbathe or go swimming.

"If you want to get acclimated for hiking up Mount Kailash, you should practice by taking the trail up the nearby mountain. Upon reaching the top there is an engraved memorandum honoring Milarepa, the Buddhist saint.

"It is near the ruins of an abandoned monastery. A trail to the left leads to a tea shop and the Buddhist monastery," said Hari, leaving their room.

"Margaret told me that she wanted to climb the mountain at dinner last night, but she can't because of her bruised toes," said Samitra.

"Maybe someone can carry her up the mountain," said Carl, reaching for his shoes under the bed.

"I can carry her up the mountain," said Kesab. "I saw that winding trail this morning. It'll only take about an hour to get to the ruins of the monastery."

Everyone got dressed with their backs turned toward the wall as they put on their clothes. Within a short time they were rinsing their hands and face outside in the bucket of fresh water. Afterwards they headed to the dining room. Upon entering they sat at a table next to Dipak, Uma, Lall and Margaret.

"After breakfast I want to walk down the beach with Uma and just relax," said Dipak.

"We want to dip in the sacred lake again and then get a sun tan," said Uma.

"Margaret's depressed because she wants to go trekking up the mountain with you guys," said Dipak.

"Hari mentioned there's a memorial to Saint Milarepa at the top of the hill next to the ruins of the monastery."

"Margaret, when the nomads were clearing your chakras they recited Milarepa's Sanskrit words, 'Aham Atama, I Am the Soul'," said Carl.

"My husband used to recite I AM prayers," said Margaret, glancing at her bandaged foot. "I wish I could go trekking with you up the mountain."

"Don't worry about that," said Kesab. "I'll carry you to the ruins and then over to tea shop and the new monastery."

"I'll give you two hundred dollars if you carry me up the mountain on your back," blurted Margaret.

"That's a lot of money," said Kesab, feeling uneasy. "How about if I carry you up the mountain for $50, and Lall carries you back down for $50, because we took turns driving you in our land cruisers."

"I will give you each $100. No more arguing with me please. I am anxious to see the ruins of the monastery where Milarepa stayed when he wasn't meditating in a cave," said Margaret.

"Here comes the waiter with our breakfast," said Carl, watching him set down plates of crispy rice donuts, spiced yogurt, fried cookies, and Nepali tea with milk and sugar.

"This is quite a meal," said Samitra, "I haven't had such wonderful breakfast for a long time."

"We're used to having, scrambled eggs, toast and coffee," said Rama, reaching for a crispy rice donut.

"Uma, do you know the recipes for these donuts and the fried cookies?" asked Samitra. "I must learn to make them when we get back."

While the women talked about recipes, Carl and Rama conversed about the book, "Seven Years in Tibet" by Heinrich Harrar, which was made into a film in 1979 starring Brad Pitt.

"That was quite a movie," said Carl. "I believe that Heinrich's still a friend of the Dalai Lama," said Carl, pausing when Hari got up to make an announcement.

"The owners of the guest house agreed to set up a large tent at the beach near the lake. All of you are invited to go there to listen to the chatting and prayers by a Brahman priest. Images of the Gods and Goddesses will be on the altar inside the tent and chairs set up for you to enjoy the service."

"It looks like quite a few pilgrims will be heading to the tent. Uma and I will be enjoying the beach since the weather is just right today," said Dipak.

"We hope you'll enjoy trekking up the mountain," said Uma, excusing herself and departing with her husband.

"Margaret, I'll help you get back to your room to change into your trekking clothes," said Samitra.

"We'll all gather at Margaret's room in a half hour before leaving on the trek," said Carl, turning toward Hari. "Do you have a computer that I can use to send an email to my wife?"

"There is no computer service for the next five days, not until we get back to Saga. I understand that you're also trekking to the top of the hill today," said Hari. "Please tell me about the monastery when you return this evening for dinner."

Chapter 44
"Going Up the Nearby Mountain"

About 45 minutes later, the group of trekkers was waiting for Margaret in front of her room at the guest house, anxious to start climbing the mountain.

"Where is she anyway?" asked Rama.

"Kesab was carrying her on his back when we left the dining room a few minutes ago," said Samitra.

"He took her to the restroom," said Carl.

"I hope the women's restroom is cleaner than the men's" said Rama. "Ours wasn't very sanitary."

"The women's rest room is a stinking mess," said Samitra. "We had such good plumbing at the hotels, but not here. It's hard for me to get use to toilets that are holes in the cement floor with no toilet paper or water to flush them."

"Hari mentioned that we should bring our own toilet paper when we go to the restrooms for the next few days," said Carl.

"Here comes Kesab with Margaret," said Carl, hurrying toward them. They stopped near the front of her door, where she washed her hands in the bucket of fresh water beneath the window.

"I'm so sorry we're late," said Margaret. "It was almost impossible for me to crouch down in that restroom without Kesab's help. I felt so embarrassed. Finally, a woman from our group assisted me. The odor in that place was terrible!"

"We all know exactly what you mean," said Carl, helping Margaret onto Kesab's back.

Rama led the way down the narrow trail toward the river bed with flat rocks forming a bridge across the water. He was followed by the others going single file across the river. Upon reaching the opposite bank, Samitra paused to admire the flowers in the meadow.

"The edelweiss blossoms are gorgeous," she said. "I didn't expect to see them here. I thought they only grew in the Alps. What are the names of the flowers over there?"

"They are blue poppies and wild irises," said Margaret.

"I'll take some pictures of the flowers for you," said Rama, removing his camera from his back pack.

Carl encouraged everyone to continue up the path, which was now wide enough for motorcycles and jeeps to bring supplies to the monks at the monastery.

Everyone was silent as they trekked up the mountain for a half hour before stopping to rest. Carl helped Margaret down from Kesab's back, supporting her arm as she limped for several yards, exercising so her legs wouldn't stiffen.

"I'm grateful that I don't have severe pain in my toes anymore. Uma changed the bandage this morning with an antibiotic ointment so that I won't get an infection," said Margaret.

"Everything looks so tiny at this altitude. Our brick guest house looks like a shrunken motel," said Samitra.

"I wonder if that's Dipak and Uma in their bathing suits heading like ants down the beach toward the lake," said Rama.

"Several pilgrims are going from the dining room toward that white tent, where there's a drum beating and chanting echoing up the mountain," said Margaret.

"After breakfast, I saw a Brahman priest setting up the altar inside the tent with statues of the Hindu gods and goddesses," said Carl.

"It's my turn to carry Margaret," said Lall, asking Carl to hoist her onto his back.

This time Kesab led the way with the others following. Within another half hour of steady climbing, they could see a white stupa at the top of the hill next to a rectangular altar made from slabs of rocks and stones.

From a distant the altar looked as if it was covered with the wings of eagles and fish tails. Upon coming closer they discovered the images were soaring antlers.

"Take a look at this huge rock with a bronze inscription, honoring the poet, Milarepa, who meditated in a cave for years before coming to live at the monastery," said Carl.

"There's nothing left of that monastery except the ruins over there," said Rama. "It was destroyed by Maoists during their Cultural Revolution in 1976 and never rebuilt!"

"Someone's camping in those ruins because laundry is hanging from a rope there," said Samitra.

"They're nomads grazing their sheep in the valley on the other side of the ruins," said Kesab.

"Carl would you please come over here?" asked Margaret, removing Nigel's note from her pocket and handing it to him.

Carl read the message about Nigel meeting his mother at Milarepa's sanctuary at the top of the hill some distance from the lake.

"It's possible that Nigel's living somewhere in that heap of ruins," whispered Carl to Margaret. "I'll go take a look while you wait here for me with Lall."

"What are you whispering about?" asked Samitra. "Rama and Kesab are waiting for us to join them at the tea shop across from those prayer flags, which stretch across those huge rocks on the other side of the road," said Samitra.

"The ropes with those flags look like a gigantic spider's

web," said Margaret. "I hope no one gets caught in them."

"Margaret please go with Samitra to the tea shop while I explore the ruins of the monastery," said Carl. "I'll meet you there in a half hour."

"No, I'll wait here with Lall until you return," said Margaret. "Carl, I really want to go with you into the ruins."

"I'm leaving you star crossed lovers here," said Samitra, annoyed because Margaret had removed her coat and was wearing a pink blouse, which exposed her cleavage.

"Margaret, I think you should come with me," said Samitra, frowning.

"I'll wait here with Lall until Carl returns," she said.

"I'm surprised that you've been exchanging love notes with Carl as if you're teenagers," said Samitra.

"I don't know what you're talking about. I asked Carl to read a note that Nigel left for in Saga," said Margaret. "I'm worried that something's happened to him."

"I…I'm sorry for being rude. I didn't sleep very well last night. I'm not used to the four people to a room. I, also, didn't get much sleep in nomad's camp, because of your screaming and the chanting all night."

"Please forgive me for causing you so much trouble," said Margaret, annoyed by her comment.

"I'll meet you at the tea shop with Rama. If we're not there, we'll be at the monastery on the opposite hill," said Samitra, hurrying across the dirt road.

Several yards away, Carl climbed through an arch to investigate the ruins, pausing so he wouldn't trip over the debris. He zig zagged among sharp rocks, protruding among the crumbling bricks, which were once a protective wall.

He continued through a collapsed room without a door, filled with crumbled plaster, bricks, and splintered wood.

While crawling over debris into the second room, he

squinted as the wind blew dust from the plaster into his face. After moving forward among shingles and broken bricks, he arrived at the third room with a closed door, which he managed to force open.

He was surprised that the interior was totally in tack. Upon entering, Carl noticed a stove with a copper tea kettle in the middle of the room and logs piled on the floor. He ignored a rattling coming from a closet, thinking it was a rat.

The room had a single bed with a neatly folded blanket and a pillow. On the nearby dresser, there was a picture of a dozen Buddhist monks next to a colorful tapestry with images of Tibetan gods and goddesses.

Carl was startled by the closet door, swinging open and someone stepping into the dimly lighted room.

"Dr. Brecht! It's good to see you again after all these years," said a familiar voice.

"Nigel! I…I didn't expect you to be here," said Carl, crossing the room to shake hands with him.

"It's been twelve years since we last met. How's your daughter, Kathy?" he asked. "My mother wrote to me that she's now a doctor."

"She came with me to Nepal and is working at Shanta Bhawan Hospital in the Emergency Room with her old boyfriend, Om, who is also a doctor."

"I'll never forget how all of you, including my mother, were held hostage in the Medicine Cave by the terrorists, who assassinated Crown Prince Dipendra," said Nigel.

"You saved our lives by helping us to escape from that cave", said Carl. "When we took off in the helicopter, we watched the villagers from the windows fleeing from the area because of the earthquake."

"I was amazed how the earthquake destroyed the mountains, but not the Tyangboche Monastery," said Nigel.

"By the way your mother's waiting for you at the stupa in front of the ruins. She wanted to come here searching for you, but she hurt her toes while wading in Lake Manasarovar."

"That's too bad," said Nigel. "I've been worried about her ever since Krishna died from that automobile accident. I hope she's not taking Zanax again to relieve her stress like she did for several years after divorcing my father. When Krishna taught my mother yoga, she stopped taking her bipolar medication and sleeping pills."

Carl informed Nigel about Margaret's stress due to the landslides, her head injury, screaming, and seizures prior to the nomads performing exorcisms, which calmed her down.

"I'm sure my mother was also overwhelmed when she read in the newspapers that I was accused of murdering a guard at the Jokang Temple in Lhasa.

"Upon seeing the corpse of the Chinese guard on the floor with a knife stuck in his back and flyers scattered on his body about liberating Tibet, I knew, I had to flee from Lhasa. I went straight to the monastery, packed a few things, and boarded a lumber truck for Saga," said Nigel.

"I made a mistake by going shopping with the abbot in the bazaar wearing my maroon robe because someone recognized me and reported me to the police. That's why I decided to come here."

"Your mother's anxious to see you," interrupted Carl. "She's with Lall, who carried her up the mountain on his back. Margaret was hoping to find you here because of the note you left her at the hotel."

"We can take a short cut by crawling through the hole in the wall. It's behind my bed," said Nigel, giving the bed a shove and then removing the board. "Just follow me through the debris to the path leading to the stupa."

As they headed away from the ruins down the trail along side of the ruins, Nigel stopped when he saw his mother standing next to Lall at the stupa in the distance.

"I'm worried about that the driver might report me to the police," said Nigel.

"You wait here," said Carl. "I'll tell him to go up the trail and wait for us at the tea shop. Our guide told us that a Tibetan family is living there with their children.

"That family was brought here by the Chinese police. They've been told to take pictures of everyone stopping at their tea shop or hiking to the monastery," said Nigel.

"Nigel, you wait here. I'll tell Lall to go to the tea shop so that I can bring your mother here to see you," said Carl.

"I'll go back to my room and wait for you to return with her," said Nigel.

Upon arriving back at the stupa, Carl told Lall that he and Margaret would meet him at the tea shop in a half hour. A few minutes later he was carrying Margaret down the path to Nigel's room, where he kicked on the board several times with his hiking boot.

Nigel removed the board and crawled out of the hole, wearing his maroon Monk's robe and sandals.

"Nigel! You're still alive!" screamed Margaret, sliding down from Carl's back and throwing her arms around him.

"Mother, I'm so pleased to see you! You haven't changed at bit since I saw you last year!" said Nigel.

"I thought I'd never see you again!" sobbed Margaret.

Carl backed away while they talked for several minutes. Finally he interrupted them saying. "Nigel we've got to figure out a way for you to come back to Nepal with us."

"We can discuss it with the Abbot at the monastery later He knows a government official in Dharsen, who issues passports to foreign trekkers," said Nigel.

"What's that noise," asked Margaret startled by the sound of motorcycles and the siren from a jeep coming up the dirt trail in front of the ruins.

"It's the police coming to check on the tourists visiting monks at our monastery on the opposite hill. They're probably looking for me!" said Nigel. "We better go inside to my room. Mother, are you able to crawl through the hole in the wall into my room?" asked Nigel.

"I'm afraid to bend down because of my injured foot," said Margaret, trembling from the siren.

"I'll go into my room and then put a rectangular rug through the hole. Mother, please stretch out on the rug so that I can pull you into my room."

Within a few minutes Nigel helped Margaret get up inside the room with Carl crawling into the room after her.

Nigel showed his mother the closet with steps leading to a tunnel, connecting to the ruins to the new monastery on the other side of the mountain.

"It took the monks ten years to build the escape tunnel in case of another invasion by Chinese guards. Mother, I want you and Carl to go directly to Abbot's quarters in the new monastery. Please don't mention my name to your pilgrim friends, travelling with you to Mount Kailash."

After the noise stopped, they departed from his room through the hole in the wall. When they were outside Nigel boosted his mother onto Carl's back.

He watched them head down the trail before returning to his room to leave for the monastery through the tunnel.

In about fifteen minutes Carl and Margaret reached the tea shop, where the shopkeeper took photographs of them to give to the police, who were at the monastery questioning other pilgrims. The shopkeeper boosted Margaret onto Carl's back and snapped more pictures as they departed.

On the way to the monastery, Chinese guards on their motorcycles stopped them. After searching their pockets and back packs, they were allowed to continue to the monastery.

Margaret was trembling after being searched, although Carl remained calm. He encouraged her to focus upon the grandeur of the clouds floating in the blue sky and the vastness of the lake below.

Within a half hour they arrived at the monastery and were informed by a monk that their friends were taking a tour of the monastery to see the statues and tapestries.

Carl informed the monk that they had an appointment to see the Abbot. He took them directly to the office. Upon opening the door, he and Margaret were both surprised to see Nigel waiting for them in the room.

Chapter 45
"From Dharsen to Base Camp"

After visiting with the Abbot for nearly an hour and discussing a possible escape plan for Nigel to meet the Dalai Lama in India, everyone left the office. Nigel, wearing his marron robe and hood, said goodbye to his mother and shook Carl's hand before joining the monks for their afternoon chanting in the temple.

The Abbot led Margaret and Carl to the dining room where they joined their friends at a table. A waiter served them barley tea and mo-mo dumplings.

"Any news about Nigel?" asked Samitra, sitting across from Margaret, sipping her tea.

"We read about him in the 'China Daily'," said the Abbot. "The police have come here twice now looking for Nigel after searching the monasteries surrounding Lake Manasarovar."

"None of us believe that Nigel was responsible for the murder of that guard in the Jokang Temple," said Rama.

"I've been worried about him during the entire trip," said Margaret, finishing her tea.

"We better get going," said Carl, noticing that about thirty hooded monks were entering the dining room to have afternoon tea.

"It's been a pleasure having you as our guests," said the Abbot, leading them out of the dining room through a side door to the exterior of the monastery. He pointed out a steep trail down the mountains, which was a short cut to the guest house in front of the lake.

Rama and Carl decided to take that trail, while Kesab and Lall went back to the wider trail, taking turns carrying Margaret with Samitra following them.

It was about 4:30 p.m. when they reached the Chiu Gompa Guest House, where they all decided to change into their swim suits and join Dipak and Uma, who were sitting under an umbrella on the beach.

Samitra encouraged Margaret not to wear her bikini so that she wouldn't attract so much attention. She took her advice and came out wearing a scarlet bathing suit.

Carl and his friends enjoyed dipping in the lake and sprawling out on their towels in the afternoon sunshine.

Later they gathered in the meeting hall for dinner, where Hari informed the pilgrims they would be leaving for Darshen after breakfast the following day.

The pilgrims stayed late in the dining room talking about the arrival of the police, who searched every room in the guest house for Nigel after coming back from their search at the monastery on the top of the hill. It was late when they finally went back to their rooms.

Carl had a restless night sleeping at the guest house in the crowded room. He got up a few times, turned on his flashlight, and walked between the beds to the door. After leaving the room, he was amazed by the grandeur of the stars and the moon illuminating the courtyard.

He headed toward the outdoor restroom, deciding to not to go inside to urinate because of the pungent odor.

Upon returning to his room, Carl noticed the others were sleeping soundly. However, he tossed and turned for quite a while before finally falling asleep.

About 5:30 a.m. everyone stirred in their beds when the

waiter knocked on the door, with cups of steaming tea. After getting dressed, they joined the pilgrims for breakfast in the dining room.

Upon returning to their rooms, the pilgrims gathered their luggage and back packs and then departed in the land cruisers for Darshen. The journey on the dirt road was long and tedious with barren mountains on each side.

Upon arrival at their guest house late in the afternoon, Hari advised the pilgrims to walk to the nearby town and take a shower at the spa for a small fee since there was no running water or toilets in their rooms.

"Where's the dining room?" asked Samitra.

There's no dining room," said Hari. "Our cooks and the Nepalese waiters will be serving dinner in that tent set up in the parking lot," said Hari.

Some pilgrims brought their plates of rice and lentils to their rooms where they sat on their beds and ate. Other ate outside in the parking lot until two huge trucks arrived, spewing exhaust from their tail pipes.

Those outside started coughing and gaging from the pollution before returning to their rooms. Others left to check out the restaurants in the nearby town, hoping to take a shower at the spa before it got dark.

After breakfast the next morning, everyone put their luggage into a storage room and went to the parking lot wearing their backpacks. They gathered around Hari in the vacant lot. All were annoyed by the lingering smell of exhaust from several trucks that had finally departed.

"My dear friends, today we'll be trekking between five to seven hours, depending how fast you can walk. I would advise you to take your time and rest along the way. We'll follow a wide trail until we arrive at our guest house in Derapuk at the base of Mount Kailash. This time dinner will be served close to the guest house. Our cooks and the waiters have already left in jeeps with the food," said Hari.

"Before leaving be sure to check your pack backs so that you have plenty of water, a first aid kit, and an umbrella in case of rain. The rest of your luggage will be in storage here at the guest house.

"Now let's begin our trek to Derapuk!" said Hari, leading the way to the trail behind the guest house with the pilgrims following him.

"We're finally on our way," said Carl, noticing that Kesab was carrying Margaret on his back with Lall walking behind with their backpacks. They were followed by Rama and Samitra.

"Maile tapailai madat dinu parcha, I must help you," said the waiter, who was left behind when the jeep departed with the other waiter and cooks.

"Purusotam, I don't need your help because I can carry my own backpack," said Carl.

"Hari sent me to be your guide," said Purusotam.

"That was kind of him," said Carl, glancing at Dipak and Uma hurrying up the trail with more pilgrims behind them.

While tying a loose string on his hiking boot, Carl said, "Why didn't you go with your friends in the jeep?"

"Hari told me to stay with you because you're the oldest man in our group," said Purusotam.

"He's wrong about that," said Carl annoyed. He hurried along, trying to catch up with the others.

Within a half hour they arrived at two large Buddhist stupas with colorful prayer flags connecting them. Some of the pilgrims were already out of breath from trekking. They had removed their back packs and were sitting on boulders in the sunshine, drinking water and eating granola bars.

Carl and his guide meandered among the stupas for a

few minutes listening to the flapping of the colorful prayer flags in the breeze before departing.

During the long trek to the guest house Carl was pleased to be able to speak in Nepali with Purusotam.

"Tapaiko parivar kaha basnu huncha? Where does your family live?" asked Carl.

"Mero srimati, twita chora ra ekai chori, mero Ama Bahabu ko gharma basdai chan. My wife, two sons, and daughter are living with my parents."

"Do they live in Kathmandu?" asked Carl.

"No, my family lives in Nuwakot, where the Shah Kings had their summer palace. My father, Gopal Upadahya, is a Brahman priest, who performs the life cycle rituals at the Hindu temple near the old royal palace.

"My father has been chanting prayers from our sacred scriptures, at weddings, funerals, and initiation ceremonies for the past fifty years," said Puruosotam, telling Carl about the Hindu sacraments as they trekked on the dirt road.

"Sometimes people come to my father, asking for prayers for family members possessed by evil spirits. When that happens he contacts the local shamans to perform the exorcisms," said Purusotam.

Carl told him about his experience with shamans because he witnessed several exorcisms as an anthropologist and published articles about them.

After trekking for an hour they stopped to admire the beauty of the mountains and the swift current of the stream.

"I travelled to Nuwakot several years ago," said Carl, as they continued trekking. "I remember going through the summer palace of the Shah Dynasty. I, also, visited the temple, where your father administers the sacraments to the people in your town.

"I have a friend, who was a Peace Corps volunteer, who

spent two years in your town, teaching at the high school. His name was John Riley."

"I know him. He was my teacher. Mr. Riley taught me how to read and write, English. Because of him, I passed my exams and graduated from high school. I wasn't able to go on to college, because my father didn't have enough money to pay for my tuition.

"I helped my father with all the ceremonies at the temple. He taught me Sanskrit so that I can read the 'Vedas' and the 'Upanisads' from ancient times."

"I'm familiar with those scriptures," mentioned Carl, as they stopped to rest after another hour of trekking.

"After I got married, and I went to Kathmandu where Hari hired me to work in the kitchen. The head chef is a Brahmin, who taught me how to cook and wait on the trekkers, who hiked from Kathmandu to Gosainkund. This is my first trip to Mount Kailash," said Purusotam.

"I earn enough money to support my wife and children and help my aging parents, who live with my family in Nuwakot."

They continued their conversation pausing every hour to drink water and eat a snack. After trekking for seven hours, they noticed dark clouds forming in the sky. It began raining a few minutes before they arrived at the guest house.

"You're finally here!" said Hari holding an umbrella and, glancing at his watch. "Purosotam, go to the tent over there and help the cooks prepare dinner for the pilgrims.

"We'll all be eating as soon as the rain stops. Carl, the pilgrims were worried that you might have been injured on the trail or murdered by renegade Khampas."

"Hari, you told us that we should take our time on the trail and rest frequently," said Carl.

"You're right. I did say that, but I didn't expect you to

take seven hours to get here. Almost everyone else got here in five hours. Only four people got here after six hours.

"Carl, here's an extra key to your room, 406. You'll be staying with Samitra and Rama and Kesab.

"Don't forget to say hello to Margaret Porter. She's staying in room 405 with Dipak, Uma, and Lall. They've been constantly asking me about you."

"Now it has stopped raining, the sun is beginning to set," said Purosotam, handing Carl his backpack, and hurrying toward the tent where the cooks and waiters welcomed him.

"Carl, I'm pleased that you got here safely, but I think you should ride a horse up the mountain tomorrow rather than trek," said Hari. "Now go inside and say hello to your worried friends!"

Chapter 46
"Trekking to Mount Kailash"

The following morning Carl was awakened by a knock on the door. He leapt out of bed in his pajamas. Upon opening the door, he saw Purosotam standing there holding a tray with cups of steaming tea.

"Namaste. Tapaile ramro sanga sutnu bhaiyo? Did you sleep well?" he asked, entering the dark room.

"Maile ramro suteko thie," I slept well," said Carl, reaching for a cup of tea. "I want to thank you again for carrying my back pack yesterday. Will you be trekking with us to Mount Kailash today?"

"I'll be taking a jeep to the guest house on the other side of the mountain with the cooks to help prepare the evening meal for the pilgrims after you come down from the mountain," said Purosotam.

The other three guests, awakened by the conversation, were now sitting up in bed as the sunlight streamed into the room from the open door.

Rama came over in his pajamas to get a cup of tea while Samitra followed him wearing a pink nightgown. Across from them Kesab sat up in bed yawning as the waiter handed him his tea.

Before leaving their room, Purosotam informed them that breakfast was being served at the tent in the courtyard at 6:30 a.m. He said that their trek up to Mount Kailash would begin at eight o'clock.

After getting dressed, they went to the tent to get plates of rice and lentils. Most of the pilgrims returned to their rooms to eat because it was cold in spite of the sunshine. Others stood outside wearing their coats, holding their plates while eating and talking. Nearly everyone watched nomad herders enter the dusty courtyard with their yaks and horses.

Hari approached Carl, while he was eating his breakfast sitting on the cement sidewalk in front of his room.

"Carl, I want you to ride a horse up Mount Kailash. You were too slow in getting here yesterday even though the trail wasn't steep," he said.

"Hari, you told us to take our time," said Carl. "So we stopped to admire the scenery and rest every hour."

"I didn't expect you to take seven hours to get here. You and Purosotam were the only ones to arrive here so late. Last night we were all worried about you because it was getting dark and starting to rain!

"Everyone got here within five or six hours except the two of you. I don't want you to be the last one climbing down Mount Kailash because it's dangerous hiking after dark," said Hari.

"Today the trail is wide for a few hours, but gradually becomes narrow and steep. Once you get to about 18,000 feet, you'll trek between huge boulders, known as Dolomyala Pass.

"After crossing the pass, you'll reach Gaurikund, the sacred lake where Parvati bathed while Shiva meditated in a nearby cave," said Hari. "She eventually became his servant then his devotee, and finally his wife.

"The trail will continue for couple hundred feet before you reach the top of the mountain to rest before descending.

"You won't ride the horse down the mountain because it's too dangerous. You'll have to trek down slowly. I'm sending a Sherpa guide to keep an eye on you while you descend. It'll take about four hours to reach the top and another three hours to come back down. We'll all gather at the base of the mountain to rest for a while before continuing to the guest house, which will take another three hours. Of course, you'll ride your horse to the guest house," said Hari.

"How much will it cost me to ride the horse?" asked Carl, finishing his rice and curry.

"It's only two hundred dollars," said Hari. "Don't worry about paying me now. You can write me a check when we return to Saga the day after tomorrow. I'll see that you get a private room with a toilet and a shower there."

"That'll be fine" said Carl. "There are eight pilgrims, mounting horses over there."

"They've all been using oxygen overnight in their rooms at the hotels ever since we came to Tibet," said Hari. "Their guides are tying oxygen tanks to the backs of their horses in case they have trouble breathing due to the higher altitude.

"Please finish eating and then meet me over there. I have a horse ready for you to mount. Don't forget to bring bottled water in your back pack," said Hari, heading toward the horses where the pilgrims were waiting for him to give them the signal to depart.

After finishing his breakfast, Carl picked up his back pack and headed toward the horses.

"Hari, which horse do you want me to ride up the mountain?" he asked, noticing that Margaret was mounting a horse with Lall as her guide.

"That brown mare over there," he said. "By the way I just received a message that a Swiss trekker was injured while descending Mount Kailash a few days ago. I want you to be extra careful coming down the mountain."

"I'm sorry to hear about that," said Carl. "How high is

Mount Kailash?"

"Our trail ends at about 18,000 feet, but the snow covered peak is 22,031 feet," said Hari, turning toward the pilgrims on their horses and shouting, "You may leave now. Good luck on the trail! I'll see you at the base on the other side of the mountain in seven hours."

"Carl, we were worried about you last night because it was almost dark when you finally reached the guest house," said Rama, approaching him.

"That's why I insisted that Carl ride a horse today. I don't want something happening to him while going up or coming down the mountain," said Hari, informing them about the Swiss trekker's accident a few days ago.

"Come on Rama," insisted Samitra. "We need to catch up with Dipak and Uma. They've already left without us ten minutes ago. They're walking at a very fast pace today!"

"We'll see you in four hours at the top of the mountain," said Rama departing with his wife.

"Carl, I want you to meet Jimpa. His name means Generosity in Tibetan. He has a reputation of getting pilgrims up Mount Kailash without any trouble. His horse is called, Pema, which means Lotus Blossom. She's nervous because she recently gave birth and doesn't want to leave her foal behind," said Hari.

Jimpa tried to help Carl mount the horse, but Pema reared up before he could get his foot into the stirrup. The guide took the mare over to a boulder, signaling to Carl to climb it.

After mounting the horse without any trouble, Carl felt relieved, sitting on the straw saddle and holding the horn with his feet in the stirrups while Jimpa held the reins.

It took several minutes before the nervous horse calmed down. It whined and moved in a circle, refusing to leave the area because of her colt.

Carl noticed that the pilgrims were trekking in small groups on the wide trail next to the stream while those riding horses were ahead of everyone else.

After riding Pema for a few minutes, Carl was worried when the horse came to an abrupt halt in defiance. Jimpa tugged at her reins, encouraging the mare to move forward but she stubbornly defied him until he slapped her on the neck with the reins.

Realizing the angry mare wanted to be with her colt, Carl clung to the saddle horn so that he wouldn't be thrown to the ground. She whinnied, rising up on her hind legs attempting to throw him off of her back. He was surprised when Pema turned her head and stared at him, reminding him that he was the cause of her distress.

Feeling tense, Carl focused upon the grandeur of the barren mountains and the beauty of Mount Kailash in the distance as they departed.

Jimpa held the reins tightly leading horse down the trail while chanting the Gayatri Mantra in Sanskrit to Lord Savitra, the Sun God, and the supporter of life on our planet.

Because of the angry mare, they were delayed, falling behind on the trail and losing sight of the other pilgrims, Carl also chanted a few passages from the "Bhagavad Gita," hoping to calm the angry horse.

As they approached a stream, the guide led Pema into the water filled with sharp rocks. When they reached the other side of the river, Jimpa told Carl to slide down from the horse.

He noticed that the mare's leg had been scratched by a rock and was bleeding. Jimpa handed Carl the reins so that he could bandage Pema's leg. The angry horse shook her head, rising up on her hind legs in rebellion.

Jimpa seized the reins and slapped her on the nose.

When she settled down again, he handed the reins back to Carl, who held them while the guide bandaged the horse's leg. Once again Carl climbed a large rock to mount the stubborn horse.

As they continued on the trail, he admired the vigor of the flowing river and the splendor of the mountains. After ascending the trail, they reached a green valley where Jimpa stopped to water the horse again.

All of a sudden they saw a horse and rider coming toward them from the meadow on their right. The stranger approaching them looked like a rugged Khampa with long hair blowing in the wind. He leapt from his horse and rushed toward Jimpa speaking roughly to him in Tibetan while holding the reins of his stallion.

Carl noticed that the stranger was wearing a shabby leather coat and worn boots. He was twice the size of his guide. As they walked along together, Pema became agitated by the stallion walking next to her. She snapped at him, nipping his neck. When he snapped back at her, she whinnied, rising up on her hind legs with Carl clinging to the saddle horn with both hands.

The Khampa struck Pema with his whip several times until she settled down. Carl wondered if he was the bandit, who attacked Margaret and knocked her to the ground at the landslide. He was worried that the stranger might pull him off his horse and steal his backpack.

After a few minutes both horses calmed down because the two men separated, leaving a wide space between them. They continued walking and talking until suddenly Pema became irritated. She rushed toward the Khampa and nipped him in the arm

Jimpa remained calm as he apologized to the wounded Khampa whose arm was bruised and bleeding. The stranger removed a first aid kit from his saddle pack and wrapped a bandage around his arm and then angrily continued walking ahead of Jimpa with his horse.

After about another hour, the stranger suddenly stopped, holding the reins of his horse with Jimpa halting Pema across from him..

Carl wondered why they had stopped. He glanced into the open meadow and saw about 40 wild dogs running toward them. He was stunned as he clung to the saddle horn, worried about the dogs attacking them.

He watched the Tibetan pickup stones from the side of the trail, hurling them with his sling shot at the pack of dogs. They howled from the pain after being hit by the stones. Rather than attacking them, the dogs rushed past them keeping their distance.

Once they were out of sight, Carl wiped the sweat from his forehead with a handkerchief, grateful that the rugged man had prevented them from being attacked by the dogs.

After another half hour more of walking, Jimpa said goodbye to the stranger, who led his stallion down a narrow trail toward a distant campsite, where sheep and goats were grazing near a stream.

Jimpa paused to rest for about fifteen minutes. He told Carl that his friend was once a Khampa, who had been arrested by Chinese guards for stealing horses. After spending several years in jail, he was released. He finally got married and settled down with his family as a nomad.

The road narrowed into a path as they continued for another hour, noticing two nomads coming toward them with a herd of yaks from another trail on their left.

They continued up the steep mountain with the yaks some distance behind them. As they approached the top of the mountain, the trail was narrow between huge boulders.

Without warning, a yak with large horns rushed toward them, pushing his hairy body against Carl's horse. Pema was forced to move to let the aggressive yak go ahead of her. A second yak approached, shoving his way past them on the narrow path.

This time Pema rebelled against the intruders by soaring upward on her hind legs, trying to stop the rest of the herd. In spite of clinging to the horn on the saddle, Carl slipped under the horse with his feet still in the stirrups. He was hanging under Pema's belly, watching the hoofs of two more yaks thunder past him.

Within seconds Jimpa pulled on the reins to calm Pema while the yak herder pulled Carl's feet out of the stirrups. Carl fell to the ground with a thud, but didn't get hurt. He got up, pressing his back against a boulder while Jimpa covered the horse's eyes with blinders so she wouldn't panic as the rest of the yak herd bolted past them.

The nomad bowed to Carl, apologizing for the rudeness of his yak herd that he was taking to the market in Dharsen.

"Now that the herd is gone, you must walk the rest of the way. We're very close to the top of the mountain," said Jimpa, removing the blinders from Pema and signaling Carl to leave.

Bewildered by the incident, Carl hurried up the trail through the boulders. He came to a halt. believing it to be the end of the trail. Glancing over the edge of the rugged cliff, he estimated that the valley below was about 2500 feet.

Carl paused wondering how the yaks managed to get across the narrow rocky ledge to his right. Suddenly he remembered Barbara's second dream about him falling off a cliff in Tibet, where he died and his body was cremated.

In her third dream, he had fallen off the cliff and broken his back. Because of the severe injury, he was taken by helicopter to Kathmandu and admitted to the hospital in Patan. Carl took a few deep breathes, thanking God that he didn't slip under the horse at the cliff's edge.

He hurried across the rocky ledge and back to the trail, pausing to watch Tibetan pilgrims standing in a clearing. They were chanting mantras as colorful prayer flags, anchored with ropes to the huge boulders, fluttered in the breeze. Carl glanced down at Gaurikund, the sacred pool about 100 feet away, where Shiva's wife, Parvati, bathed.

A few moments later Jimpa caught up to him with his horse. He handed Carl his backpack, telling him they would meet him at the base of the mountain in three hours.

Carl continued walking up the shaded path between massive boulders, leaving the narrow trail behind. He paused to rest in a spacious area where the sun shining, noticing that the trail going down the mountain was steep and slanted.

While gulping down a half bottle of water, he was approached by a Sherpa named Choejor (Spiritual Wealth).

"Here's a walking stick for you," he said. "Please let me carry your back pack. Hari hired me to go with you down the mountain."

"Thanks," said Carl, accepting the cane and handing him his backpack. Since it was hot, he took off his coat and tied it around his waist.

Within a few minutes, Carl began the trek down the mountain. He glanced over his shoulder, noticing that Choejor was helping Jimpa with his stubborn mare, which refused to be led down the trail.

In the distance he saw Margaret being carried by Lall with Dipak and Uma following him. They were forced to step aside, when the herd of yaks charged past them.

Further down the mountain, he saw small groups of

Hindu pilgrims carrying their back packs, looking like miniature camels on a safari.

In front of them Samitra and Rama were walking behind the seven horses being lead in single file by their guides.

Carl continued down the trail, supporting himself with the cane. After trekking for a half hour, Jimba hurried toward him leading Pema carrying Carl's backpack. He gave it to Carl. Then Carl paused to eat a granola bar and drink a bottle of water. A few moments later, Choejor caught up with him, carrying a pilgrim on his back.

"Three pilgrims from our group fell from their horses before reaching the top of Mount Kailash. Only one was seriously injured and her name is Maya."

"Namaste, Maya, tapailai kasto cha? Greetings! How are you doing?" asked Carl.

"Mero khuta dherai dhukdai cha kina bane bhanceko, My leg hurts a lot because it's broken," said Maya.

"I'm sorry to hear about your injury," said Carl, helping her down from Choejor's back.

Maya moaned from pain as she sat down on the grass and stretched out her legs.

"Carl, I was talking to Hari before leaving our guest house this morning about the Swiss trekker, Heinrich Salzmann, who had in a severe accident while going down this mountain three days ago," said Choejor.

"His hiking companions from Switzerland left him behind. They said that he was going too slowly. The truth is that Heinrich passed out from drinking alcohol because he wanted to celebrate trekking to the top of Mount Kailash.

"A yak herder found Heinrich unconscious on the trail. After bandaging his wounds, he tied him onto the back of his horse and led him down the mountain to the guest house.

"The clerk at the desk contacted the local police in Dharsen to send an ambulance to take him to the hospital.

"The clerk tried to reach Heinrich's Swiss companions but they had taken a bus back to Kathmandu," said Choejor.

"We better get going," said Carl. "Maya also needs to see a doctor when we get to the guesthouse."

"I've already notified the clerk at the guest house to have an ambulance waiting for her at the bottom of the mountain," said Choejar.

After trekking for over four hours, they arrived at the base of the mountain. The ambulance was there with the attendants waiting to take Maya to the hospital.

Dipak and Uma approached them, and said "Hari, told us it was a three hour trek down the mountain. This time you're only an hour late."

"We were delayed because of Maya's injury," said Carl, walking toward the ambulance where the attendants put her into the back of the vehicle.

"I'm riding with Maya to the hospital in Darshen," shouted Hari. "I'll see you all tonight at the guest house."

"By the way Carl, Margaret's waiting for you in the shade of that tree over there," said Hari.

"Have a good trip to the hospital," said Carl, hurrying toward Margaret.

"Carl it's so good to see you again!" she cried. "Would you mind lifting me back onto the horse? Loll's exhausted from carrying me down the mountain."

"Of course not," said Carl, helping her mount the horse.

"Thanks for your help, Carl," said Loll leaving the area.

"We'll see you at the guest house," shouted Margaret, looking over her shoulder and waving to him.

Carl headed back Jimpa and mounted Pema by using the stirrup, rather than climbing onto a rock.

Chapter 47
"Overnight at the Guest House"

Carl was about to depart for the guest house when Rama and Samitra hurried toward him. Jimpa pulled on the reins and stopped Pema.

"We're so pleased you took a horse up the mountain and trekked down without having an accident," said Samitra. "I almost lost my balance several times coming down the trail this afternoon."

"We were worried about you trekking without a guide because you arrived late with Choejor, who was supposed to be carrying your back pack. Instead he was carrying Maya. What happened to her?" asked Rama.

"Maya told me that her horse panicked when a herd of yaks were coming up the trail, causing her to fall to the ground. While she was struggling to get up a yak rushed past her, stepping on her leg" said Carl.

"Did you hear about Heinrich Salzmann, the Swiss trekker? He was, also, injured while coming down Mount Kailash three days ago," said Rama.

"A yak herder carried him down the mountain and brought him to the guest house, where we're going to spend the night," said Carl.

"I was told that Heinrich's still recovering at the hospital in Dharsen, where the ambulance took Maya," said Samitra.

"How's Margaret doing?" said Rama.

"I only spoke to her for a few minutes before she left for the guest house," said Carl.

"I thought Margaret would be depressed because of

Nigel's strange disappearance," said Rama. "She hasn't said one word about him since we left Chiu Gompa Monastery on the hill above Lake Manasarovar."

"Margaret's been getting quite a bit of attention from Lall and Kesab. Everyone's been wondering about which one will be her next husband," said Samitra.

"Some of the pilgrims believe that you're number one on Margaret's list because you've spent time with her in a medicine cave some years ago," said Rama.

"Margaret and I weren't alone in that cave. My daughter was there and so was her boyfriend, Om. We had been captured by terrorists who tied our hands so that we couldn't escape." said Carl. "Nigel came to our rescue and freed us before the earthquake struck the mountains behind the Tyangboche Monastery," said Carl irritated.

"Most of the pilgrims have already left," said Rama, changing the subject.

"I'm sorry, Carl. I didn't mean to offend you. We'll see you later," said Samitra turning toward her husband. "Rama, I wish you had rented me a horse. I'm exhausted from walking for seven hours. We still have three more hours to trek to get to the guest house."

"Samitra, why don't you ride my horse. I don't mind walking with Rama," said Carl.

"I'm sure Hari will be angry if he found out that you gave me your horse to ride," said Samitra.

"I don't think he'd mind if you rode Pema," said Rama. "I don't want you fainting from heat exhaustion along the way to the guest house."

"I do feel as if I'm going to faint," said Samitra, wiping her forehead with a handkerchief.

Carl spoke to Jimpa in Nepali, explaining the situation. Within a few minutes, Samitra mounted his horse, following the other horses down the wide road toward the guest house.

While walking along, Carl admired the scenery on the trail for several miles with the sun shining. After two hours of trekking, dark clouds drifted toward them from the peak of Mount Kailash.

As they approached the guest house it began to rain. This time it wasn't a gentle shower, but a deluge. Having left his water proof coat in his back pack, Carl was drenched from the unexpected storm.

Upon reaching the guest house, the manager gave him a key to the room, while Rama waited outside with his umbrella for Samitra to arrive.

Carl entered the room and changed into dry clothes, pulling back the drapery to look out the window, noticing the rain had suddenly stopped. He was in awe at the sight of the reverse side of Mount Kailash. From where he stood, he could see the snow-covered peak at 22,031 feet.

He glanced across the road where Jimpa had arrived with Samitra, drenched from the rain. Rama was there helping her get down from her horse.

Carl left his room, leaping around the puddles toward them. He handed Jimpa a crisp twenty dollar bill, thanking him for being his guide.

Jimpa bowed his head with gratitude and stuffed the money into his pocket. He then took Pemba to the corral across from large red brick restroom.

Having leapt around the puddles, Carl returned to the entrance of his room. He stood with the door open. Within a few minutes, Rama arrived with Samitra and went inside to change their clothes.

Carl stood outside watching four horses arrive at the corral with their riders wearing their blue and orange waterproof coats. Among them was Margaret, clinging to the saddle horn with her hair soaked from the rain and shivering from the cold.

Lall helped her down from the horse and onto his back. Within a few minutes he zig-zagged around the puddles coming towards him from the muddy road.

Before Carl could speak to them, the manager arrived with his clipboard to check their names on the list. After handing Lall the key, he pointed to the location of their room two doors away.

"Put me down next to Carl," insisted Margaret, releasing her grip from Lall's neck. She slid down from his back onto the concrete sidewalk in front of his door, moaning because of her bruised toes.

"I'll get you a towel so you can dry your hair," said Carl, returning from the room with a chair and a towel.

"I'm freezing cold," said Margaret, shivering as she removed her waterproof coat.

"Here's the towel," said Carl, distracted by her low cut blouse.

"Thank you so much," she said, leaving a streak of makeup on the towel. She turned toward Lall, who was staring at her figure while holding her back pack.

"Please put my back pack in our room," said Margaret, noticing that Dipak and Uma had arrived and were speaking to the manager across the road.

"Did you have any trouble coming down the mountain?" asked Carl, watching Margaret rummage through her back pack, searching for her makeup kit and mirror.

"The wild dogs tried to attack us as we came up the mountain," said Margaret, trembling. "Thank God for Lall. He held down my horse and threw stones at them.

"Oh Carl!" gasped Margaret, hugging him. "I can't find my makeup kit! Someone stole it from my back pack!"

Carl felt uneasy with Margaret clinging to him while several pilgrims stared at them as they weaved through the puddles and headed toward their rooms.

"Margaret, please sit down while I get you a blanket from the room I'm sharing with Samitra and Rama."

Upon returning, Carl wrapped the blanket around her, reassuring her that the storm was over.

"A Khampa arrived on his horse and walked with us on the trail for quite a long time," said Margaret. "I'm sure he stole my makeup!"

"I also met a Khampa on the trail. His horse nipped at mine when he first arrived. He also helped Jimpa drive away the wild dogs with his sling shot," said Carl.

"The Khampa told Lall that he wanted to take me back to his camp to spend the night with him. I was terrified by the way he was looking at me. I saw Lall reach into a backpack and give him a few yuans so that he'd leave us alone," said Margaret.

"What's going on here?" asked Dipak, coming across the road with Uma, drenched from the rain.

"Margaret's had a rough trip because she rode on a horse up the mountain and was carried down by Lall," said Carl.

"I was threatened by a Khampa. He wanted to take me back to his camp for the night!" gasped Margaret. "My guide gave him my makeup kit so he'd leave me alone."

"We'll help you get to our room," sighed Uma. "We're just as exhausted as you are Margaret."

"Margaret, I found your makeup kit and mirror," said Carl, removing it from a side pocket of her back pack.

"Oh! Then that Kampa didn't steal it after all," said Margaret, letting the blanket slip from her shoulders

"The manager told us that Lall has the key to our room, said Dipak. "Carl, I'll carry Margaret to our room if you will put her on my back."

"Of course I'll help you," said Carl, feeling relieved once they left. He took a deep breath, noticing that the manager was still standing across the road, checking his clipboard as the last of the pilgrims arrived. He paused as Samitra and Rama came out of their room wearing dry clothes.

"What was all that commotion about in front of our room?" asked Samitra .

"Margaret was stressed out from the outburst of rain," said Carl. "It's been a difficult trip for her."

"We were, also, delayed getting here because fourteen pilgrims from India were blocking the trail. They were following their leader by bowing and then prostrating onto the ground," said Samitra.

"When the leader gave the signal, they got up and then walked a few yards before stretching out again on the ground," said Rama.

"They were doing penance for their past karma," said Samitra. "I spoke to the leader in Hindi about us going past them on the narrow trail. He was annoyed because we interred with their prayers, but he ordered his group of pilgrims to step aside so that we could go up the trail."

"Now that the sun is shining again, I'm amazed by the splendor of Mount Kailash," said Rama.

"Those pilgrims doing penance are going to have to camp in wet grass tonight," said Samitra.

"I hope Margaret isn't stressed out again because of Nigel. We haven't talked to her since we left the guest house about 11 hours ago," commented Samitra.

"Nigel seems to have a way of appearing and then disappearing," said Carl, not mentioning that he had seen him in the ruins of the monastery on the hill.

"It looks like the sun's starting to go down," said Rama,

"The manager told us that dinner would be served tonight in our rooms since there is no dining room here."

"We're tired of being served rice and lentils nearly every meal," said Samitra.

"Hari told me that we were going to have spaghetti for dinner tonight, but I don't know what kind of sauce they'll be making since almost everyone is vegetarian," said Rama.

"He also said that a bus will be arriving to take us to Darshen tomorrow right after breakfast," said Carl.

"Don't tell me we have to stay another night in that filthy town," said Samitra. "The pollution from the trucks in the parking lot of our guest house in Dharsen was terrible."

"We're only stopping there to pick up our luggage in storage. After that we'll be heading for Saga," said Carl.

Chapter 48
"Travelling from Dharsen to Saga"

The next morning everyone was up early. The waiters came with trays of tea, rice and lentils. After finishing their breakfast, the pilgrims left their rooms and brought their back packs to the bus. Upon boarding everyone patiently waited for the driver and stray pilgrims to arrive.

"I can't believe, we'll soon be on our way back to Dharsen. I hate to leave this beautiful view of Mount Kailash," said Samitra, sitting next to Rama.

"Look who's boarding the bus without being carried by Lall or Kesab," said Rama.

"Why Margaret, you're walking without anyone helping you!" said Carl, seated next to Dipak in the front row.

"The manager's son's a doctor from Beijing. He's visiting his parents at the guest house. Last night he gave me an injection in my foot to stop the pain. For the first time since we left Lake Manasarovar, I was able to sleep the whole night," said Margaret.

"Dipak, would you mind if I sat next to Carl. It's only an hour's ride to Darshen."

"Uma has reserved a window seat for you in the back of the bus," said Dipak. "Carl needs to write a letter to his wife and mail it once we get to Dharsen."

"He can use a computer once we get to the hotel in Saga," said Margaret.

"We can talk for a while at Dharsen when we retrieve

our luggage from the storage room," said Carl, noticing that all eyes were on Margaret as she walked toward the back of the bus wearing a low cut red blouse, black slacks and sandals with her hips swaying.

Lall and Kesab followed her, carrying her leather purse and satchel, which they put on the ledge above her seat before sitting across the aisle from her.

"Margaret, I can't believe that you're finally walking on your bruised toes," said Uma.

"Doctor Chang told gave me an injection last night that released the tension in my foot," said Margaret, sitting down next her.

"Some of our pilgrims are debating whether you're having a love affair with Lall, or Kesab. A few of them believe you'll probably marry both of them like Tibetan nomads who practice polyandry," said Uma.

"They've both been very kind to me, but I'm not interested in marrying either one of them," said Margaret.

Once everyone was seated, Hari boarded the bus and walked down the aisle, checking that everyone was aboard. He then went to the microphone to make an announcement.

"My dear friends, I want to thank you for your patience and tolerance during this pilgrimage. You've all been wonderful in spite of the wild dogs, yak herds, servings of rice and lentils, and steep trails on Mount Kailash.

"Our injured pilgrim, Maya, was taken by jeep to the guest house last night, where Doctor Lee Chang diagnosed her condition as a compound fracture. Afterwards I travelled with her to the hospital in Dharsen, where her foot will be put into a cast. Hopefully, she will join us and travel with us to Saga. The doctor, also, treated Margaret Porter's injury, and she's finally walking without limping or being carried by one of our drivers.

"Once we reach the guest house at Dharsen, please go to the storage room and retrieve your luggage. Then put them into the trunk of your land cruisers. We'll be departing for Saga as soon as possible," said Hari, taking his seat across the aisle from Carl and Dipak.

Within a few minutes, the bus departed from the guest house down the rugged dirt road. As they travelled the pilgrims talked about the difficulties they had while trekking or riding up and down on Mount Kailash. In less than an hour they reached Dharsen.

Everyone left the bus to retrieve their luggage and then returned to the land cruisers, lined up in the parking lot.

Samitra and Rama were sitting in backseat of their vehicle, while Carl was standing near the trunk with his luggage. He paused as an ambulance arrived.

Hari hurried toward the ambulance, opening the back door to help Maya out with her leg in a cast. Using a walker, she hobbled toward the land cruiser, joining Uma in the back seat with Dipak in the front across from Lall.

All eyes turned toward Hari helping a stranger out of the ambulance to sit down into a wheel chair. His neck, chest, and head were bandaged like an Egyptian mummy, and his right arm and leg were in casts. The driver pushed him through the dusty parking lot and halted at a land cruiser.

Hari made an announcement on his megaphone. "My dear friends, I'd like you to meet Heinrich Salzmann. He'll be travelling with us to Kathmandu where his parents are waiting to take him on the next flight to Switzerland.

"We want Heinrich, who was seriously injured, while descending Mount Kailash, to sit in the back seat of the land cruiser sideways with his leg elevated, which means I'll have to rearrange the seating."

Hari announced that they would be leaving within a half

hour, encouraging everyone to be ready to depart.

After placing his luggage in the back of the land cruiser, Carl paused as Margaret approached him.

"I'm worried about Nigel. Will you come with me to the manager's office to see if he left a message for me at the desk?" she asked.

"I promised Maya that I'd go into town and get her a copy of the 'China Daily' for her to read during the ride to Saga," said Carl.

"Margaret, I'll go with you to the desk," said Samitra, overhearing her.

After the women left, Rama said, "Carl, please get me a copy of the 'Times of India'. I'm going over to say hello to Heinrich Salzmann."

Within twenty minutes Carl returned to the parking lot, noticing that Margaret was sitting in the back seat of the cruiser sobbing with Samitra consoling her.

"What's wrong, Margaret?" asked Carl, handing Rama his newspaper.

"I…I didn't receive a message from Nigel. I have a feeling something terrible has happened to him. The manager told me that the police will be coming to ask us questions before we leave Dharsen!"

"There's nothing on the front page about Nigel in the 'Times of India'," said Rama, leafing through the newspaper.

"The 'China Daily' has warnings by seismologists of earthquakes taking place in Nepal due to the melting of the glaciers in the Himalayas," said Carl.

Upon turning the page, he glanced at the headline, "Buddhist Abbott Murdered in Eastern Tibet." His eyes widened upon seeing a picture of Nigel in his maroon robe while shopping in the market place with the Abbot and monks from the monastery in Saga.

"Carl, you look like you've seen a ghost," said Margaret, coming out of the cruiser. "That article's about Nigel. Isn't it! Please let me see that newspaper!"

"I'll give you the paper but if you get depressed you must take your medication."

"I promise you I won't get hysterical," said Margaret, taking a deep breaths and pacing in front of the cruiser

"All right, here's the newspaper," said Carl, handing it to Margaret, who was startled by the headline.

"Oh my God! It's a picture of Nigel with the monks at Saga. It says the Abbot and all the monks were arrested and that the monastery was shut down by the Chinese guards for harboring a criminal."

She continued reading, "After murdering a Chinese guard at the Jokang Monastery in Lhasa, Nigel fled to Saga on the back of a truck. The Sikh driver was arrested but set free because he didn't know that Nigel was the murderer.

"No! I can't believe it!" cried Margaret. "The Chinese guards also discovered that Nigel was living in the ruins of the monastery destroyed by the Maoists during the Cultural Revolution across from the Chiu Gompa Monastery."

"After a careful investigation, the monks confessed that Nigel came daily to their monastery from his room in the ruins to chant and meditate. They were all shocked when they found the Abbot dead in his office with a knife in his back! They believe that Nigel murdered him and escaped from the monastery after knocking out a monk and stealing his motor cycle.

"That Abbot promised to help Nigel escape because he believed he was innocent," cried Margaret, pausing when Hari came toward them with two Chinese guards.

"Please have your passports ready for inspection," said

Hari. "We'll depart for Saga after the guards see them."

The Chinese police moved swiftly from vehicle to vehicle, inspecting the passports of the pilgrims in their land cruisers, lined up for departure.

After meeting Heinrich Salzmann, who was stretched out in the back seat of a cruiser, they approached Hari and asked him why the Swiss citizen had a new passport issued by the authorities in Darshen.

Hari explained to the officers about Heinrich's accident on the mountain and his credentials being stolen. After the police returned his passport, they headed toward the next land cruiser.

The officers went back to Hari and asked for the names of the pilgrims who trekked from the Chiu Gompa Guest House to the ruins and the monastery where the abbot had been killed.

Hari told them that Carl had gone up the trail with Samitra, Rama, and Margaret Porter, who had been injured and was carried by Lall and Kesab to the ruins and then to the monastery.

The Chinese Police informed Lall and Kesab to go directly to the manager's office while the others waited in their land cruisers. Those who didn't go to the monastery were free to depart in their cruisers for Saga.

"What's all this commotion with the Chinese officers?" asked Dipak. "We were about to leave for Saga when Lall told us he had to go to office to talk to the police."

"Our driver was also being questioned about Nigel," said Carl. "Only those of us who trekked up to the ruins will be interrogated."

"Here come Kesab and Lall. They weren't in the office very long," said Carl.

"We told the guards that we knew nothing about Nigel,

living in the ruins. We've never met him or even saw a picture of him," said Lall, entering his cruiser and departing with Dipak next to him and Uma and Maya in the back seat.

After waving to them, Rama and Samitra hurried together toward the office. Within twenty minutes they returned to their cruiser.

"Margaret, the police want to talk to you first and then to Carl," said Rama, sitting next to Samitra in the cruiser.

"I'm sure the Abbot was murdered because he helped Nigel escape to India," said Margaret, noticing that all the land cruisers had departed expect theirs.

"We all know that Nigel is innocent," said Carl. "I believe he's safely with the Dalai Lama at Dharmasala."

Carl watched Margaret hurrying toward the office with her hips swaying. When she finally came out of the office an hour later, she burst into tears.

Margaret threw her arms around Carl and sobbed for a few minutes before entering the back seat of the cruiser and sat next to Samitra, who encouraged her to take deep breaths.

An irritated Chinese guard came out of the manager's office to get Carl After being interrogated for nearly 45 minutes, he left the office feeling tense and angry.

Carl entered the land cruiser and was relieved when they left the parking lot for Saga. He glanced at Margaret asleep in the back seat between Rama and Samitra.

Chapter 49
"Overnight at Saga"

It was after dark when their land cruiser arrived at Saga. Carl was surprised that Margaret slept for four hours and was perfectly calm during the rest of the trip. She talked a great deal about her husband, Krishna, and their cruises on the Rhine, Danube, and Nile Rivers.

Upon reaching their hotel, Carl and his friends went directly to the dining room, which was deserted except for Heinrich Salzmann sitting in a wheel chair, drinking coffee and talking to Hari

After greeting them, the late arrivals went to the kitchen to get their food before it shut down for the night. When they returned to the dining room, Hari was leaving the room pushing Heinrich in his wheel chair.

Upon finishing dinner, Carl hurried to the front desk of the hotel, realizing the computer room was only open to 10:00 and it was already 9:30 p.m.

Carl checked his email and was pleased to see a letter from Barbara.

Dear Carl,   August 17, 2013

I've missed you terribly since you left for Nepal. I've been worried about you travelling to Tibet and hiking because of my terrible dreams about you falling off the mountains. I was horrified when I saw the headlines of the "Chicago Tribune" yesterday, "Trekker Injured on Mount Kailash in Tibet." I nearly fainted, thinking it might be you.

I was surprised to see pictures of Heinrich Salzmann before his accident and after he was treated at the hospital, wrapped up in bandages like a mummy. Apparently his trekking companions abandoned him on the mountain because he was drunk.

A rescue team went in an ambulance to the base of Mount Kailash, where they met the Yak herder, who carried Heinrich down the mountain. They took him directly to the hospital in Dharsen, where he received treatment. The doctors were amazed that he survived. The article also stated that Hari Sharma, your tour guide agreed to take Heinrich back to Nepal in a land cruiser.

I hope that you climbed Mount Kailash and descended without any problems and that my horrible dreams about you falling off the cliff didn't come true.

This past weekend my mother, Renee, and I took Emily and Sammy in her limousine to Springfield, Illinois to the Lincoln Museum.

A woman, dressed like Mary Todd took us to the reconstructed log cabin in the museum, where Abraham Lincoln studied law at night in front of his fireplace.

We then visited rooms, which were replicas of the White House, where he lived with his family, the Balcony of the Ford Theater, where Lincoln was assassinated, and the Capitol Rotunda, where he was laid in state.

The kids were impressed with "The Ghost Theater" with holograms floating on the stage. After the performance we went to the children's section of the museum, where Emily and Sammy played with toys and drew pictures.

Upon leaving the museum, Renee's driver, Bill, took us to Lincoln's Home in Springfield. We had a good time touring the two story house.

While leaving the house, I accidentally tripped and fell

down onto the sidewalk, flat on my face. Sammy and Emily cried when they saw my nose bleeding and bruised face.

A nearby Park ranger administered first aid and stopped the bleeding. After getting up from the sidewalk, I was so stiff that I could hardly walk. The driver, Bill, helped me get into the limousine with my mother and the children. He then took us to St. John's Hospital in Springfield.

Renee read stories to Sammy and Emily in the lobby while I went to the Emergency Room. I left the hospital three hours later with a brace on my right leg and a bandage on my hand. After returning to our house in Arlington Heights, I couldn't sleep that night because my leg was swollen.

I limped over to Renee's room leaning against the wall for support. My mother called an ambulance which arrived within ten minutes. The attendants strapped me down and drove me to Northwest Hospital.

The Emergency Room doctor told me, I had a blood clot in my leg. I was given medication and kept in the hospital overnight. The following day, I was discharged because the swelling had gone down.

I'm so grateful that Renee's staying with me for the summer to help out with the grandchildren. While I was recovering at home with ice packs on my leg, Renee took the kids to the Shed Aquarium in downtown Chicago.

Tomorrow they'll be going to the Waterpark to swim in the pool since it's been so hot here the whole month of August. I want to go with them to the Museum of Science and Industry this weekend, but I'll probably need to use a walker to see the exhibits.

Carl, I haven't heard from Kathy. She emailed me that Greg was leaving Quito, Ecuador after being there only two weeks at the hospital, because of marching and protesting in the streets.

He's planning to fly to Kathmandu to stay with Kathy during her time off from work at the hospital in Patan. Her old boyfriend, Om, wants to take them both to meet his family in Pokhara.

Please write to me as soon as you get to Saga. I'm still a nervous wreck over Mark's divorce. Nothing has been finalized about the custody of Sammy and Emily.

Mark will be flying home from Philadelphia with Sam and his lawyer for a hearing with Corrine and her lawyer next week. I hope everything gets settled before school starts for the children. With all my love, Barbara

Carl paused, glancing at the clock on the wall. He still had few minutes before the computer room shut down.

Dearest Barbara,   August 18, 2013

I'm relieved to know that you're recovering from your injury after falling down at Lincoln's house. I'm worried about your blood clot. I hope you'll follow the doctor's instructions by putting ice on your leg to reduce the swelling.

We arrived late here in Saga. Some of us were delayed because we were questioned by the Chinese police over the murder of the Abbot at the Chiu Gompa Monastery.

I had a chance to meet Heinrich Salzmann, who's travelling with the pilgrims back to Kathmandu in a land cruise.

Nigel's disappearance is still a problem for Margaret Porter. I'm sure that he's staying with the Dalai Lama in India. I wanted you to know, I managed to ascend and descent Mount Kailash without injuring myself.

The desk clerk is here to shut down the computer room. I'll email you, once we get to Kathmandu. Please say hello to Renee, Sam, Mark, Sammy, and Emily. With love, Carl

Chapter 50
"Arrival at Zhangmu"

Everyone was eager to leave Saga the following morning after breakfast. The land cruises were lined up with their drivers inside waiting for the pilgrims to arrive with their luggage.

Hari informed them that upon arrival at Zhangmu, they should go to the customs terminal, where their passports and luggage would be inspected.

As they travelled along everyone enjoyed the vastness of the blue sky, the grandeur of the snow covered Himalayas. They were all surprised when the scenery changed as they headed south where nomads were grazing their herds of goats and sheep in the green pastures.

Carl and his friends were in awe when they entered a vast tropical rain forest. As they ascended the paved road going up the mountain they saw a roaring river below and cascading waterfalls.

"The mountain on our left is covered with green moss and shrubs growing between the waterfalls!" said Samitra, gazing out the open windows.

"I've never seen so many waterfalls in my whole life," commented Margaret.

"The waterfalls are gushing down from the top of the mountain about every two hundred feet," said Carl.

"It's starting to rain!" said Margaret, listening to the water splashing onto the top of their land cruiser.

"That's not rain," said Rama. "It's a waterfall pouring

down on us from the right side of the mountain."

"Hamro jane batoma pani dherai chiplo cha, The water on our road is very slippery" said Kesab, slowing down to avoid skidding from the puddles.

"The Chinese engineers certainly did a good job building this road," said Carl. "It's well paved at this altitude."

"I was amazed by the quality of the service by the Chinese staff at the hotels and guest houses. They were always considerate and helpful," said Margaret, pausing to listen to the water splashing onto the roof as they drove through another waterfall.

"I was surprised that our rooms were kept so clean, especially our sheets and blankets," said Samitra, gasping from fright as the water thundered on the roof of the cruiser.

"The hotels with indoor plumbing at Saga and Nylam were immaculate," said Rama, noticing the women were trembling from the roaring of the next waterfall..

"It was difficult to get used to the outdoor toilets," said Carl. "Wow! I hope the road doesn't get washed away by the next waterfall."

"This pilgrimage is beautiful but dangerous!" gasped Margaret. "The road ahead is flooded!"

Kesab slammed on the breaks as the cruiser skidded on the flooded road and crashed into the railing, denting the doors on the left.

Margaret screamed when he slammed his foot onto the gas pedal and lunged forward away from the gushing water onto the dry road ahead.

Everyone took deep breaths feeling relieved as they continued on through the rain forest.

"We're fortunate that we'd didn't break through the railing. It's must be at about a thousand feet to the river below!" gasped Rama, sighing with relief.

"The engineers took a risk building the road so close to the waterfalls on this side of the mountain," said Carl.

"No doubt it was difficult for the laborers to cut through the solid rock to make the road," said Rama.

"I hope we don't have to drive through any more waterfalls," said Margaret sighing.

"I'm grateful the railing was solid cement; so we didn't go over the cliff," said Carl.

"I wish we could stop so that I could go for a walk," said Margaret, taking deep breaths with her eyes closed.

"It looks like we're leaving the rain forest," said Carl

"It won't be long now before we reach Zhangmu," said Rama, looking at a map from his guidebook.

Everyone settled down as they continued their journey. It was late in the afternoon when they reached the border. They were surprised to see several empty land cruisers parked across street from the terminal.

"Here comes Hari," said Rama, unable to open the dented door on the left side of the cruiser while Samitra and Margaret got out on the right side.

Kesab, who couldn't get out from the dented driver's side, slid across the seat, following Carl out of the passenger side.

"I see you've damaged your land cruiser," said Hari. "Heinrich Salzmann's vehicle was also damaged from the waterfalls. He and Maya will be the only ones travelling back to Kathmandu in cruisers. They're waiting with the rest of the pilgrims to leave.

"The bus is already waiting for us on the other side of the terminal. Please go directly through customs and then board the bus for Kathmandu," said Hari.

"I'll carry that suitcase for you, Margaret," said Carl, leading the way across the street. Once inside the terminal, they stood in line with their luggage.

"I'm so grateful that I can walk on my own," said Margaret, pacing up and down and taking deep breaths.

"The Chinese official at the desk stamped Rama's, Kesab's, and Samitra's passports and returned them. They hurried through the turntable where their back packs and luggage were waiting for them.

"I'm sorry to detain you, Mrs. Porter. Our records show that you are married to Doctor Krishna Manandhar although you aren't using his name on your passport. Please come this way. Our manager wants to speak with you for a few minutes," said the Chinese guard.

"Margaret said, "I renewed my passport prior to marrying my second husband, Krishna Manandhar. I forgot to change my name on my passport."

"Our records show that you attempted to contact your son in Saga where he was given asylum by the monks at the monastery there."

"I...I never met him at Saga," said Margaret, trying to control the tremor in her voice.

"Mrs. Margaret Manandhar Porter kindly follow me to the office," insisted the guard.

"Carl, I'll see you on the bus," said Margaret, looking over her shoulder. "Please save me a seat so we can ride back to Kathmandu together," entering the office.

"I'll do that," said Carl, following behind her with a Chinese officer leading him.

"Our customs manager would also like to speak with you, Dr. Carl Brecht," said the officer. "You have a history of being involved with Margaret and her son, Nigel. You may sit down over there on the bench and wait your turn."

An hour later, Margaret came out of the office with her makeup smeared from crying.

"Carl, I'm so sorry for the delay," she sobbed, eager to talk to him. She was interrupted by the guard, who led her through the turntable, where her luggage was waiting.

"This way Dr. Brecht," said another officer, leading Carl into the room to be questioned. After forty minutes of interrogation, he returned to the desk and was handed his passport. After putting on his back pack, he picked up his luggage and hurried through the terminal.

Within ten minutes they both crossed the border into Nepal and hurried toward the bus, where Hari was pacing waiting for them. Upon boarding the crowded bus, the weary pilgrims were annoyed by the delay.

Margaret was sitting in the front of the bus across from Hari, with Carl sitting next to her.

When the driver started the bus, two Chinese photographers arrived taking their pictures for the "China Daily." As soon as they departed, a Nepalese photographer arrived from the "Nepal Daily" to take more pictures.

Once their pictures were taken, the bus driver departed for Kathmandu while Hari made an announcement.

"My dear friends, I want to thank all of you for being so tolerant and patient while waiting for Carl and Margaret to board the bus.

"I didn't expect newspaper reporters to question so many of you right here on the bus before our friends returned. Some of you believe that Carl and Margaret are Star Crossed Lovers, but Margaret explained to me that they've had a platonic relationship that goes back several years.

"Be sure to get copies of the 'China Daily' and the 'Nepal Daily,' tomorrow and find out what the press has to say. Please relax for the next four hours and enjoy the scenery in rural Nepal. Gita will lead the chanting while we begin our journey back to Kathmandu."

Chapter 51
"Back to Kathmandu"

"Oh not that chanting again," said Carl. "I wish I had my ear plugs with me, but they're in my suitcase in the luggage compartment."

"I'm so sorry that I've caused you so much trouble during the trip. Your friends from the University of Chicago, Rama and Samitra, and her relatives Dipak and Uma, have tried their best to keep us separated during the whole trip."

"It's because of Barbara. She got very angry when she found out that you were going on the pilgrimage with us to Mount Kailash. I have to admit that I've always been attracted to you, Margaret, because you remind me of Marilyn Monroe."

"Oh for heaven's sake!" said Margaret. "Our relationship has always been platonic. You've been such a good friend ever since I met you in the fall of 1976. You're like the older brother that I never had when I was growing up.

"I was an only child and abandoned when I was five years old after the divorce of my parents. My father was an officer in the British army, and he had no time for me after my mother died from pneumonia.

"I stayed in orphanage until I was nine years old. My mother's sister, Aunt Margo adopted me. I got relief from her nagging, when I began taking piano and voice lessons at the best studio in London. I used to practice for three or four hours every day on my aunt's grand piano.

"Aunt Margo invited her friends to her mansion for lunch

every week. They always asked me to play for them. Her women friends appreciated my music and gave me money which I used for my music lessons.

"The biggest mistake of my life was marrying Jim Porter because he was wealthy not because I loved him. It resulted in a disastrous marriage," she said, pausing as the chanting continued.

"My other mistake was getting involved with the London Coven, where I offered Nigel to them when he was an infant. When I realized my error, I tried to flee from the coven, but no matter where I went, Yorg followed me."

"You've had difficult life. I remember that you were taking medication when I first met you."

"Yes, I was taking tranquilizers when I met you on the flight to Kathmandu."

"That's when you were fleeing from the coven with your sons, Nigel and Christopher," said Carl.

"Leaving London was difficult for me. I fainted from shock after Christopher death in the garden at Kathmandu Guest House," said Margaret.

"That pomelo tree is still there, along with a snack bar behind it's now called 'The Pomelo Tree Café'," said Carl.

"It took me years to get over Christopher's death," said Margaret. "You were very supportive of me, while I was in the hospital. I'm so grateful to you for helping me find Nigel after he was kidnapped.

"After my divorce, I devoted my time to giving music lessons and playing with the symphony orchestra in London. Later I married Krishna, and we returned to Nepal numerous times to visit Nigel after his conversion to Buddhism."

"The last time that I met you in Nepal was twelve years ago when Nigel was living at the Royal Palace during the assassination of the Royal Family," said Carl.

"I went into shock again when Nigel was arrested and put into jail because he was a good friend of the Crown Prince," sighed Margaret. "I was horrified when he was accused of murdering the Chinese guard in Lhasa and the Abbot at the Chiu Gompa Monastery."

"You and I know that Nigel had nothing to do with the assassinations then or now."

"Instead of reliving the past, I would suggest that when we arrive in Kathmandu that you go to the British Embassy and have them contact Dharmasala to see if Nigel is staying there with the Dalai Lama. You could easily get a flight to India to visit him before returning to London," suggested Carl, relieved that the chanting had stopped.

"My dear Hindu friends," said Gita, finally out of breath from leading the chanting. "I would like to invite Margaret Porter to sing her favorite English hymn to us."

Margaret was surprised by the invitation. When she got up from her seat, she took the microphone and said, "Gita, thank you so much for inviting me to sing my favorite hymn, 'How Great Thou Art'."

"O' Lord my God when I in awesome wonder, consider all the worlds thy hands have made. I see the stars and hear the rolling thunder, thy power throughout the universe displayed. Then sings my soul, my Savior God to Thee, how great Thou art, how great Thou art!"

After finishing the next three stanzas, Margaret paused while everyone clapped. She bowed to the pilgrims and said, "I want to thank you for your patience with me for causing delays during this trip.

"I was questioned by the Chinese police about my son Nigel's involvement with the murder of a Chinese guard in Lhasa, and the Abbot at the Chiu Gompa Monastery.

"I am convinced that my son is innocent of these

accusations. By now he is safely with the Dalai Lama in India. I hope that you will ignore the publicity about him in the newspapers," she said, handing the microphone to Hari.

"My pilgrim friends, we'll be back in Kathmandu by about 3:00 p.m. today, unless there is a delay due to traffic," said Hari.

Margaret sat down next to Carl and asked "Did you have a chance to talk to Heinrich Salzmann? Hari sent him back to Kathmandu in a land cruiser, where he'll meet his parents, who will take him back to Switzerland."

"Heinrich told me that his Swiss companions abandoned him at the top of the mountain because he had been drinking. A Yak herder carried him down the mountain on the back of his horse and brought him to the guest house," said Carl.

"The desk clerk called an ambulance, which took him to the hospital in Dharsen," said Margaret, removing from her purse, "The Power of Now."

"I was impressed by Eckhart Tolle's comment that most people live in the past with anger and resentment or the future with fear and anxiety," said Carl.

"The real problem is the ego can never get enough. It thrives on the belief that more is better."

"Many people ruin their health by drinking, overeating, or taking illegal or prescription drugs to relax because they are unable to set boundaries," said Margaret.

"How about if we rest for a while because in a few more hours we'll be arriving in Kathmandu," said Carl.

"I agree," said Margaret. "Being in the present moment connects us with the Universal Spirit."

As they continued their journey, many passengers slept, or read books or newspapers.

Four hours later, Hari announced, "We are in Kathmandu; taxies and family members are waiting for us."

Chapter 52
"Arrival in Kathmandu"

Upon reaching Kathmandu, the Hindu pilgrims were anxious to retrieve their luggage and depart for their homes. Most of them were weary from traveling. Some welcomed family members coming to greet them. Others headed toward taxies wearing their back packs and carrying their suitcases.

Dipak and Uma sons' waited for them in front of their family cars. Chandra rushed toward his parents and gave them hugs.

"I'm so happy you're back in Kathmandu! I've been worried about you trekking down Mount Kailash ever since reading about Heinrich Salzmann," said Chandra.

"Your mother and I didn't have any trouble going up or down the mountain," said Dipak.

"Where's your brother?" asked Uma. "We were expecting him to drive your uncle and aunt back."

"Surya, is standing behind the Toyota with the trunk open next to your Honda. Uncle Rama and Aunt Samitra are heading toward him right now," he said.

"How about you, Dr. Brecht? Are you coming back to my house with my parents." asked Chandra. "I've got room for one more person in my car."

"I'll be staying with friends in Patan for a week and then the Kathmandu Guest House before leaving Nepal with my daughter Kathy and her boyfriend, Greg."

"Will you be coming for dinner this evening?" asked

Dipak. "We're having a 'Welcome Back from Mount Kailash Party' hosted by our relatives."

"No, I will be meeting my daughter, Kathy, and her boyfriend for dinner at the Kathmandu Guest House. Margaret Porter will be joining us. She plans to stay there overnight and then fly to India to meet her son, Nigel, in Dharmasala," said Carl, introducing her to Chandra.

"Your son, Nigel, has made the headlines in our newspapers for several days now. I'm sorry that he's caused you so much grief," said Chandra.

"I'm not worried about him," said Margaret. "I'm sure the Dalai Lama in India is taking good care of him!"

"I hope you enjoy your trip to Dharmasala. I must go now. My parents are anxious to get home," said Chandra.

"Oh, I almost forgot I got an email this morning from your daughter, Kathy," said Chandra, giving it to Carl and then departing with his parents.

Carl read the email to Margaret. "Dad, I hope you arrived safely in Kathmandu from Tibet. Greg got here a few days ago from Quito. I introduced him to Om, who took us to visit his family in Pokhara. It was a long taxi ride to his village where we stayed overnight and visited with his parents, wife, and three children. We had a good time even though none of them spoke English except Om. The trip back to Kathmandu was long and tedious.

"Greg and I would like to meet you for dinner around 6:00 p.m. at the Kathmandu Guest House this evening. He's working at the Emergency Room with Om and me. If that's not possible, please call me on my cell phone and leave a message. Take care for now, your daughter Kathy."

"It's already 4:15," said Carl, picking up his luggage. "Margaret, I hope you can join us for dinner tonight at the guest house."

"I'd love to join you. I can't wait to see Kathy again and meet her boyfriend, Greg, but I'm so tired from travelling. As soon as I check into my room, I'll rest for a while. After dinner tonight I must get a plane ticket to Dharmasala." said Margaret.

They both headed toward a taxi, where the driver was waiting with his trunk open for the luggage. Within minutes, they were heading from the bus station to Tamel in Kathmandu.

"Tapai ko nam ke ho? What is your name?" asked Carl.

"My name is Lakshman", said the driver.

"In the Hindu epic, 'The Ramayana', Laksman helped Rama slay the Demon King, Ravana," said Carl.

"You must be a professor," said the driver.

"I teach anthropology part-time at the University of Chicago even though I'm retired," said Carl.

"Lakshman, where did you learn to speak English so well?" asked Margaret, disturbed by the heavy traffic.

"I attended Saint Xavier's in Patan for grade school and then went to the Jesuit high school in Godavari. I'm only driving a taxi for the summer. I'll continue with my education at the university in September, where I'm studying engineering."

"Nepal has a surplus of engineers," said Carl.

"I've already been offered a job in Australia after I graduate next spring," said Lakshman.

"Would you please stop at a Travel Agency? I want to book a flight to India. I would also like to get a copy of today's newspaper," said Margaret.

"Of course," said Lakshman, slowing down due to the heavy traffic. "Most of our roads in Kathmandu need to be repaired, but there's not enough government funding to finish the work."

"The country's still recovering from the Maoist Revolution," said Carl, as they crawled along in traffic.

"There's a newsstand on the corner near the Himalayan Travel Agency. I'll park on the side street," said Lakshman, swerving the taxi out of the traffic.

"While you're getting the newspaper, I'll book my flight from Nepal to Dharmasala at the travel agency," said Margaret.

"That won't be necessary. Please wait here because of the pollution. I'll get you a flier with the schedule of the flights to India. The staff at the Kathmandu Guest House can make the booking for you by telephone with your credit card. I'll get you the newspaper," said Lakshman, leaving the taxi and hurrying down the crowded sidewalk.

"I'd prefer the 'China Daily'," shouted Margaret, rolling down the window.

"I'm pleased that you'll be meeting Nigel in the near future," said Carl. "He'll be so glad to see you."

"What will I do if he's not there?" asked Margaret.

"Stop worrying! Krishna taught you how to meditate. Just relax now and take a few deep breaths."

After inhaling polluted air, Margaret began coughing. She rolled up the window, reaching for a handkerchief to cover her mouth and nose.

"It's hard to breathe here in Kathmandu," said Carl. "The rush hour traffic's thick with exhaust!"

"I've never seen so many trucks, buses, and motorcycles, clogging the street. The pollution's awful in comparison to Tibet," said Margaret coughing.

Within a few minutes, Lakshman returned with the schedule and the newspaper. Margaret thanked him with a crisp $10.00 tip.

Margaret read the headline on the front page to Carl

involving pilgrims being rescued in the Himalayas due to the collapse of the roads during the monsoon rains.

"I'm so relieved that the Prime Minister Mohan Singh took action and sent dozens of helicopters to rescue the pilgrims over the past two months," said Margaret.

"Earlier in the summer over 60,000 people were stranded in the Himalayas, because entire towns with guest houses and hotels were destroyed due to mountains collapsing in India," said Carl.

"There's also been a peaceful march here in Kathmandu by LGBT protestors. Most of them are high school or university students, demanding equal rights."

"They're often criticized by traditional family members and relatives because of their sexual orientation. Sometimes they're bullied by students, policeman, and even tourists," said Margaret.

"Is there any news about Lhasa?" asked Carl.

"Not on the front page," said Margaret opening the paper to the inner section and reading the headline, "Shopkeeper Arrested in Lhasa near Jokang Monastery."

"That's where Nigel was accused of murdering the Chinese guard!" said Margaret trembling. She handed the newspaper to Carl. "Please read it to me."

"A Tibetan shopkeeper, Vajra, was arrested for selling rubber masks of Crown Prince Dipendra and Nigel Porter, the prince's Buddhist mentor from Tyangboche Monastery in Eastern Nepal.

"Vajra denied that he knew anything about the rubber masks, confiscated by the Chinese police. He pleaded with them that he was innocent.

"The police agreed to set the shopkeeper free if he told them where he got the masks with labels, Made in Beijing, May 4, 2001," read Carl. "That was a month before the assassination of the Royal Family by terrorists from India.

"The shopkeeper informed the police that two men from Bombay sold him a cardboard box filled with the rubber masks about three weeks ago. One worked at the night club, 'The Pink Flamingo' and the other at the cabaret, 'The Wheel of Life', in downtown Lhasa.

"The police found the men and arrested them for selling cocaine and heroin to the customers and tourists. After a week of interrogation, one of the drug dealers from Bombay confessed to wearing a mask of Nigel Porter and murdering the Chinese policeman at the Jokhang Temple.

"The other drug dealer followed Nigel to Saga and then to the Chiu Gompa Monastery, where he ransacked the office while wearing a mask of Nigel and stabbed the Abbott," read Carl.

"Nigel's innocent! Thank God! I can travel to Dharmasala without being questioned," shouted Margaret.

"Nigel will be free to return to his monastery here in Nepal," said Carl.

"I want to take him back to London for a few weeks. I wish he would stay permanently at the Tibetan monastery in Switzerland. Then I could visit him more often."

"Be sure to mention it to Nigel. He might agree to stay for the some months to study the scriptures there," said Carl.

"It says here that The Chinese police shut down the nightclub and the cabaret in Lhasa after arresting the Chinese owners, waiters, and chorus girls," continued Carl.

"The drug dealers refused to disclose names to the police. However, a chorus girl told the police that the dealer at the cabaret was Raktavija, which means Hero of Blood.

"A waiter from the Pink Flamingo informed the police that other dealer's name was Ravana, the King of the Demons," read Carl.

"The editor of 'The China Daily' apologized for posting pictures of Nigel Porter in the head lines over the past few weeks. He stated that Nigel was probably at the Dalai Lama's monastery because he was falsely accused of murdering a Chinese guard and the Buddhist Abbot.

"The Chinese government agreed to free the monks arrested in their monasteries at Lhasa and Saga. For restitution each monastery will be given a new jeep and reimbursed with a thousand yuans for their time lost.

"The Chinese government invites Nigel and his mother, Margaret, to return to Lhasa and stay a year there with all expenses paid by the government so that Nigel may finish his studies of the Buddhist manuscripts," read Carl.

"I'm so relieved that Nigel is safe, but I doubt whether he'll go back to Lhasa," said Margaret. "Look Carl! We're driving past the Royal Palace, now a museum. I had lunch there twelve years ago with Queen Aisvarya and her relatives before their assassination by terrorists wearing rubber masks."

"We're now in Tamel," said Lakshman, driving past the former palace with palm trees wavering in the breeze and fruit bats hanging from the branches like closed umbrellas. The curio shops, restaurants, and clothing stores were filled with tourists entering and leaving with shopping bags.

"Tamel is quite crowded," said Carl, as the taxi slowed crossing New Road, where pedestrians, taxis, and rickshaws filled the crowded street.

Lakshman honked the horn at the tourists and Nepalese shoppers warning them to move out of the way.

Chapter 53
"The Kathmandu Guest House"

"We're finally here at the Kathmandu Guest House," said Margaret, sighing with relief as the taxi went through the arched entrance, where several other taxis waited for guests going out for the evening.

After the driver parked, he opened the trunk and removed the luggage and backpacks, handing them to the bell boys, who rushed from the lobby to bring them inside.

Carl gave Lakshman a generous tip, wishing him well during his studies in engineering at the university. He then accompanied Margaret through the outdoor café, where erotic wooden carvings of rampant lions drew the attention of the tourists having dinner.

Margaret checked in at the front desk while a bell boy carried her luggage to her room on the third floor in the southern wing overlooking the garden.

"Please join Kathy, Greg ad me for dinner tonight. We will meet you in the garden at 6:00 o'clock. It's already almost five o'clock," said Carl, reading the note he got from the clerk at the desk.

"Thanks for the invitation. I'll be there for dinner. I can't wait to see Kathy after all these years," she said, heading up the stairs with her hips swaying.

Carl introduced himself to the clerk and asked if he could leave his luggage and back pack behind the desk because he would be departing for Patan after dinner to stay with his Nepalese friends for a week and then return to the guest house before leaving Nepal.

A bell boy took Carl through the outdoor dining room, where he wove through a labyrinth of tables with waiters carrying plates of steaming food toward the computer room.

The area was filled with tourists from Europe and America speaking in French, English or German. He overheard elderly women talking about the vulgar erotic wood carvings on both sides of the entrance.

After nearly bumping into a waiter with a tray of food, Carl followed the bell boy down a hallway and into the computer room. A few minutes later he opened his email.

Dear Carl,

Kathy emailed me from Shanta Bhawan Hospital and told me that you were arriving in Nepal from Zhangmu and would be having dinner with her and Greg at the Kathmandu Guest House tonight. I was hoping you'd get this email since I've been pacing the floor every night since you've left for Mount Kailash, worrying about you.

I'm so relieved that you got back from Tibet without falling down and breaking your back. I wanted to tell you that Mark will have custody of Emily and Sammy for the school year in Philadelphia, provided he goes to an Outpatient Treatment Center for a month after work each night for the next two weeks and then attend AA meetings regularly. My father, Sam, agreed to pay for all of his expenses.

I'm very pleased that our grandchildren will be going to school in Philadelphia. Sam has already enrolled them in a private school in the suburbs close to his mansion.

Corina will have custody of Sammy and Emily during Christmas and Easter holidays and for the entire summer. I don't think we'll be seeing the children very much unless Mark brings them home with him now and then for a weekend.

Sammy testified at a private hearing that Grandma Margo drank heavily and beat him with a belt, leaving black and blue marks on his body. Because Margo was so brutal, she's forbidden to see them during the summer and holidays. Fortunately, the lawyers settled the case without it having to go to trial.

Carl, I know you must be exhausted from travelling all the way from Mount Kailash. I wish I could join you, but I'm still recovering from that fall at Lincoln's Home. I'd like to meet you again under the Pomelo Tree in the garden at the Kathmandu Guest House.

Please write to me again soon. I miss you terribly, especially at night. With love, Barbara

Carl glanced at his watch, realizing it was almost time for dinner. He quickly wrote a message to Barbara, telling her that he missed her, especially at night. He, also, said he was staying with friends in Patan for a few days before returning to the guest house for a week before leaving Nepal with Kathy and Greg on September 4th.

Carl left the computer room and hurried past the erotic carvings of the rampant lions in the outdoor dining room. He paused in the lobby, noticing that Margaret Porter was waiting for him at the desk.

He was surprised to see her wearing a modest, green silk dress with a red scarf around her neck. She hurried toward him with her high heels echoing on the wooden floor.

"That's a nice outfit that you're wearing," said Carl.

"Thank you, Carl. I looked down at the pomelo tree in the garden from my room on the third floor." said Margaret, taking Carl by the arm. "My husband, Krishna, and I always stayed here when we came from London to visit Nigel. We arrived during Tihar, the Festival of the Lights.

"To be very honest, I've been afraid to go into the garden because of Christopher's death. I visualized him hanging from the tree with that rope around his neck with Nigel standing there dazed from drugs that Yorg gave him."

"Just take a few deep breaths and count to ten," said Carl, opening the double doors leading into the garden.

"I hate to think about Yorg kidnapping Nigel and forcing him to stay with him in that coven for months," said Margaret, clinging to Carl's arm as they walked down the path lined with rose bushes.

"There's the pomelo tree with fruit hanging from the branches" said Carl. "Would you like to sit at a table some distant from the tree?" asked Carl.

"No, Carl, I'd rather sit at the table under the tree next to the walkway, leading to the Pomelo Tree Café."

After sitting down, Margaret reached for the menu, deciding to have tea before dinner.

The waiter came down the steps from the café and took their order. While they were waiting for their tea, Carl glanced down the aisle where he saw the bandaged head of someone reading a newspaper.

"Margaret, guess who's only a few tables away from us," said Carl, pausing as the man set down the newspaper.

"Why it's Heinrich Salzmann! No one said that he was staying here at the Guesthouse," said Margaret.

"Hari mentioned that his parents were waiting here to take him back to Switzerland," said Carl. "They're probably out shopping for gifts for their relatives."

Ignoring the waiter, who had returned with tea, which he set down on their table, Margaret pushed her chair back and went over to visit Heinrich. Carl followed her.

"Why Heinrich, you look so relaxed drinking that soda with a straw," said Margaret, approaching him. "You and

Maya both came back in land cruisers! The rest of us rode in the crowded bus! I'm so please that you got here safely!"

"I'm happy to see you and your friend, Carl Brecht," he mumbled. "Would you kindly help me remove the tape from the bandages on my head and around my neck? I need to take a shower when I get back to my room. I haven't had a bath since leaving Dharshen."

"Are you sure it's safe to remove those bandages?" asked Margaret, backing away from him.

"Maybe you should go to the Emergency Room at Bir Hospital, where a nurse can clean your wounds. It's only a couple of blocks from here," said Carl.

"I asked the manager at the desk to send me a doctor to remove my bandages and casts here in the garden. That was over an hour ago!"

"Why Heinrich! That's not such a good idea!" said Margaret. "You might start bleeding from your wounds if a doctor removes them before you're healed."

"Please sit down at the table with me and drink your tea before it gets cold," said Heinrich.

Carl brought the two cups of tea from the other table and sat down next to Margaret, who was trying to convince Heinrich to go to the hospital. While they were talking, the double doors from the lobby swung open.

Kathy came hurrying toward them with Greg following her with a black leather medical kit.

"Oh Dad, it's so good to see you," said Kathy, giving her father a kiss on the cheek. She then turned to Margaret and gave her hug before introducing her boyfriend to them.

"And you must be Heinrich Salzmann," said Kathy, shaking his bandaged hand.

"You look familiar! You're Doctor Kathy Brecht," said Heinrich.

"Just call me Kathy," she said, turning toward her father. "Dad, I wanted to show you my engagement ring. Greg and I are planning to get married next year in June."

"Ah...Ah...Congratulations to both of you!" said Carl.

"We were working in the emergency room hospital, when we received the message that Heinrich wanted us to remove his bandages in the garden of the Kathmandu Guest House. We can do it if he signs a paper saying that he won't sue us if something goes wrong."

"I'll sign it with my right hand," said Heinrich, noticing that the waiter had returned to take their order.

"Waiter, please bring us a basin and kettle of steaming water?" asked Kathy. "We'll start by removing the bandages around your head, neck, and chest. It looks like you've been wearing them for several days now. Didn't the nurses change them for you when you were at the hospital?"

"Yes they changed them before I departed in the land cruiser for Saga," said Heinrich.

As Kathy removed the bandages on his head and neck, she didn't expect Margaret to scream. "You're not Heinrich! You're Nigel!"

Margaret threw her arms around him hugging and kissing him in spite of the pungent odor wafting from his skin.

"You're here! Thank God, you're safe! What happened to you! Did someone push you down the mountain?" asked Margaret.

"No, mother, no one pushed me down the mountain. The Abbot arranged for me to be bandaged by a doctor in Dharsen, who put a cast on my arm and leg."

"You mean they're not broken!" cried Margaret, backing away because of the odor.

"No, they're not broken, Mother," he said.

"Nigel! I haven't seen you since you rescued us from the

Medicine Cave twelve years ago!" said Kathy, looking over her shoulder. "And here comes the waiter with the kettle of hot water and a bucket with a sponge."

Once the water cooled off Kathy began washing Nigel's face, neck and chest while Greg removed the plaster castes from Nigel's arm and leg with a small electric saw. He then washed and dried them with a towel.

Nigel stood up and walked slowly up and down the path in the garden with Margaret holding him by the arm. They then headed across the grass toward the statue of Buddha, where they bowed and offered prayers.

"Let's get this mess cleaned up," said Kathy. She and Greg picked up the bandages and the splintered castes and put them in a garbage bag, which they handed to the waiter for disposal.

All heads turned to the desk clerk coming through the double doors with a cell phone. "Dr. Carl Brecht, here's a call for you from Arlington Heights, Illinois."

"It must be Barbara," said Carl, thanking the clerk.

"Carl? Are you all right! Kathy woke me up in the middle of the night and told me that you would be meeting her and Greg for dinner at the Kathmandu Guest House! She told me that she and Greg are engaged to be married."

"That's right, Barbara. We're all here in the garden of the Kathmandu Guest House!" said Carl.

"I had a terrible dream about you staying at the guest house and spending the night with Margaret Porter because you tried to comfort her over the loss of her son. I read in the New York Times that Nigel's probably with the Dalai Lama in India."

"Barbara, I'm not staying here tonight. I'll be leaving after dinner to stay with my Hindu friends in Patan for a few days. I'll call you later this evening when I get there. Kathy and Greg arrived a little while ago."

"Something has happened! I can tell by the tone of your voice," said Barbara.

"Yes, something good has happened. Margaret won't have to go all the way to India to meet Nigel."

"Don't tell me Nigel has been arrested by the Chinese police?" asked Barbara.

"Do you remember Heinrich Salzmann, the Swiss trekker?" asked Carl.

"Of course I do. He made the front page of the 'New York Times'," said Barbara.

"Well there's no such person as Heinrich. Here comes a photographer from the 'Nepal Daily'. He's taking pictures of Margaret and Nigel, standing in front of the statue of Buddha here in the garden of the Kathmandu Guest House. Kathy and Greg are also having their pictures taken next to them," explained Carl.

"Don't tell me Nigel came back to Kathmandu all the way from the Dalai Lama's monastery in Dharmasala!" said Barbara.

"No, Nigel was disguised as Heinrich Salzmann."

"You're kidding!" gasped Barbara. "Carl, I'm so glad you're back in Kathmandu. You call me later from your friend's house in Patan."

"I wrote down Surya Narayan's telephone number. It's on the pad next to the phone in the hallway."

"Yes, it's right here," said Barbara. "Carl, I love you! Say hello to Margaret, Nigel, Kathy and Greg for me!"

"I'll do that. I love you Barbara," said Carl, "Please say hello to Renee, Sammy and Emily for me. I'll talk to you later this evening."

Carl handed the cell phone back to the clerk, who was patiently waiting for it in the garden. He, also, noticed that the photographers had left the garden. However, he saw a bell boy hurrying down the path carrying a suitcase.

Nigel opened the suitcase in front of the statue of Buddha and put on his maroon monk's robe while Margaret took pictures of him with her cell phone.

"Let's go to the dining room. I'm starving," said Kathy, leading the way toward the double doors with Greg at her side followed by Margaret and Nigel.

As Carl followed them down the path between the roses, he glanced at the pomelo tree, noticing that most of the grapefruit size pomelos were green, but a few of them were beginning to ripen.

Biographical Information

Nick Cibrario joined the Peace Corps after completing three years of college. Upon arrival in Nepal, he taught English and General Science (1962-1964) at high schools in Bhimphedi in the mountains the first year and in Kalaiya near the Indian border during the second year.

Upon returning to the U.S. he entered a Jesuit novitiate in Milford Ohio and stayed for two years. Upon leaving, he completed a Bachelor of Arts Degree from the University of Wisconsin-La Crosse in 1969 and then a Master of Science Degree from the College of Racine in 1974.

Nick also received a fellowship from the University of Pennsylvania (1969-1970) in South Asian Studies. In 1976 attended Marquette University for the summer.

He taught English at William Horlick High School in Racine Wisconsin (1970-1976) and returned to Nepal, where he wrote the manuscript of his first novel, *The Pomelo Tree*.

After returning to teaching, he married Geraldine, who helped him edit his manuscripts. He continued writing before his two sons and daughter were born.

In 1982 Nick was asked to teach Latin by the principal of the high school in Racine. After retiring from teaching in 2000, he began updating his manuscripts for publication.

Since retiring Nick's six novels and two children's books were published. He continues to study painting and sculpture and exhibits his work in Racine and Kenosha as a member of Kenosha Art Association and the Racine Art Guild. His books are available on Amazon and Kindle.

Contact Nick Cibrario

He speaks to groups interested in his Himalayan Adventures or purchasing his books

Please send him an email

nickcibrarioracine@sbcglobal.net

or

google his website,

www.pomelotree.com   (Nick Cibrario)

Bibliography

1. "The Story of Tibet: Conversations with the Dalai Lama," Thomas Laird, Grove Press, New York, copyright, 2006. **Chapter 1**

2. "The Art of Happiness," His Holiness the Dalai Lama and Howard C. Cutler, M.D. Riverhead Books, New York, copyright 2009. **Chapter 2**

3. "Sherpa: Reflections on Change in Himalayan Nepal," James F. Fisher with forward by Sir Edmund Hillary, University of California Press, Berkeley& Los Angeles, copyright 1990.

4. "Tibet: Abode of the Gods, Pearl of the Motherland", Barbara Erickson, Pacific View Press, Berkeley CA. 1997

5. 'Tibet: The Secret Continent", Michael Peissel, Thomas Dunne Books, St. Martin Press, New York, 2002

6. "Nepal Trekking and the Great Himalaya Trail: A Route & Planning Guide", Robin Boustead, Trailblazer Publication, and Pinhead Surrey, UK

7. "The End of the Revolution: China and the Limits of Modernity", Wang Hung, Verso, London, New York, 2009.

8. "In the Himalayas: Journeys Through Nepal, Tibet, and Bhutan", Jeremy Bernstein, Simon & Shuster Inc., New York, New York,1989.

9. "Tibet, Tibet: A Personal History of a Lost Land", Patrick French, Alfred A. Knopf, a division of Random House Inc. New York. 2003.

10. "The Soul of the Rhino", Hemanta Mishra, The Lyons Press, Guilford, Connecticut, 2008.

11. "Bones of the Tiger: Protecting the Man-Eaters of Nepal", Hemanta Mishra, Lyons Press, Guilford, Connecticut 2010.

12."Hindu Epics, Myths and Legends in Popular Illustrations", Vassilis G. Vitsaxis with forward by A.L. Bahsam, Oxford University Press 1977, Printed in India, New Delhi.pp.89-91

13. Kali-Wikipedia-the free Encyclopedia, "Etymology of Kali, Kala", en.wikipeidia.org/wiki/kali "The Goddess Kali of Kolkata" by Shoma Chatterji, "Dictionary of Hindu Lore and Legend". **Chapter 21**

14. "The Festivals of Nepal," Mary Anderson, Chapter 8: Naga Panchami, pp. 85-92, George Allen & Unwin Ltd. Ruskin House, Museum Street, London. **Chapter 19**

15. "The Birth of Kumara", Kali-Dass, Translated by David

Smith, copyright, 2005, New York University Press, JJC Foundation, Introduction pp.15-16, Quotations pp. 287, 291, 299, 301. **Chapter 21**

16. "Talks on Upadesha Saram (Essence of the Teaching) of Raman Maharshi", Swami Dayananda, 1987, Sri Gangadhareswar Trust, Publication Division, Mangalam, Opp: Nehrunagar S. M. Road, Ahmedabad -380 015
Chapter 22

17. "Devastating earthquake strikes Nepal", "The Journal Times", Racine, Wisconsin, and Sunday, April 26, 2015 p.3A, Bhrikuti Rai and Julie Mkinen, Los Angeles Times **Chapter 22.**

18." The Kathmandu Post", Tuesday, August 13, 2013, P.IV, "Imports of Heavy Equipment: Soar Amid Building Frenzy". **Chapter 23**

19. "The Himalayan Times", August 9, 2013, "Locals demand early road construction", Submit memorandum to Kathmandu District Development Committee, Himalayan News Service, and p.2. **Chapter 23**

20. "The New York Time", http://nyti.ms/1E2phKz, May 1, 2015 "Nepal's Fast Urbanization and Lax Enforcement Add to Quake's Toll," by Chris Buckley. Stuff.co.nz "Nepal Earthquake Offers Chance for Safer Future," pp.1-2
Chapter 23

21. "The Festivals of Nepal," Mary Anderson, Chapter 9, "Janai Purni or Raksha Bandhan, The Sacred Thread Festival", pp. 93-98, George Allen & Unwin Ltd. Ruskin House, Museum Street, London, **Chapter 24**

22. Official Nepal.Com, Website, Blog, "The Spectacular Kumbeswar Temple". **Chapter 24**

23. http://mantrapower.blogspot.com/Resources: "Bagala, Muki, Ajima, The Mother's Face that Controls Evil Forces" **Chapter 24**

24. "Dancing with Siva, Hinduism's Contemporary Catechism," By Satguru Sivaya Subramuniyaswami, Copy write 1997, Published by Himalayan Academy, India –USA. See www.hindu.org/ashram/ **Chapter 25**

25. "Nepal Mandala A Cultural Study of the Kathmandu Valley", by Mary Shepherd Slusser, Volume 1: Text "Origin of the Pashupatinath Temple, Lord of the Animals". pp. 226-228. Shiva taking the form of a gazelle **Chapter 25**

26. "The Presence of Shiva," by Stella Kramrisch, , Appendix: "The Great Temple Of Shiva On The Island of Elephanta", pp 443-468, Princeton University Press, 1981,**Chapter 25**

27. "The Nepal Cookbook," Association of Nepalese in the Americas, Illustrations by Palden Choedak Oshoe, Snow

Lions Publications, New York, copyright,1996. **Chapter 26**

28. "Tibetan Buddhism and Research Psychology: A Match Made in Nirvana?" by Sadie F. Dingfelder, Monitor Staff, December 2003, Vol. 34, No 11, Print Version p.46. www.apa.org/monitor/dec3/Tibetan.aspx **Chapter 30**

29. "The Bhagavad Gita, Vibhuti Yoga," Chapter 10, Verse 28 by Srimath Swami Chidbhavananda. Sri Ramakrisha Taoivanam, Tirupparaithurai -639 115 Tiruchirappali Dt. Copyright 2008 **Chapter 30**

30. "Sakala Daevataa, Gayatree Mantras", Translated by Sri. P. Ramachandra Sekar, Printed by M. B. Publishers, #95 T.S.V. Koil Street, Mylapore, Chennai -600 004 India Translation into p.6 – Sanskrit p.7 **Chapter 28**

31. "Wheels of Life: A User's Guide To The Chakra System", Anodea Judith, PhD, 2000, Llewellyn Publications, St. Paul, Minnesota, USA. Copyright 1987/1999 pp.42-44

32. "The World of Tibetan Nomads", Daniel J. Miller, 2007. This text will be used in a forthcoming book, "DROKPA: Nomads of the Tibetan Plateau and Himalayas", Vajara Publications, Kathmandu, Nepal. **Chapters 35-36**

33. "Sprit Possession in the Nepal Himalayas", Edited by John T. Hitchcock & Rex L. Jones, Vikas Publishing House, New Delhi, 1976 pp.141-151 **Chapter 36**

34. "Foundations of Tibetan Mysticism," Lama Anagarika Govinda, Rider and Company, 3 Fitzroy Square, London, First published, 1960, Fourth Publication 1973. Chapter 9 "Psycho-Physical Process in the Yoga of the Inner Fire...Milarepa". **Chapter 36, 37, 40.**

35. "Sakala Deavataa, Gayatree Mantras, Om", translated by Sri P. Ramachandra Sekar, M.B. Publishers, 10 Lakshman Apartments, Mylapore Chennai-600 004, and 1st Edition Dec. 2005. **Chapter 43**

Made in the USA
Lexington, KY
19 May 2017